The Life and Loves of
Grace Kelly

JANE ELLEN WAYNE

ISIS LARGE PRINT

Oxford, England
Santa Barbara, California

First published in 1991 by Robson Books Ltd

First published in the U.S.A. 1990 by St Martin's Press
under the title "Grace Kelly's Men"

Published in Large Print 1992 by Clio Press,
55 St. Thomas' Street, Oxford OX1 1JG
by arrangement with Robson Books Ltd and St Martin's Press

British Library Cataloguing in Publication Data
Wayne, Jane Ellen
The life and loves of Grace Kelly.
I. Title
944.9490092

ISBN 1-85089-417-5

Printed and bound by Hartnolls Ltd, Bodmin, Cornwall
Cover designed by CGS Studios Ltd, Cheltenham

CONTENTS

ACKNOWLEDGMENTS

As the author of *Gable's Women* (1987) and *Cooper's Women* (1988), I interviewed people who were acquainted with Grace Kelly before she gave up her movie career. I was fascinated by Grace's romances with Hollywood's most desirable leading men. More intriguing was their devotion to her.

It was screenwriter-producer Bob Slatzer who urged me to do a book about Grace's men. She was a newcomer in Hollywood when he met her in 1951. Bob was in love with Marilyn Monroe (they would marry briefly a year later) and Grace was carrying a torch for his pal, Gary Cooper. "We cried on each other's shoulders," Slatzer says today.

Thanks for prodding me, Bob.

My gratitude also to "Brian Evans" (not his real name), a close friend of Grace Kelly who prefers to remain anonymous. His reflections run deep and lend a touching aspect to Grace's psyche.

I want to express my appreciation to author James Spada for allowing me to use portions of his 1987 best-selling book, *Grace: The Secret Lives of a Princess.*

As always, I am indebted to editor Pat Wilks Battle at the *New York Post* for providing me with clippings from national and international news files and to movie historian Philip Paul for his valuable help with research.

Sincere thanks to my editor, Toni Lopopolo, for her guidance and patience.

I am forever grateful to my old friends who worked behind the scenes in Hollywood. Joan Crawford referred to them as the "little people who are bigger than life." They contribute without credit or fanfare, and I respect their anonymity.

INTRODUCTION

Grace Kelly and I had a few things in common. We were both born in Philadelphia; we both attended the American Academy of Dramatic Arts in New York City; and we both lived at the Barbizon Hotel for women. Grace preceded me by three years and had, by then, appeared with Gary Cooper in *High Noon* (1952). As the saying goes, she had become a star overnight and was the topic of conversation at the academy. "She slept her way to the top" was the gist of it. As an aspiring actress, I had heard all about the casting couch but did not consider Grace the type to keep it warm.

Everyone at the school was talking about the tall, slim, flat-chested actress who fitted the image of Marshal Kane's prim and proper Quaker wife in *High Noon*.

Another coincidence was my dating a close acquaintance of hers. "Brian Evans" is a Canadian tycoon who was a long-time friend of Howard Hughes. As it was with Grace, I met him on a blind date. Brian was a distinguished middle-aged man-about-town and a backer of Broadway plays. He preferred dating young actresses and was genuinely interested in helping them get a break in the theater. A good listener and not one to brag, he never mentioned Grace Kelly until we ran into her at the Stork Club. While on the dance floor, she spotted Brian and came over to our table with her arms outstretched. "*Where* have you been?" she asked.

"I *know* where you've been," he said, beaming. "Do you like California?"

"Not really."

Brian introduced us and mentioned that I was attending the American Academy of Dramatic Arts. She and I exchanged an amusing story about one of the instructors who spied on us from an inconspicuous balcony every morning to see if we were walking properly. In the meantime, Grace glanced at Brian with glowing affection. They talked about her trip to Africa for *Mogambo* (1953) with Clark Gable. "I'm learning Swahili," she said in earnest.

"Aren't you the least bit nervous going all that way alone?" he asked.

"My mother's doing the worrying for both of us. I'm very excited. After all, I made a lot of sacrifices for *Mogambo*."

"You'll drop me a line?"

"I always do," Grace said, getting up from the table. She wished me well at school, kissed Brian, and left.

"How long have you known her?" I asked him.

"Three years."

"How did she get the breaks so fast?"

"Grace's type is rare in Hollywood these days. She's a natural beauty with class and refinement . . . the gal from the right side of the tracks. She's ambitious and determined and has a way with men without being obvious. Grace is the most affectionate girl I've ever met — an adorable and amorous python."

"Python?" I laughed.

"Oh, she wraps her arms around you and won't let go. She makes a man feel like king of the world. Wonderful feeling. The first night we were together, I did not have the urge to take a shower afterward. That never happened to me before."

"Do you love her, Brian?"

"I could but I don't."

Grace Kelly became a star in *Mogambo* and dated such famous men as Clark Gable, William Holden, and Bing Crosby, but she kept in touch with Brian, who was gradually spending more time in Canada tending to his business ventures there. He and I corresponded over the years. Grace's name came up only when she won an Oscar and later when her engagement to Prince Rainier of Monaco was announced.

I spoke to Brian about this book and asked if Grace had ever met his pal, Howard Hughes. "Yes," he replied. "Twice that I know about." It was before *High Noon*. She had wanted to meet Hughes because he owned RKO Studios and was known to be a possessive lover. Grace, the adventurous type, was intrigued with his cloak-and-dagger meetings on deserted side streets, in the Hollywood Hills, or on the beach. She was not aware that Hughes had his favorite girls watched twenty-four hours a day; Ava Gardner knew the names of his hired guards and invited them in for a drink. It is doubtful Grace fit into this category, however. She was starved for more affection than Howard was capable of giving, and he was a "breast man" who liked brunettes.

William Holden said, "Grace's romances were always serious. She put her heart and soul into love affairs."

In later years, Grace explained: "As an unmarried woman, I was thought to be a danger. Other women looked on me as a rival, and it pained me a great deal. The worst was when Hollywood gossip columnist Hedda Hopper started to persecute me with her hatred. She warned all producers, directors, and actors against me. Hedda called me a nymphomaniac."

Hollywood was and is one of the smallest towns in America. Everyone knows everyone else's business — who's gay, who's sleeping with whom, who's had a face-lift, who's going to be a has-been, and who's going to be a star. They resented Grace, the daughter of a millionaire and a neophyte, who had come to Hollywood, hypnotized director Fred Zinnemann, Gary Cooper, and Alfred Hitchcock, almost broke up a few marriages, and won an Oscar that she carried off wearing white gloves and a virginal smile. Grace may not have been popular in Hollywood but the friends she had there were powerful and loyal. One was Hitchcock, who had been mesmerized by her in *Mogambo*. He saw fire underneath the lily-white skin. There was something about her sex appeal that fascinated him. She was his concept of the angel-whore. It was Hitchcock who taught Grace how to smolder for the camera, and it was she who made him smolder from the first moment he saw her. Hitchcock became a Grace-watcher, a smitten voyeur whose fantasies about her were never quite fulfilled. The author of his biography referred to it as "unrequited love."

Romanticists were not as impressed with Grace's Prince Rainier as they were with Rita Hayworth's Prince Aly Khan, who was known throughout Europe as the greatest lover of the century. He had more magnetism than Clark Gable and more charm than Cary Grant. Aly's father, the Aga Khan, was the richest man in the world. Rainier was cash-broke.

When Grace Kelly's engagement was announced,

America asked, "Prince who?" The mother of the bride-to-be thought he ruled Morocco. When she was promptly corrected, she appeared baffled and inquired, "Where *is* Monaco, anyway?"

The royal weddings of the two actresses occurred seven years apart. By the time Grace took her marriage vows, Rita was divorced and making movies again. Ironically, it was Princess Grace who yearned to be back on the screen and Rita who wanted nothing more than a faithful husband. Her daughter, Princess Yasmin, said that Rita was never the same after Aly was killed when his speeding Lancia collided with another car head-on.

Grace had dated Aly Khan after his divorce. Columnist and party-giver Elsa Maxwell, who had introduced him to Rita, said, "An affair with Aly was the chic thing to do. You hardly counted if you'd not been to bed with him."

Aly and the Shah of Iran gave expensive presents to Grace, according to Brian, who was amused that he was ignored when she was in the company of these royal gents on the nightclub circuit. "Grace dated a variety of men," he said, "... actors, producers, directors, and even head-waiters from swank restaurants who got her invitations to exclusive parties. The Kellys did not have *that* much influence in society."

Grace's father, Jack Kelly, was a self-made millionaire from Philadelphia who, as a former bricklayer, did not qualify for the Social Register. Grace had the physical characteristics of a debutante, however, and sprinkled her polished voice with a British accent. One of her attributes was her posture. Edith Head, the renowned Hollywood costume designer, once listed the perfections of the famous actresses she dressed: Marilyn Monroe's nose, Ingrid Bergman's mouth, Sophia Loren's eyes, Audrey Hepburn's waist, Shirley MacLaine's legs, and Grace Kelly's carriage. "Tall women tend to slump," Miss Head remarked, "but Grace, who is five-feet-seven, stands erect. Her peers show up for work in jeans, but she always wears white gloves and carries a hankie."

Grace emerged a species apart from the athletic Kellys. Susceptible to head colds, she was a sickly child who played with dolls or curled up with a book. Unlike her rambunctious brother and two sisters, Grace was soft-spoken and shy but nevertheless the first sibling to leave Philadelphia. Her father predicted she would come running home in a week. When Grace became a movie star, he didn't know what all the fuss was about; regarding her engagement to royalty, he said, "The Prince comes up to Gracie's titties." Her mother, Margaret Kelly, a staunch Irish Catholic, did a series of newspaper articles about her daughter's romantic life. It was a long time before Grace forgave her mother, who had always preached the importance of putting on a good appearance at all costs and yet who had revived the dark rumors about Grace's flings with Bing Crosby, Bud Palmer, Ray Milland, Clark Gable, William Holden, and Gary Cooper, many of whom were married men.

In tears, Grace asked her mother, "Why?"

Mrs. Kelly responded innocently, "But I'm donating my royalties to charity!"

Grace had given and proclaimed her love for many men except the one she chose to marry, a man she had met only twice. Alfred Hitchcock said about her proposed marriage to a prince, "Grace has bounced around with the ease of a girl on the trapeze. Whether the platform on which she has landed is too narrow, I don't know."

News of a quiet wedding in Philadelphia led her friends to suspect Grace was pregnant, which had been Rita Hayworth's predicament. Others took it for granted that the marriage had been arranged by the Kellys. A few considered Grace an opportunist but her former boyfriends had their own opinions: Couturier Oleg Cassini thought she was escaping from the turmoil of life; Brian was certain that it was Grace's attempt at winning over her father; and Clark Gable thought she was a smart girl to retire at her peak in movies: "Actresses age on the screen and even faster in their own mirrors."

Grace said, "I met Rainier at the right time. A few years earlier would have been too soon. I will learn to love him." It was obvious that a strong physical attraction existed between them, but observers did not detect the emotional attachment she had shown for Don Richardson, her former instructor at the American Academy, or for Cassini, the front-runner. Both men had been humiliated by the Kelly clan and Grace had not come to their defense. They suspected she had planned it that way to avoid committing herself. One wonders what might have happened if she had brought Clark Gable home for approval!

The late actor Gene Lyons, best known for his supporting role in the "Ironside" television series, was one of Grace's boyfriends who drank himself to death. She might have been partly responsible for Gene's downfall, but their affair was doomed when Mrs. Kelly discovered that he was trying to annul his marriage. She also investigated Richardson and was shocked to find out he was separated from his wife. Despite her mother's stern objections, Grace continued to see both men.

That she played a childish and fickle game cannot be

denied, but Grace was a love addict and afraid of losing her sweethearts. She did not have many close friends other than a small circle of Hollywood intimates whom she later entertained at the palace in Monaco. Rainier found the movie crowd overbearing and dull but liked David Niven's quiet continental manner and sense of humor. The Prince knew that Niven had been quite the ladies' man at one time and asked, "Who was your favorite?"

"Grace," Niven replied without thinking. ". . . er . . . Gracie . . . Gracie Fields!"

"Grace was very serious about her work . . . had her eyes and ears open," Gary Cooper said. "She was trying to learn. You could see that, and she was very pretty. It did not surprise me when she was a big success. She looked like she could be a cold dish with a man until you get her pants down and then she'd explode."

Cooper was separated from his wife and having a serious affair with actress Patricia Neal when he was making *High Noon*. Gary had misgivings about working with a girl who was twenty-five years younger until he saw Grace, who was in awe of the Montana cowboy whom flapper Clara Bow had nicknamed "Studs." On location in California's Sonoma Mountains, Gary succumbed to Grace's youth, beauty, and innocence and she fell head over heels in love with him. It was her first idolistic affair, and she followed Coop everywhere, moving her chair close to him or sitting on his lap. When rumors of an affair persisted, Mrs. Kelly rushed to California and chaperoned her daughter's last dates with Cooper.

Clark Gable was almost thirty years older than Grace

when they costarred in *Mogambo* on the Dark Continent. She resembled his late wife, Carole Lombard, who had called him "Pa," so Grace borrowed from Swahili and nicknamed him "Ba." She accompanied Clark on dangerous safaris and followed him around like a puppy dog. "The King" was a womanizer between wives facing six months of filming in Africa without seeing a white woman other than Grace and Ava Gardner, then Mrs. Frank Sinatra. At the onset, Gable asked a friend, "What the hell am I going to do with her?" Grace persisted and fell in love again. They finished *Mogambo* in England, where they kept a low profile until reporters followed them to the airport and caught Gable, who was staying in London, trying to comfort a sobbing Grace. He made light of it, but when he returned to Hollywood, they resumed the relationship that eventually faded. One reporter quoted Grace as saying, "His false teeth were too much."

Ray Milland was forty-eight years old and had been happily married to the same woman for two decades until he worked with Grace Kelly in Hitchcock's *Dial M for Murder* (1954). Ray had enjoyed brief flings, but he was serious about Grace and she felt the same way. *Confidential* magazine exposed the affair, and Ray left his wife. The Kellys were appalled and Hollywood was disgusted. Hushed about in studio circles was that Grace was "hot stuff," "an easy lay," and a home wrecker. "I felt like a streetwalker," she said. The gossip hurt her deeply, but she stayed at Milland's apartment and the romance lasted for almost a year. Various reasons have been given for their painful parting. Mutual friends said it all added up to Milland's wife having control of their money. Ray's close acquaintances insisted he could not bear to give up his wife after all. Metro-Goldwyn-Mayer press agents worked overtime to save Grace's reputation, insisting she "ran like a thief" when Milland filed for divorce.

William Holden, the extraordinarily handsome "Golden Boy," was married to beautiful actress Brenda Marshall. Shortly before making *The Bridges at Toko-Ri* (1954) with Grace, he was in love with his leading lady in *Sabrina* (1954), Audrey Hepburn, who chose Mel Ferrer instead. To punish her, Holden threatened to travel around the world and "screw a girl in every country." He accomplished his mission but looked forward to meeting the blonde actress from Philadelphia everyone in Hollywood was talking about. Bill was not disappointed and neither was Grace. The romance overlapped into their next film together, *The Country Girl* (1954), with Bing Crosby. The fifty-year-old crooner had a man-to-man talk with Holden. "I'm smitten with Grace," he said. "Daffy about her, and I was wondering if . . ."

"If I felt the same way?" Bill asked, grinning. "What man wouldn't be overwhelmed by her? But look, Bing, I won't interfere."

Grace and Crosby had been previously involved, according to Sue (Mrs. Alan) Ladd: "While his wife Dixie was dying of cancer, Bing would drop by late at night with Miss Kelly. I caught them more than once nestling on our couch."

Crosby had been a widower for a year when he deluged Grace with marriage proposals. Feeling pressured, she began very discreetly seeing Holden again; but spies from *Confidential* magazine were hot on their trail and the notorious Kelly girl found herself involved in another scandal with a married man: "Behind that frigid exterior is a smoldering fire . . . In the Hollywood of the chippies and the tramps, a lady is a rarity. That makes Grace Kelly the most dangerous dame in the movies today."

Holden said he wanted to marry Grace but could not be dictated to by any church. Crosby carried a torch for Grace the rest of his life. They remained close friends because she never actually turned his proposal down and kept her distance from Holden on *The Country Girl* set out of respect for Bing. Grace then began dating dress designer Oleg Cassini, who had been married to actress Gene Tierney. Grace used Cassini as a shield during the final months of her affair with Holden but got caught up in her own web of deceit by falling in love with Oleg.

Jean-Pierre Aumont, the good-looking French actor, had been married to actress Maria Montez, who had died of a heart attack in 1951. Twenty years older than Grace, Aumont got her on the rebound from Clark Gable. They had met in 1953 as costars in a television drama, had had a brief fling, and parted company when he returned to work in France. Two years later, their romance blossomed again at the Cannes Film Festival. Photos of the couple kissing and holding hands prompted Elsa Maxwell to predict marriage. Grace and Jean-Pierre spent a week in Paris together, but she returned to New York alone. Maxwell wrote that there were career conflicts, ". . . his in France and hers in America."

Prince Rainier III assumed Monaco's throne in 1949 and was the last heir of the royal Grimaldi family. A lonely and unloved child, he attended schools in England after his parents were divorced. His most outstanding quality being a quiet charm that appealed to the ladies, he was a shy man of medium height with dark hair and a mustache.

In 1947, Rainier fell in love with the stunning French actress Gisele Pascal. Six years later, he approached his advisers about marrying her. Without a Grimaldi heir, Monaco would become a French principality, but Gisele failed the fertility test and Rainier was forced to give her up. The Prince told his advisers, "If you ever hear that my subjects think I do not love them, tell them what I've done today." (How sad it was for Rainier when Gisele got married and had a child.)

Shipping magnate Aristotle Onassis, who had financial interests in Monte Carlo, was arranging for Marilyn Monroe to meet the Prince. She said, "Give me two days alone with him and of course he'll want to marry me." A few days later, Grace Kelly's engagement to Rainier was announced. Onassis's mistress, opera diva Maria Callas, and Grace became friends and remained close even after Onassis married Jacqueline Kennedy, who bowed to no one, including the Princess of Monaco.

Grace's first meeting with Rainier in the spring of 1955 was publicized, but pictures of her nibbling Jean-Pierre Aumont's fingertips took precedence. When she returned to New York, reporters were anxious to know more about the Frenchman, not the Prince. She resumed her relationship with Oleg Cassini, dated Frank Sinatra and David Niven, and was linked with Spencer Tracy, much to the distress of Katharine Hepburn.

When Grace won an Oscar for *The Country Girl*, she thought Jack Kelly would finally acknowledge her worth, but her father told the press, "I can't believe it! I simply cannot believe Grace won. Of the four children, she's the last one I expected to support me in my old age."

With the world at her feet, Grace had yet to satisfy the man she cherished most of all, her father. During visits to Philadelphia, she wanted his attention, some words of praise. She was ignored.

Brian was in Los Angeles at the same time Grace was finishing *The Swan* in December 1955. "We were having some champagne to celebrate the holidays," he said. "Grace was unusually quiet, drifting in and out of another world. When I kidded her about it, she said, 'I'm debating with myself whether to go home for Christmas this year.'"

Grace hesitated because Prince Rainier had been invited to the Kellys' for the holidays and she suspected he was going to propose marriage. She had told no one about their correspondence or his intentions. She thought about Oleg Cassini, with whom she had almost eloped in defiance of her parents, who refused to accept him. The romance was held together by a thread, but Grace gave him every reason to be optimistic.

She flew home to Philadelphia for Christmas and ten days later asked Oleg to meet her on the Staten Island ferry.

"For various reasons that should be apparent," Grace said, "I have decided to marry Prince Rainier of Monaco."

"But you hardly know the man!" Cassini protested.

"I will learn to love him," she said with conviction.

In a fairy-tale wedding on April 18, 1956, the Girl Who Had Everything married her prince and sailed off into the Mediterranean sunshine on the royal yacht. Nine months later, in January 1957, Princess Caroline was born. Jack

Kelly shrugged, "Aw, shucks. I was hoping for a boy."

He got his wish in March 1958. Grace gave birth to Prince Albert, but Rainier and the people of Monaco showed more enthusiasm than Grandpa Kelly, whose only satisfaction had been lauding Grace's crown over members of the Social Register and Main Line society. He hated the palace in Monaco and visited only twice. His sudden death in 1960 nearly destroyed Grace, who told a confidant that there was nothing she would not have done for her father ". . . but I got nothing in return."

After the birth of her third and last child, Princess Stéphanie, in February 1965, Grace wanted more freedom. She found an apartment in Paris and then joined the board of Twentieth Century-Fox, which required her to be in Los Angeles four times a year. According to Rock Hudson, "Her Royal Highness and I were at a Hollywood party, drinking until we were ripped to the tits."

Richard Burton was also amazed. "Grace let her hair down — literally and figuratively. She confessed that she never knew she had it in her. She danced wild Hungarian dances and the conga. I was goggle-eyed . . . Grace in the middle of all. Unbelievable."

Close friend Ava Gardner said, "Give her a couple of dry martinis and Her Serene Highness Princess Grace becomes just another one of the girls who likes to dish the dirt."

Those who knew her well enjoy telling about Grace's grand appearance at an elegant dinner party. After a few too many, she sneezed and popped all the buttons off her evening gown. Grace couldn't leave the table for repairs because she was laughing so hysterically.

These were the good times with friends she loved, but

they also remember the sad occasions at private gatherings when Grace was drunk and unkempt. It wasn't the bloat or smudged mascara or the slip that hung below the dress. It was the unhappiness in her eyes and Grace's valiant attempt to pretend she was contented.

Alfred Hitchcock knew she missed Hollywood and begged her to work with him again, but the people of Monaco protested en masse. Grace turned to Cary Grant for consolation and began seeing him in New York, Paris, and Los Angeles. When they had made *To Catch a Thief* (1955), it had been taken for granted that the two stars were having an affair because Grant fit into the pattern of Grace's men; but his wife, Betsy Drake, Oleg Cassini, and Mrs. Alma Hitchcock were on location, too, making it a family affair. Cary gave Grace the poodle she carried on her triumphant arrival in Monaco for the royal wedding and was invited to the palace five years later. She broke protocol by meeting Grant at the airport and kissing him while photographers took pictures from every angle. Monaco officials were displeased with their Princess flaunting her affection for the debonair actor.

Their romance began in the late sixties after Grant's divorce from actress Dyan Cannon. In Monaco, it was common knowledge that Grace and Rainier no longer shared the same bedroom, and his rumored flirtations wounded her deeply. She told a close friend in Hollywood, "Maybe I should have married Cary because he's the only man who understands me." The confidant had told no one and so was shocked to find out William Holden knew about it, too.

Brian said, "Grace mentioned that Grant was her salvation during those lonely and troubled years back in the seventies, but I didn't delve into the relationship."

Viewing *To Catch a Thief* is eerie today — Grace speeding in a white convertible with Cary on the Riviera's winding Corniche, the road that led to her death in 1982, and their steamy love scene at a picnic near the site in the background where her car would years later crash.

On September 18, 1982, Cary and his fifth wife, Barbara, attended the state funeral of Princess Grace of Monaco. Devastated and weak from grief, he had to be assisted during the services and to his car, where he finally broke down. Hearts also wept for a shattered Prince Rainier, whose sorrow was so pathetic that Grant said, "Can there be any doubt that he loved Grace with all his heart?"

Grant: Tell me, what do you get a thrill out of most?

Kelly: I'm still looking for that one.

Grant: You know just as well as I do this necklace is imitation.

Kelly: Well, I'm not!

From *To Catch a Thief* (1955)

CHAPTER
ONE

Images

Grace's invitation to her fortieth birthday party was quite unusual for royalty, referring to herself as the "High Scorpia." It was a weekend celebration commencing with dinner and dancing on Saturday, November 15th, and Sunday brunch at the posh Hotel de Paris swimming pool.

Grace believed in the stars, read her horoscope every day and frequently consulted an astrologer.

Those born under the sign of Scorpio are secretive, psychic, manipulative, passionate, stubborn, well-organized, deceitful, resourceful, vindictive, and tenacious. They have a strong sexual drive and great personal magnetism. Grace Kelly felt she gained a better understanding of herself through astrology and was therefore able to deal more effectively with her strengths and weaknesses.

She was captivated by the tarot cards, and as a young girl had gone to a gypsy fortune-teller in New York. Though Grace was a religious Catholic, she believed in destiny — but all the while paving the path of life as if it were in her own hands.

Nearing her fortieth birthday, she said in an interview, "I'm an absolute basket case. I can't stand it. It comes as a great jolt. It really does. It hits one right between the eyes.

For a woman, forty is torture, the end. I think turning forty is miserable." These were not the thoughts of a princess, but of Grace the movie star. During her carefree days in 1955, she said that marriage was a full-time job. "I'm afraid that all the rest of my life I'd be fretting about what a great actress I might have been."

Elizabeth Taylor wore the famous 33.19-carat Krupp diamond around her neck for the first time at Grace's birthday party. She was living the good life then, making movies at her leisure and madly in love with husband Richard Burton. Three years later, she invited Grace to her fortieth celebration in Budapest and was redecorating hotel rooms for the guests. Elizabeth told the designer, "Make a royal one for Grace . . . pretty enough for a princess, but remember she's just like us." Indeed, she was, living vicariously through them the exciting and unpredictable years as an actress. The adventurous Princess envied her Hollywood friends and told them wistfully, "I know where I'm going to be every single day of my life."

Grace's fortieth birthday was a reminder that if, by some miracle, she could make a comeback in films, there was not much time, though her chiseled features blended delicately with a more rounded face and her figure was well-shaped by motherhood. But the sexual mien was no longer an element of Grace's attractiveness.

The battle that raged within her was a hopeless one. She had given up the right to be a free spirit when she married the Prince, but Grace wanted desperately to be creative and to have her own identity.

Brian recalled a telephone call from her in 1970 that caught him by surprise. She was waiting for a connecting flight at the airport in New York and was bored, apparently.

Jokingly, he said it was obvious she hadn't been able to reach anyone else and had tried him as a last resort. She laughed, but it was forced. Then out of the blue, Grace told Brian she was considering therapy again. Twenty years earlier, both had undergone therapy. "We were both seeing a psychiatrist at the same time," Brian said. "She was trying to pull herself together after the Bill Holden fiasco and I had family problems. Today shrinks are fashionable, but in the fifties, it was a sign you were on the brink of insanity."

Brian said that Grace had a difficult time accepting Freud's theory that our insecurities stemmed from childhood, but on the phone in 1970 she said that having children of her own had changed her way of thinking. "I want them to feel loved," she said, "and not search for it later."

Brian had commented, "Love is like money because we can never get enough."

"We're never satisfied, are we?"

"Are you going back into therapy?" he asked.

"A caged animal doesn't need a psychiatrist."

Their conversation was getting too deep for Brian, who suggested they have lunch on her return trip. Instead, Grace called again from California because her schedule was indefinite. He wanted to know if she was seriously considering going back into therapy. "I get down in the dumps," she said, "but being in California usually cheers me up. I love the aura of imagination and fantasy, the productive minds and ingenuity. Do you think I'd feel the same way if I hadn't given up my career?"

Brian said he missed New York and the challenge of investing in Broadway shows, but there was no turning back. It was all or nothing.

"I can't agree," she said. "You have the freedom to do as you please."

"But you don't. Is that what you wanted to talk about?"

"It's been very, very difficult for me because I can't face the fact that resuming my career is impossible." Grace went on to say how much she admired mature actors whose faces expressed their thoughts. "Gary Cooper, for example," she said, "and Cary Grant. I've reached that stage in life and I'm not able to take advantage of it."

"Have you any idea how many great actresses can't find a decent movie script?" Brian bellowed into the phone. "They're more frustrated than you are! Even my favorite, Barbara Stanwyck, is doing a TV Western series. Barbara Stanwyck! And Joan Crawford, who said any movie star who appeared on television was a traitor. Well, she's a traitor!"

"But they're doing what they love the most — acting."

Brian was losing patience, pointing out to Grace that she had security for the rest of her life while other mature actresses needed to work for a living. He understood her dilemma, knowing she hated confinement. Her big sacrifice for *Mogambo* and Clark Gable had been signing a seven-year contract with Metro-Goldwyn-Mayer (MGM), and she had hated it. While most actresses would have jumped at the chance, she wanted to blaze her own trail. "I couldn't possibly have known as much about Grace if we hadn't confided in each other during therapy," Brian said. "As far as I was concerned, she was right back where she started as the middle Kelly sister in Philadelphia — looking for love, searching for her own personal identity. At forty, Grace reminded me of the optimistic girl I met in

New York on a blind date with one exception. Her dreams were in the past."

Grace's friends believed in this theory, too. Judith Quine, who was a bridesmaid at the royal wedding, makes the premise that everything was in vain because Grace could never get the only thing she wanted — the love and approval of her father. How far is it in soul miles from the brick house that Jack Kelly built in Philadelphia to the Grimaldi Palace in Monaco?

Woolworth heiress Barbara Hutton said in a 1937 interview, "Maybe the rich are different. If we didn't have all this money we wouldn't even be in the Social Register." Her name was dropped from the bible of the blue bloods a year later because she was too frequently in the news. "And what is the Social Register anyway, if not a glorified telephone directory?" she exclaimed. With $50 million in the bank, Barbara could afford to care less.

Jack Kelly was rich but not eligible for the Social Register because he was the son of an Irish immigrant. Society, with a capital S, in Philadelphia was known as Main Line, consisting predominately of white Anglo-Saxons.

The shunned Kellys were in good company, however. Also excluded from the Social Register was millionaire Joseph P. Kennedy, another Irishman who had settled in aristocratic Boston. His son John's marriage to debutante Jacqueline Bouvier gave the Kennedy name social prestige.

Jack Kelly expected one of his three daughters to marry a blue blood, giving him the same distinction and gratification that his millions could not buy. There was another deep-seated reason: Kelly hated the English, whom his Irish ancestors had rebelled against in Ireland.

5

Another rub was his first employer, an Englishman from Yorkshire whose family was prominent in Philadelphia. The Irish Catholics were considered the working class or, as Jack Kelly put it when his application for a prestigious rowing event in England was denied, "I was turned down because I worked with my hands. In other words, I wasn't a gentleman and didn't qualify." This was not the reason for his disqualification, but it was Kelly's way of striking out at the British and the WASPs (white Anglo-Saxon Protestants) who dominated high society in America.

Joe Kennedy often said the Irish should stick together, but he was proof that Jack Kelly might have been his own worst enemy. Kennedy made his money in banking, the motion picture industry, and real estate. A man of great vigor and drive, he settled in Boston, married the mayor's daughter, and was appointed ambassador to Great Britain. Joe's sense of humor overshadowed any bitterness he might have had toward class distinction, unlike Jack Kelly, who failed in local politics and put the blame on religious discrimination.

The old adage, "It's a small world," is used appropriately here. Barbara Hutton married and divorced Cary Grant, the only one of her eight husbands who refused alimony. Joe Kennedy was her good friend but hoped for a closer relationship. Barbara wasn't interested in being the mistress of someone else's husband when she could afford eight of her own. She sent Joe back to his longtime mistress, Gloria Swanson. Before her death in 1979, Barbara settled in Los Angeles and went into seclusion at the Beverly Wilshire Hotel, where Cary met with Grace during their romance. Odd that he would choose that particular hotel.

Joe Kennedy was also chummy with Oleg Cassini, whose

courtship of Grace was wobbly after the Kellys rejected him. Joe offered to help, but over lunch he referred to Oleg as a "donkey" and tried to make a date with Grace! His son Jack liked to embarrass Cassini at informal White House gatherings by asking him to tell the story "about how Dad screwed you up with Grace Kelly."

Cassini was Jackie Kennedy's dress designer until her husband was assassinated in 1963. Five years later, she married Aristotle Onassis, who controlled Monte Carlo's casino in Monaco's backyard. The Princess and Jackie socialized but were never close. Alert journalists wrote that the former First Lady never forgot the candid photo of Grace looking at the President seductively and had been suspicious of an affair. Jackie held the aces, however. She was a blue blood and represented high society wearing blue jeans or emeralds. In 1947, Jackie had been nominated Debutante of the Year by Cholly Knickerbocker, the society columnist. Grace Kelly could only dream of wearing a sweeping gown at her own coming-out party and to the Assembly Ball for Main Line daughters. What the two women had in common was deep and utter devotion to their fathers. Jackie saw little of "Black Jack" Bouvier III after her parents were divorced. Handsome and roguish, he was very much the ladies' man, which might have been one of the reasons Jackie was drawn to a Kennedy who was irresistible and flirtatious. Grace's friends felt much the same way about her attraction to Rainier. As ruler and defender of Monaco, he bore the fatherly image of protector and guardian. She would belong to and follow a man of great accomplishment like her own father.

There had not been a meeting of the minds between Grace and Jack Kelly until he was on his deathbed. There

7

are no photos of them sharing a moment of mutual love and admiration nor could Grace's friends recall seeing him hug her with genuine affection or speak of her fondly. He was a proud and distant man and yet he fawned over the eldest daughter, Margaret, and brought up her name whenever Grace was mentioned. It was always Peggy, Peggy, Peggy — her wit and enthusiasm, her jokes and pranks. She was Jack's pride and joy. He never made it quite clear who came in second, but it wasn't Grace.

There was a son, John Brendan II, called "Kell," whose life was dictated by his athletic father; defeating the British at rowing was the first order of business. When he lost his first Henley race, Kell's defeat was so humiliating that his hands had to be pried from the oars. Nevertheless, he went on to win the Diamond Sculls at Henley not once but twice, victories that Jack Kelly claimed as his revenge.

Grace said she should have been a boy because of her father's obsession with sports, but Kell never had a chance to find himself as she did. "The old man pushed the hell out of me," he confessed. His first marriage that was held together by mama and papa for twenty-five years finally ended in divorce, and Peggy suffered through two failed marriages. Only Grace and her younger sister Lizanne maintained their marital status.

While Jack Kelly made snide remarks about his famous daughter surreptitiously, brother Kell went out of his way to prove that his sister was only one of the gang, regardless of a royal title, by slapping her on the back and calling her "Gracie." She took it in stride, as she had done when he made fun of her boyfriends to their faces. As her older brother, Kell might have been the father substitute for Grace, but there was a lack of communication in their relationship, too. He made one revelational remark about Grace: "She did the smart thing by leaving home."

Jack Kelly had his faults but he was a man of vision who worked hard and made a name for himself in business and as a 1920 Olympic Gold Medal champion in rowing. A strong believer in heredity nurtured by environment, he was blind to the possibility that one of his children might be more interested in the arts rather than striving for a Gold Medal. Yet his brother was a Pulitzer Prize-winning playwright who had the characteristics of a well-bred gentleman. George Kelly was a creative and witty snob who refused to discuss his impoverished childhood as the son of a common Irish laborer. He was disgusted and bored by the loud and raucous household of his brother Jack. With his encouragement, Grace was able to navigate her dream of becoming an actress. Uncle George was a discreet homosexual, but the family considered him merely a bit eccentric because he never married. It seemed, for a time, that fate might have the same in store for Grace, who was an aunt several times over and godmother to her girlfriends' children before the Prince came along. She feared living alone for the rest of her life and had doubts that she would find the right man who would meet with her parents' approval. Jack had made it clear to Grace that she would not be welcome in his house again if she married Oleg Cassini, and the same threat most likely applied to the other married or divorced men with whom she became involved.

Brian's knowledge of the Kelly family came from mutual acquaintances and what little Grace revealed when she was seeing a psychiatrist. "It seemed rather odd that her father never had much to say about her," he said. "He was described to me as a blowhard, but he didn't brag about

Grace in any of the articles that I read. One of his business associates said Jack wanted total recognition because he was the one who made it all possible. The hard way."

"He wanted the glory?" I asked.

"A man like Kelly who has nothing and makes his fortune doing manual labor has little respect for the writer, the actor, or the painter. They're sissies who don't have the guts to do anything worthwhile. Jack didn't toil and sweat day and night to watch his kids take it easy, and that, in his opinion, is precisely what Grace did. Why would anyone compare the Oscar to an Olympic Gold Medal, for God's sake? If you want my opinion, father and daughter were unknowingly in competition. She was out there to win and, as judge and jury, he proclaimed her the loser. One of his racetrack buddies relayed this to me, among other things."

"Such as?"

"Jack Kelly's extramarital affairs. It was common knowledge that he had a mistress at one time. She was a Philadelphia socialite."

"I was told he had many women."

"His friend intimated that," Brian said, "but defended Jack because he was such a handsome, strapping guy with a fine sense of humor and a good deal of charm, especially with the ladies, who did the chasing and he didn't run so fast."

"Do you know anything about his wife, Margaret?"

"She was a German hausfrau. Grace called her "my Prussian mother" because she was the disciplinarian in the family. Apparently Jack wasn't home very much."

From Brian's description, Margaret Majer Kelly sounds little more than a dowdy housewife, but she was, in fact, a beautiful woman who had earned her degree in physical education at Temple University. She had been a cover girl for respectable magazines, such as *The Country Gentleman*, posing in refined sporting attire while holding a rifle. It was from "Ma" Kelly that Grace inherited her chiseled features and blond hair.

Margaret was in no hurry to settle down; she ignored Jack's attention for almost ten years. Finally, the lovely Miss Majer agreed to go out with Kelly, and they were married a year later.

Not only did Margaret pass on her looks to Grace, she was also determined to pursue a career; she was the first woman to teach physical education at the University of Pennsylvania, quite a feat in the early twenties. After she had proven herself, Margaret was ready for the responsibilities of marriage. As a former swimming instructor, she shared Jack's enthusiasm for sports, his competitive nature, and the all-consuming will to win.

A friend of the Kellys said, "Jack has money to burn but his wife doesn't like to smell the smoke." Grace wore hand-me-downs that were altered by Margaret, who had household help but frequently did the cooking herself. Her daughters were taught needlepoint, knitting, and sewing, and they were expected to keep their bedrooms neat and clean. Jack took complete charge of Kell from the first day he could walk. Margaret, well-organized and efficient, devoted very little time to playing with the children and, like her husband, was not an affectionate person. They were both uncomfortable with and unaccustomed to displays of love and tenderness. Only in later years did Jack feel the need for attentive and romantic companionship. One of Grace's cousins said, "there never has been a good Kelly marriage."

CHAPTER
TWO

The Early Years

Grace Patricia Kelly was born on November 12, 1929, in Philadelphia. Her grandparents were immigrants, one an Irish farmer and the other a German squire.

No one knows for sure why John Henry Kelly migrated to America in the late 1860s. It might have been crop failure or his taking part in the uprising against the British. How he managed to settle in Rutland, Vermont, is also a mystery, but John was in the right place at the right time. There he met and married another Irish immigrant, seventeen-year-old Mary Ann Costello, in 1869. John did odd jobs in New England until Mary Ann's cousin, who was a foreman at Dobson's Mill in Philadelphia, arranged a job for John. With their two sons, Patrick and Walter, the Kellys settled in the Falls of Schuylkill in northeast Philadelphia. John Henry had escaped the British in Ireland, but he found himself working for two Englishmen, James and John Dobson, owners of the textile mill.

The Kellys had ten children, six boys and four girls. Grace's father, John Brendan ("Jack"), was born on October 4, 1889. When three of her sons gained prominence, Mary Ann said in an interview for *American Magazine* ("Oh, For a Million Mothers Like Mary Kelly!"), "I had to be cook, baker, laundress, scrubwoman, dressmaker, milliner, valet, lady's maid, waitress, and chambermaid. Yes, and I've been the banker that received the money, the accountant that kept the books — in my head — the cashier and paymaster. I had to know groceries and dry goods, fuel and light, plastering and papering and carpentering. That is what it means to be the wife of a poor man and the mother of ten children.

". . . but I never stopped reading and studying. I've stood by the stove hundreds of times, a baby under my left arm and a book in my left hand, while I made pancakes with my right one."

Mary Ann had a hunger for learning. She was interested in history and read Shakespeare aloud to her son George, who became a Pulitzer Prize-winning playwright. His quick-witted brother Walter mimicked himself to stardom in vaudeville. Before they could pursue their chosen professions, however, all the Kelly boys worked at Dobson's Mill. Their sisters went to school at night learning bookkeeping and stenography. By 1900, Patrick was working in construction as a bricklayer, but at twenty-eight he wanted to go into business for himself and entered "The Most Popular Town Employee" newspaper contest. The prize was a $5,000 house. Patrick won, sold the property, and formed the P. H. Kelly Building Company. When Jack was old enough, he worked for Patrick as an apprentice bricklayer; his favorite brother, Charles, managed the office.

During World War I, Jack was turned down as an aviator because of his poor eyesight. He volunteered for the Ambulance Corps and was sent to France. When he returned home, he pursued his two ambitions — to be in business for himself and to win the national single sculls title. "As a kid," he said, "I was always on the banks of the

Schuylkill River, and if I could watch the oar or hold the sweater of one of the great oarsmen, my day was complete." He rose early every morning, practiced on the river for an hour, went to work until five o'clock, and then rowed until it got too dark. Jack won the national title in 1919 but wasn't satisfied until he had conquered the Diamond Sculls at Henley, England. Alas, his entry was rejected. "I remember," he said, "reading that cable over and over and seeing the tears drop on the paper and realizing that all my castles were tumbling down about my ears. The letter that was supposed to follow never came, so I assumed the old rule that a man who worked with his hands could not compete was the reason. As I looked through the tears, I felt that my grandfather, who really hated the English, was right and all the disappointment that I felt was turned into bitterness towards the English."

The real reason for his rejection was a feud between Henley stewards and Jack's sponsor, but he preferred the original version of class discrimination — the poor Irishman who worked with his hands versus England's conception of a gentleman. In later years, he admitted the truth to reporters just in case the press delved into the Henley files, but Jack Kelly wanted to believe that he had been blackballed, to substantiate the prejudices that he was forced to endure.

His daughter Grace recalled, "Did you ever know an Irishman who would take a thing like that lying down? So Jack Kelly, grandson of an Irish pig farmer, two months later won the 1920 Olympic singles Gold Medal. And whom did he beat? The English champ! So he sent his victorious green rowing cap to the King of England with his compliments!"

Jack and his cousin Paul Costello won the doubles Gold Medal on the same day.

At the North Philadelphia railroad station, the mayor and town officials were waiting to welcome their Olympic hero. Jack and his mother rode in an open car through the streets lined with cheering crowds waving in tune to the policemen's and firemen's bands. Later a banquet was held in his honor at the old Tissot's Inn, known now as the Fairmount. Kelly was moved by the tribute, but his insides were still curdling from the Diamond Sculls incident; revenge was in his soul.

He had, however, proven his athletic skills. Now it was important that he make a name for himself in business. To accomplish this, he needed money and borrowed $5,000 from Walter, who had become a successful vaudeville star, and $2,000 from George, a promising playwright. In 1921, Jack went into competition with brother Patrick by forming his own company, Kelly for Brickwork, and taking Charles with him. This caused a serious breach in the family even though Patrick was in his middle fifties, very rich, and living in an opulent stone mansion complete with a ballroom. Without Charles to oversee his finances, Patrick eventually died broke, leaving nine children. There is no doubt that it was Charles who made Kelly for Brickwork a multimillion-dollar concern by overseeing every aspect of the business, as he had done for Patrick.

Jack focused on sports and having a good time. At the age of thirty-four, he was considered one of the most eligible bachelors in North Philadelphia. Though sculling and business had taken up most of his time, he dated many women who were his for the asking — all except one, that is.

He had met Margaret Majer in 1914 at the Philadelphia Turngemeinde, an athletic social club. She said, "He was nine years older than I, so we didn't take each other very seriously." But Jack was obviously attracted to the lovely sixteen-year-old, often picking her up after school until World War I broke out. Returning from France, he concentrated on the Diamond Sculls and the Olympics while Margaret attended college. Jack took it for granted she would be on hand for the parade and banquet to celebrate his Gold Medals, but he received only a brief note of congratulations from her. He was irked and disappointed. She consented to an occasional date but kept her distance, a frustrating first for the dynamic and very popular Jack Kelly.

Margaret Katherine Majer was born in Philadelphia of German immigrants whose ancestry could be traced back to sixteenth-century nobility. Her father Carl was born in 1863 in a castle, Schloss Helmsdorf, near Lake Constance in the German state of Württemberg. Squire Johann Christian Carl Majer, Margaret's paternal grandfather, lost his fortune and came to America with his son Carl. They settled in Philadelphia and, in 1896, Carl married Margaretha Grossmutter Berg, the daughter of a saddle and harness maker, at St. Paul's Independent Lutheran Church. As a designer of carpet textiles, Carl Majer could afford to live in a respectable middle-class neighborhood in North Philadelphia.

Margaret pursued a career as a swimming instructor, graduated from Temple University, and became the first woman to teach physical education at the University of Pennsylvania. She also did some casual posing for an artist friend, and her picture appeared on a number of magazine covers.

If she had tried, Margaret could not have done a better job of taunting Jack Kelly. "She asked for waivers on me, as she couldn't compete with my boat," he said. Afraid of rejection, he stopped asking her to go out but showed up wherever he thought Margaret might be. "She treated me as if I had BO," Jack said. Then one day they met accidentally on the street and he asked for a date. She accepted; "— but I was fifth on her list," he said. Within the year, however, Margaret had converted to Catholicism and married Jack on January 30, 1924, at St. Bridget's in the Falls.

Mary Ann Kelly was opposed to her son marrying a German Protestant and assumed that the independent Miss Majer would not give up her faith. Margaret, who was also stubborn and strong-minded, converted because she chose to do so, not to placate her future mother-in-law. Though the religious aspect bothered Mary Ann, the thought of losing her influence over Jack was more distressing. She had met her match in Margaret. Ironically, it was this similarity in personalities that had attracted Jack to his wife. One can only speculate how the two women might have compromised because Mary Ann died two years after the wedding.

The newlyweds rented a small apartment, but when Margaret became pregnant, Jack hired an architect to build a seventeen-room colonial brick house at 3901 Henry Avenue, not far from the Dobson estate. Following the birth of Margaret ("Peggy") in June 1925, the Kellys moved to their new home in Germantown where John Brendan II was born in May 1927. With Jack's first glance at his son came a pledge that "Kell" would someday win the Diamond Sculls.

The Kellys' third child was Grace, named after Jack's sister, who had been studying to be an actress when she died at the age of twenty-two. In June 1933, Elizabeth Anne, nicknamed "Lizanne," was born, the last of the Kelly clan.

Margaret was the disciplinarian, never threatening "Wait until your father comes home!" because Jack had no set schedule. He went to work six days a week, began a string of extramarital affairs, and delved into politics. He was rarely seen without a hat because his hair was thinning out. Friends said he was a proud man. His critics thought of him as vain. Assuming he was both, Jack took charge of his son's scull training, and when the boy was only seven years of age, he was rowing the river. Kell was a born athlete and wanted to participate in other sports, especially football, but his father wouldn't allow it. One goal was a sure goal. As a teenager, Kell had no time for his school buddies or for dating. Sadder yet was his lack of enthusiasm for sculling, but he would eventually achieve his father's revenge.

When Jack was home, which was seldom, he romped with Peggy, the apple of his eye. Observers were bewildered and yet fascinated that he barely acknowledged Grace and Lizanne. A family friend said, "Jack always bragged about Peggy. If she smiled, he said, 'Look at that!' If she told a cute story, he roared with laughter. If she wore a new dress, Jack's eyes glowed with pride, 'Isn't she something!' If I brought a stranger to the Kelly house I told him to compliment Peggy, for God's sake! That was a sure way to win over Jack. He proved himself capable of being a warm and loving father but only with one of his children. Poor Grace and Lizanne sat on the sideline waiting for an invitation to join in, but that happened infrequently. If Jack's pride and joy had been his son, I could understand it, but Kell was ignored, too, when he wasn't in training."

Margaret indulged Lizanne, the baby of the family, and did not have the time or patience for a clinging Grace, who said in reflection, "We were always competing. Competing for everything — competing for love." Grace was a frail child in a family of robust and energetic athletes. Susceptible to allergies, lingering colds, and ear problems, she did not play and wrestle out-of-doors with her tomboy sisters. Margaret, however, did not pamper Grace, but when one's daughter becomes famous, the past is modified, particularly if you are the mother of a princess. Margaret told the press that Jack's mother accepted the death of her granddaughter Grace philosophically. "The namesake will have the talent," Mary Ann Kelly predicted, referring to her own daughter, Grace, who had died in the midst of her study of acting. Margaret claimed they all knew there was something different about Grace . . . her tranquility and quiet resourcefulness: "The other children were handsome, but Gracie was truly beautiful." She failed to mention her husband's comment: "I don't get that girl. We're an athletic family, very good athletes, and she can barely walk!"

Those who knew the Kellys well were either amused or nauseated by Margaret's description of how she was more conscious of Gracie's wants and needs than those of her other three children, and of how Jack wanted to protect and take care of his sickly little girl when he was actually disenchanted with her. "What's Grace sniveling about now?" he asked his wife. On one of her birthdays, no one in the family noticed the wrong number of candles on her cake. As the middle sister, she had no identity, but as a Kelly, she did not reveal her slights and disappointments. Born with a vivid imagination, Grace made up little plays with her dolls and learned to be quite content alone in her bedroom. As if they were devoted friends, she kept her doll collection into adulthood as a reminder of the many hours of happiness they had shared when there was no one else. When asked about the early years, Grace replied, "My older sister was my father's favorite, and there was the boy, the only son. Then I came, and then I had a baby sister, but I was never allowed to hold it. So I was always on my mother's knee, but I was pushed away."

Jack Kelly was annoyed that Grace refused to fight back. "Most kids do," he said. "Eventually, they get tired of being teased and abused, but our youngest could beat her up!" To his way of thinking, the children had to learn how to defend themselves — among themselves. Peggy wasn't punished for dragging Grace by the hair across the front lawn. She was rewarded instead. "I ordered her around," Peggy said, "told her to do this or get me that, and she did." Was Grace a weakling and a coward? She answered that question in an interview. "I don't like yelling and fighting, and I can't quarrel. Getting angry doesn't solve anything. I'd rather give in because bitter words tire me out. I'm not one to forget easily, and the hurt lasts for a long time."

Grace eventually outgrew her illnesses. She was a fine swimmer and played a good game of tennis. Her only desire to excel in sports was to please Jack, but she would never live up to his standards. He made a remark that Grace did not have the Kelly determination to win, win, win because she was enjoying herself too much. According to a friend of the family, "Jack Kelly was a firm believer that if you didn't want with every fiber of your heart and body to win at sports, you would never be a winner at anything. I felt sorry for Kell. Regardless of how many medals he won, his father expected one more or the kid was a total failure. I take a more optimistic view of Grace's situation because Jack didn't expect the impossible of her. In fact, she didn't exist. The first time I met the whole family, Jack forgot to introduce Grace, and she was the one I noticed first because of her ethereal quality that the others didn't have."

Grace was five when she was enrolled at Ravenhill, a convent school only a few blocks from home. The nuns remember her as quiet, poised, and dainty. Maybe they referred to her as "Princess." It's easy to look back and believe they did. Actually, Grace was not an outstanding child. In comparison to the other Kelly siblings, yes, but in school she was an average, well-behaved little girl with a cute face and sweet smile.

She spent summer holidays and weekends on the Jersey shore at the Kellys' Ocean City house, thriving in the salt air and building castles in the sand. She loved to swim and dived into the ocean waves without hesitation. Over the years, Grace looked forward to vacations in Ocean City and brought her own children there often.

Though all three sisters took ballet lessons, only Grace was inspired by the dance after seeing the Ballet Russes with her family in Philadelphia. She never expressed a desire to become a ballerina, but her enthusiasm in dancing class undoubtedly helped Grace get through the awkward transition of growing into her spindly legs.

With the other children at Ravenhill, she took part in school shows. Grace Kelly's first role was as the Virgin Mary in the annual Nativity play. Her performance consisted of walking on stage and laying down Baby Jesus with reverence. It seemed unlikely that the timid and quiet Grace would be at ease on the stage, but taking on the role of someone else was gratifying to her. As many actors have testified, becoming the character they were portraying was an escape from themselves. For Grace, this was the fantasy world that she had shared with her dolls, and she could make the transition with little effort. It was this inborn talent that eventually made her a fine actress.

After seeing a production at the Old Academy Players in East Falls, Grace decided to join the group. "I was eleven when I told my father I wanted to become an actress," she said. "He looked at me for a long time and then said, 'All right, Gracie, if that's what you want to do — go ahead.'" She made her stage debut the following year in *Don't Feed the Animals*.

It was Uncle George who gave his favorite niece encouragement though he confessed to her, "Your Aunt Grace wanted to go on the stage and I tried to discourage her because it's a hard life plagued with disappointments. As a struggling playwright, I wanted to protect her, but if I had it to do over again, I would have given her my blessings. Mother said my sister's namesake would have the talent, Grace, so give the theater a try or you'll wonder for the rest of your life what might have been."

In 1922, Grace received her first review in George's play, *The Torch Bearers*, for the Academy Players in Philadelphia: "Miss Kelly came through this footlight baptism of fire splendidly. From where I sat it appeared as if Grace Kelly should become the theatrical torch bearer of her family." When Jack was asked to comment, he emphasized that the Kellys were athletes. "Grace wants to act," he said, "and when she gets up on the stage, I

22

get a kick, but otherwise . . ." and then he shrugged it off. Margaret was not overly impressed either: "In her teen years, she was nothing but a giggly somebody with a high nasal voice. Her enjoyment of food gave her a little extra weight. And, like her father, she was nearsighted, which made it necessary for her to wear glasses. All in all, she was nobody's Princess Charming in those days."

Grace did not have fond memories of her teens. "I was shy," she said, "never much of an extrovert. They were wonderful years and terrible years. Anxious years. Not very happy."

When she enrolled in the ninth grade at Stevens School in Germantown, Grace had blossomed into a very pretty, willowy young lady with soft blond hair. Her clear white skin, compared to the acned and pimpled complexion of so many classmates, was her most outstanding attribute. Because Grace was tall for her age, older boys were attracted to her and she quickly cultivated a flirtatious response. She took advantage of this sudden attention that was foreign to her by going to dances with juniors and seniors. Her nervous giggle should have been a sure giveaway that Grace was only fourteen, but she was able to balance the silly laughter with her serious approach to life.

Many of Kell's buddies from William Penn Charter School were also interested in Grace. They had other excuses to visit the house that Jack built because the backyard had a tennis court that could be converted into a rink for ice hockey plus a swimming pool. The Kellys were well-acquainted with Kell's friends and their families, so Grace was allowed to attend football games, proms, and fraternity parties. One of these Penn Charter boys was Harper Davis, the son of a Buick salesman. He asked permission to take Grace on a double date with Kell. Margaret was taken aback because her daughter was only fourteen, but ". . . off they went, Gracie in her first long dress. Because she was so young, I waited until they got home." After that, they dated on a regular basis. Harper, according to Grace, was her first love, but in 1946, he became ill with multiple sclerosis. Before Harper entered the hospital, she visited him at home daily, and when he died in 1953, Grace flew from Hollywood to Philadelphia for his funeral. During her engagement to Prince Rainier, reporters asked Grace if she'd ever been in love before. "Yes," she replied, "I was in love with my first boyfriend. His name was Harper Davis, and he died."

Grace had many other boyfriends, according to her mother. "Men began proposing to her when she was barely fifteen. If she had added a charm to a bracelet for each proposal, she could scarcely be able to lift that bracelet today."

One of Grace's classmates at Stevens said, "She was a wild teenager." Another commented, "There was nothing cold about Grace. She was a normal girl on a date."

Her 1947 yearbook prophesied: "Miss Grace P. Kelly, famous star of screen and radio." Her ambition was — Broadway!

After Grace's graduation, the Kellys crossed the Atlantic to watch Kell row at Henley. They stayed at the old Red Lion hotel and had the great satisfaction of seeing him win. Kell would repeat this victory in 1949. "At last," Jack cheered. "After twenty-seven years of waiting and hoping, the name of John B. Kelly is on the Diamond Sculls!"

Though George Kelly hoped Grace would attend the

American Academy of Dramatic Arts in New York City, Jack wanted her to go to college, but there had been so much emphasis on Kell's winning the Diamond Sculls that no one gave Grace's future education much consideration. To appease her parents, she applied for admission to Bennington College in Vermont; she was turned down because she had only one year of high school mathematics. Grace added, "We applied too late, anyway. By then, the boys were coming home from the war and given preference." With that obligation behind her, Grace expressed the desire to enroll at the American Academy. Margaret was afraid for her little girl all alone in the big city, but Jack was so sure his daughter wouldn't qualify that he gave his consent. "I give her two weeks and she'll be back home," he said.

Grace faced a similar problem at the American Academy as she had with Bennington College — the enrollment books were closed for the 1947-48 session. However, when Emil E. Diestel, Secretary and Treasurer of the Academy, found out George Kelly was her uncle, he offered to "look into the matter." She was given thirty pages of script to learn for an audition the following day. Some sources claim that Grace would have been accepted regardless of how well she read. Others are adamant that her uncle's name merely gave Grace an opportunity to audition. After that, she was on her own.

George Kelly's first Broadway hit, *The Torch Bearers* in 1922, was followed two years later by *The Show-Off.* In 1925, he won the Pulitzer Prize for *Craig's Wife*, which was made into a well-received 1936 movie starring Rosalind Russell and which was later remade into a 1950 movie with Joan Crawford entitled *Harriet Craig*. This was not

George's first Hollywood encounter. *The Show-Off* was revised for the screen in 1926 with Louise Brooks, in 1934 with Spencer Tracy, and again in 1946 with Red Skelton. The noted playwright had little respect for Tinseltown compared to the theater, and his niece felt the same way for a long time.

On August 20, 1947, Grace auditioned at the Academy, located in the Carnegie Hall building on 57th Street and Seventh Avenue. She read from her Uncle George's play, *The Torch Bearers*. Emil Diestel noted in his report that she was a lovely child and thought that Grace had dramatic instinct, imagination, and intelligence, but her voice was too nasal. As a result, she was enrolled as a junior and would begin classes in October.

Grace told her mother, "At last, I'm really going to do what I've always wanted to do."

It has been said that the Academy was the best finishing school in America. As a former student, I can verify that. My own father did not recognize my voice on the telephone after two months of diction lessons. We were told from day one that before we set foot on stage, we had to learn to walk, talk, and breathe all over again. It was basic training for the theater and a rebirth for anyone who wanted a new start in life. Though I did not pursue an acting career, the fundamentals I learned at the Academy remained with me. I continue to walk with my knees slightly bent, which gives the body balance and relaxes the legs. If I'm nervous before giving a speech, I go off by myself and rotate my head very, very slowly with my mouth open and my tongue hanging loose. Doing this in class was embarrassing at first, needless to say. Breathing from the diaphragm was a most important lesson. Touching the back of the upper and lower teeth with the tongue is excellent for good pronunciation. We were also taught the art of applying make-up, how to open the door and enter a room gracefully, how to sit down and get up again, how to walk up and down the stairs, how to get in and out of a car, how to put on a pair of gloves, and how to smoke a cigarette.

We had to be dressed properly every day and act accordingly. Charles Jehlinger, vice-president of the Academy, was the director of plays in the second session but kept an eye on the decorum and manners of all the students. Jehlinger, nicknamed "Jelly," was directing Colleen Dewhurst and said, "Do it like a lady!"

"What's a lady?" she asked.

"A lady is a woman who would do anything, but only as a lady would do it!"

He might have said that to Grace Kelly, who surely made it her credo. Observing life outside the Kelly cocoon, she said, "I had to find out who I was." Her parents made sure, however, that Grace did not have too much freedom. The Barbizon Hotel at 140 East 63rd Street was the proper place for wealthy young ladies to live in the late forties. No men were allowed in the hotel after 10 p.m. and never in the girls' living quarters. I lived at the Barbizon but can't say I ever got used to the matrons checking my room on their "manhunt" once or twice a day. My roommates said that the living quarters were so small that it was impossible to hide even a small man, and even then, ". . . one of us would have to go." We eventually moved to the Rehearsal Club, a very proper boarding house for women in show business. Re-created for the 1937 movie *Stage Door* with Katharine Hepburn, the Rehearsal Club was a charming brownstone. Men were permitted in the living room until 10 p.m. and the rules were strictly enforced. We could, however, chat with our dates on the front steps provided we didn't neck or linger too long.

I asked Brian if he had mentioned the Rehearsal Club to Grace. "As a matter of fact," he said, "I always recommended the Club because all the girls who stayed there were studying opera, ballet, drama, and art. The older ones helped out the newcomers, gave them advice and, above all, confidence. I found the Barbizon to be rather cold, but it's all a matter of taste."

"The girls at the Rehearsal Club were more mature," I said.

"Precisely. The Barbizon catered to daughters of the rich who had never been away from home. Many of them were like silly coeds trying to get away with something. Did you find this so?"

"Quite often word got out that someone smuggled a man in just for a prank. I'm told by a Barbizon girl who knew Grace at the time that she got away with it."

"She joked about it later on," Brian said. "I didn't believe her because Grace would have been risking everything. Had she been caught, the Kellys would have dragged her back home. But I went along with the story and asked Grace how she could take a chance like that. She said, 'There's only one reason why a woman would risk everything for a man. To be with him, of course.' Hogwash! She wasn't a virgin, but that's immaterial. The idea that girls are protected from men by residing at the Barbizon is ludicrous. They're free to go to a man's apartment or hotel room. On my first date with Grace, I was prepared to take her home right after dinner, but she said it was too early. We went to my suite at the Warwick and talked for hours about the Academy. She put on a few skits. As I recall, she was supposed to be a squirrel. Then a palm tree. Grace was doing her homework."

Anyone else might have snickered, but Brian sat through many of my pantomime assignments. He was an attentive audience, and his comments were taken seriously because he was closely connected with the theater. I can identify with Grace practicing her next day's assignment in his hotel suite because my first meeting with Brian was similar. We had met on a blind date. I wanted to be an actress and he knew Howard Hughes. Simple as that. As for intimacy, Brian allowed nature to take its course. In the fifties, young girls were assumed (and expected) to be virgins. The ones who were not pretended they were.

Once Grace got to know and trust Brian, she told him about her frustrating teen years. It was impossible to go all the way with her dates because she knew that few boys could keep a secret.

"Grace made it happen," Brian said. "Apparently, he was an older man and married, but they weren't involved. She didn't want to come to New York and not know what sex was about." Brian couldn't help telling her it was very sad that someone as soft and pretty as she did not have the love and romance that ought to be part of a girl's first sexual encounter. Grace patted his hand and said, "It wasn't all that bad."

Before she finished the first year of school, there was no trace of her Philadelphia accent and she spoke in a lower and gentler tone of voice. When the Kelly brood made fun of her new manner of speaking, Grace retorted, "I *must* talk this way for my work." She was breaking away from the family and was very anxious to be financially independent of Jack, who was anything but generous with her allowance. Seemingly, it was another battle of the wills between father and daughter. Having predicted that she would come running home, he challenged Grace by giving her little spending money; but she became even more determined to be on her own in New York, a city that gobbled up attractive young actresses who needed a job. Grace was just another pretty girl with one exception — she had a "scrubbed" look that was hard to find in our generation of black-lined eyes and defined brows. Big breasts were the rage, too, thanks to Marilyn Monroe and Jane Russell. If we didn't have the busty look, we bought it. Not Grace. She never wore falsies or heavy make-up. This wholesomeness got her on the covers of *Redbook, Ladies Home Journal,* and the original *Cosmopolitan* that catered to housewives before Helen Gurley Brown revamped it for the single working girl. Grace was also in advertisements for a variety of products that included Old Gold tobacco and Electrolux. She was a candidate for Miss Rheingold and lost, but her picture was plastered all over New York, giving Grace some credibility. She was soon earning more than $400 a week, which would relieve Jack Kelly of his "financial burden."

Photographer Ruzzie Green was skeptical about Grace's future in modeling. "If she lacked anything, it was sex appeal," he said. "She was what we called 'nice clean stuff' in our business. She wasn't a top model and never would be. She was the girl next door. No glamour, no oomph, no cheesecake. She had lovely shoulders but no chest." Grace hated modeling, anyway, and was doing it only for the money until she graduated and could concentrate on getting a part in a Broadway play.

As I mentioned in the Introduction, there was a good deal of talk about Grace when I was a student at the Academy. The brother of one of her classmates sat next to me on our first day at school and we were bonded by fear for a month or so. He was trying hard to be impartial about Grace but said, "My sister thought she was a cold snob who came from a rich family and that she got through school because her uncle was George Kelly. I saw Grace in a few plays at the Academy and she was only fair. Sis was worse, though. They were both outclassed. Grace was involved with one of the directors and should have had the edge. That was another thing that annoyed my sister."

All writers who review Grace Kelly's life include her first love, Harper Davis, also her first boyfriend from New York who was invited home to be scrutinized by the family. Now, Mrs. Kelly noted not only a change in her daughter's speech, posture, and manners but also a starry-eyed look. "There's a man in your life, isn't there?" she asked Grace.

"Yes," was the dreamy response.

"Do you want to talk about it?"

"He's a director at school."

"Older?" Ma Kelly asked.

"A few years . . ."

"Catholic?"

"No . . ."

"Are you in love with him, Gracie?"

"Yes."

Most mothers would have been in a dead faint, but not Margaret Majer Kelly. She wanted to meet the city slicker who was *not* going to marry her daughter.

CHAPTER
THREE

In Love with Passion

Though Grace was dating several men at the Academy, she was seriously involved with one of the instructors. To appease her parents, she was also seeing a wealthy young athlete from Philadelphia. Ma Kelly was becoming more and more aware of a new Grace emerging. "But during the second year of school," Margaret said, "she had that faraway look. I knew the symptoms only too well and asked if there was a man. Gracie told me about him. She was beguiled by the fact he was going to make her a big star. I tried to convince her that she could make it on her own, but when she talked about this director, Gracie was carried away. There were all these big things they were going to do."

Don Richardson was Jewish, separated from his wife, and nine years older than Grace. Even if he hadn't had these three strikes against him, the Kelly clan was prepared to throw him out of the game anyway. He was invited for the weekend to the house that Jack built on Henry Street. Margaret told Kell to bring over three of his biggest athletic friends on that Friday evening. "I got the word this guy was a creep," Kell related in an interview. "When he came in with Grace, we gave him the grip and he landed on the floor. She wouldn't speak to me after that." Richardson apparently went through the tortures of the damned. During dinner, Grace said nothing while Kell's buddies made sarcastic remarks directed at Don.

Ma Kelly asked him, "How is my daughter doing in school?"

"She's going to be a great movie star," he replied.

Jack, from the other end of the table, commented, "She'll get over that nonsense and settle down."

The next morning, Margaret had the nerve to go through Richardson's belongings. Not only did she find legal papers pertaining to his forthcoming divorce but several prophylactics as well. It seems that Grace had forgotten to mention her boyfriend was married. The condoms spoke for themselves. Kell said his mother told Richardson to leave the house, and Grace was forbidden to see him again.

Back in New York, Brian was concerned because she wasn't returning his phone calls. He knew her graduation from the Academy was approaching and hoped she'd have dinner to celebrate. "At first, the Barbizon operator told me Grace wasn't in," he said, "but after a while, I got suspicious and went to the hotel only to discover she had checked out. For all I knew, she was dying or dead. I called the Kelly house in Philadelphia and her mother answered the phone. I pretended to be the father of a classmate who wanted to invite Grace to a graduation party at the Plaza Hotel. Mrs. Kelly was very sweet, very gracious. 'I must decline on Grace's behalf,' she said, 'because she'll be in New York only for graduation.' I thanked her and hung up fast before she asked me to repeat my name. Grace sent me a postcard from the Jersey shore saying she'd see me in the fall. Four or five months later, we had dinner and she said simply that her parents were upset that she was dating a married man and forbade her to come back to New York except for graduation."

The summer of 1949 was a turning point for Grace. She had been torn from the man she loved, denied the right to look for a job in the New York theater, and was more distant than ever from her family. Discussions about New York were tinged with Jack's threatening to have her followed. There were rules and regulations set forth that made the future look very bleak. The alarming possibility that Grace was no longer a virgin cast a dark shadow over the trusting relationship she once had with her parents. Grace did not try to defend herself because she could not forgive them for the horrid way they had treated Richardson without giving him a chance. The breach in the family was never completely mended, and Grace would never be the same again. As her twentieth birthday approached, she wanted more latitude. She had loved and been loved and had experienced the height of passion that no college boy from Germantown could offer. Like her Uncle George, she had needs and desires far removed from the regimented dictates of Margaret and Jack Kelly.

Grace had every intention of seeing Richardson again, but looking for a job in the theater after graduating from the Academy was uppermost in her mind. Sitting on the beach in Ocean City was a waste of valuable time and, apparently, the Kellys thought so, too. Grace was allowed to audition at the Bucks County Playhouse in New Hope, Pennsylvania, not far from Philadelphia. That Jack knew the owner might have had something to do with Grace's getting a job. The Playhouse cast suspected George Kelly used his influence because she made her debut in *The Torch*

Bearers playing the role of an amateur actress. Grace had to cope with jealousy and resentment from the other players, but she came through like a professional.

In the fall of 1949, Grace returned to the Barbizon in New York and defied the Kellys by seeing Richardson, who told biographer James Spada that her father had tried to bribe him with a Jaguar. When that had failed, there had been threatening phone calls warning him to stay away from Grace or "we'll break every bone in your body." Despite these obstacles, the romance lasted for another few years. Richardson, who has since been married six times, claims he broke up with Grace because she was seeing men "who I found unworthy of her," but their friendship endured and they corresponded until her death. His observations of Grace coincide with what Brian said: "She came back to New York like a kid who'd been through basic training at Fort Dix. Ready for action on all fronts."

Grace began to make the rounds of theatrical agencies and auditioning for plays. She said, "My height, five-feet-six-and-a-half, was a handicap. 'You're very good, my dear, but too tall.'* Lack of experience was another drawback. The American Academy of Dramatic Arts had credibility, but my degree was worthless without experience." Grace read for thirty-eight parts and was turned down. Brian used his connections in the theater and told me frankly that Grace was not a good stage actress. "She didn't have the voice or the presence," he commented. "Casting directors said she needed extensive training in voice projection. That was

---

*Margaret Kelly gave Grace's height as five-feet-seven-and-a-half. Edith Head said she was five-feet-seven even.

nonsense. She simply wasn't meant for the stage."

Noted actor Raymond Massey did not agree. "I auditioned twenty-one girls," he said. "Grace was my second choice and by the time she left, the part was hers." Massey was directing and acting in the Broadway play *The Father*, a harsh story about a Swedish cavalry captain who is driven to madness by his evil wife's accusations that their daughter is not his.

Grace called her mother and gushed, "Guess what? I'm going to be in a Broadway play with Raymond Massey! I think I got the part because he's taller than I am."

The Father tried out in Boston and opened at the Cort Theatre in New York on November 16, 1949. *The New York Times* said in its review, "Grace Kelly gives a charming, pliable performance as the bewildered, broken-hearted daughter." The acclaimed playwright George Jean Nathan wrote, "Only the novice Grace Kelly, convincing as the daughter, relieves the stage from the air of a minor hinterland stock company on its off days."

The Kellys were in the audience on opening night, but Jack was more enthusiastic over Kell's winning the Diamond Sculls again. Raymond Massey, who used to row in Toronto, was surprised to see Jack at the cast party.

"What on earth are you doing here, Kelly?"

"My daughter's in your play."

"Grace? Grace Kelly?" Massey exclaimed. "I had no idea you were her father. What a delightful surprise!"

Jack changed the subject. "Did you hear about my son scoring an easy victory at the Henley Regatta?"

The Father closed after sixty-nine performances. Grace said in an interview, "I had to wait two years for another play. People were confused with my type, but they agreed on one thing — I was either too tall, too leggy, or too chinny."

Still, she had caught the attention of television producer Fred Coe and a close friend of the Kelly family, Isaac Levy, who was the founder of CBS. Grace did a series of television shows, including "Philco/Goodyear Playhouse," "Studio One," "Lux Video Theatre," "Hallmark Hall of Fame," "Robert Montgomery Presents," "Lights Out," and "Playhouse 90." Doing live television was no easy task. The actors had only one chance, camouflaging errors and blunders as they went along. Facing a TV camera was do or die in the early fifties but was also an excellent breeding ground for young actors. Grace appeared in more than sixty television shows, affording her enough money to get out of the Barbizon and into an apartment of her own.

"Grace was very excited," Brian said, "but her parents were not. Living at the Barbizon represented a temporary arrangement, but signing a lease was entirely different. She was adamant with or without permission. Mrs. Kelly insisted she find a respectable roommate. 'My mother's concept of respectable is a girl from a fine family who's attended the best schools,' Grace laughed. 'I had Sally in mind, anyway.' What tickled me was Mrs. Kelly's reason for liking Grace's choice. It seems the roommate could speak French fluently and mama wanted Grace to learn a prestigious language. I was amused because the two girls were actresses and hardly ever home at the same time. Obviously, Mrs. Kelly was concerned more about appearances than reality."

Grace's new apartment was located on the ninth floor of Manhattan House at East 66th Street and Third Avenue.

There was one bedroom, a kitchen, a bath, and a terrace facing south. Margaret took more of an interest in the furnishings than her daughter, and the place was usually strewn with books, scripts, and clothes. "Oh, Gracie," she said, bending over, picking up, and straightening up. "I hope when you get married you have someone to clean up after you!" Margaret related this story often when her daughter became a princess and had a multitude of servants at her beck and call.

Grace's roommate, Sally Parrish, was a Southern girl from Virginia. After two years studying drama at Sarah Lawrence, she transferred to the American Academy of Dramatic Arts, where she met Grace. Sally worked in stock plays and did some television, but when the right man came along, she gladly gave up her career for marriage in 1954. Two years later, she was one of Grace's bridesmaids at the royal wedding. Ironically, Sally's married name is Richardson, but her husband is no relation to the Academy director who some people think was the love of Grace's life. Don might have given the impression he was filling her head with stardust, but he introduced Grace to agent Edith Van Cleve of MCA (Music Corporation of America), one of the most powerful talent agencies in the world. Van Cleve knew at first glance that the elegant blonde would be perfect for Hollywood but kept this to herself because her new client was determined to make it in the theater.

In the early months of 1950, Grace did some modeling, worked on television, and dated a variety of men, including the Shah of Iran, who was in New York for only a week. He and Grace went out on the town every night. She said one of the Secret Service men asked her if she would please stay home one night because they were exhausted. Grace had no intention of doing any such thing, and the Shah was just as enthused and energetic. At the opera, she was spellbound when everyone stood up as they entered. The Kellys browsed through the newspapers daily to find out all about the wonderful time their daughter was having with the Shah of Iran but were horrified over an article that mentioned he had given her very expensive jewelry from Van Cleef and Arpels. Margaret rushed to New York and confronted Grace.

"What did he give you?"

"Oh, Mother . . ."

"Where are the jewels?"

"In my dresser drawer."

"Get them!"

Grace showed the jewelry to her mother — a pin in the shape of a gold cage with a diamond bird inside, a gold vanity case with thirty-two big diamonds on the clasp, and a bracelet watch with a dome of pearls and diamonds covering the face.

"Well!" Margaret bellowed. "You'll give them back."

"That would be rude."

"Your father says they have to be returned."

"It just isn't done, Mother. I can't."

Grace either defied her parents or convinced them that it would be an insult to the Shah if she sent back his gifts. She kept the jewelry until shortly before her wedding in Monaco. "I can't wear them after I'm married," she told a friend.

Brian does not recall seeing Grace's elaborate jewelry. "Whatever she wore," he said, "was expensive and subdued. She wasn't the type to wear anything that was obviously given to her by a suitor. The Shah of Iran lavished Grace with more gifts than reported, and I'm sure he was very close to her during his stay in New York."

"How do you know?" I asked.

"Because she was mesmerized by him. Their relationship wasn't serious. It was brief and beautiful. The story of Grace's love life. I knew she dated Prince Aly Khan because I saw them together. He gave her jewelry, too, but you must understand that this sort of generosity was common in those days."

Aly Khan is best remembered today for his marriage to actress Rita Hayworth, but there is much more to tell about this charismatic man. When he was eighteen, his father, the Aga Khan III, ruler of a Muslim sect called the Ismailes, sent Aly to an Arab doctor in Cairo to learn and perfect *Imsák*. It is a philosophy of the Orient that proper lovemaking is scientifically taught and not a result of overwhelming passion. Only when a woman is completely satisfied does the man allow himself to achieve a climax, if then. Aly mastered this art, called *Imsák*. Though he was known to be with several women in one night, his reaching a climax was the highest compliment a woman could receive from Aly. He was particularly attracted to tall, slim women with small bosoms. Grace's posture and the way she walked caught his eye right away. Though Aly was only five-foot-eight, a bit chubby, and balding, his appearance did not detract from his charm. He flirted unmercifully, but each affair was precious to him. "There will never be anyone to replace you, my love," was one of his brief farewells. When a lady assumed she had been forgotten, Aly would send hundreds of flowers to "my lost love."

International party hostess Elsa Maxwell, a close friend of Aly's and the one who introduced him to Rita Hayworth, said, "In Europe, a woman was déclassé, démodé, nothing, if she hadn't been to bed with him. If Aly was part of her past, a lady had a better chance of marrying a man of substance."

In the January 1989 edition of *Celebrity Plus*, Don Richardson is quoted in an article about Grace: "She called me up and invited me to come and have dinner," he said, "and then she brought out the bracelet. I recognized it. When Aly Khan had a date with a girl, he used to give her a cigarette case with one emerald in it. When he slept with her, he gave her the bracelet. I dropped it into her fishbowl and left in a huff. That was the end of our romance. I thought her values had gone gaflooey, you know."

One of my roommates at the Rehearsal Club went out with Aly Khan and was in a state of euphoria for several weeks. She didn't brag or name-drop. In fact, Carole said very little about it until one evening when we were sitting on the front steps people-watching. "He made me feel as if I were the only woman in the world," she said.

"Who?" I asked.

"Aly."

"Was it worth it for only one night?"

"Forever, my dear. Forever."

"I pity the other men in your life, Carole."

"You're missing the whole point," she said with a glowing smile. "I know now what I *won't* settle for."

"A commoner who can't make love?"

"No, a commoner who doesn't give a shit."

We had almost forgotten about Aly Khan when Carole received a huge bouquet of flowers. The note read, "I'll never forget you. Love, Aly."

Carole did not take the note seriously, but it was a

romantic gesture after so many months. "Aly has a long list of names, most likely," she laughed, "and someone else sends the flowers."

I was intrigued now more than ever. "What was he like, Carole? What did he talk about?"

"Me," she replied. "Aly was very attentive at dinner. In the limousine on the way home, he was romantic and amorous. I feel sorry for any girl who falls in love with him."

"I've been dying to ask you one question, Carole."

"What was he like in bed? Aside from his staying power, Aly knows how to arouse a woman. He knew more about me than I did. It was a lesson in lovemaking that I shall never forget. I told him as much, and Aly said, 'Guide your gentlemen friends or tell them what you want.'"

"And did you?"

"Yes, and only the creeps took it as an insult to their manhood. If it hadn't been for Aly, I might never have known myself as a complete woman."

Since Aly Khan's lifetime, sex has been talked and written about freely in our society, emphasizing the male's selfishness and the female's ignorance in the bedroom. It's old hat now, but forty years ago the woman was merely a receptacle.

I don't know if Carole received one of Aly's famous bracelets. It's too late to find out because she died ten years ago. Instead of pursuing ballet, Carole was happily married to an engineer from Pasadena.

Why this discourse about Aly Khan? Because he has been overlooked in the telling of Grace Kelly's romantic life. The Shah of Iran is always mentioned because they were seen together in public and his gifts to her received a good deal of notoriety; but he's insignificant compared to Aly Khan, whom author Leonard Slater referred to in 1964 as "Prince, adventurer, diplomat, deity, and perhaps the greatest lover of our time."

Grace, who had all the qualities Aly admired in a woman, met him at an exclusive party in New York. She was consumed with curiosity about his reputation with women. The trick was *not* to fall in love with him. "Aly wasn't her type," Brian said, "but I thought he bore a striking resemblance to Prince Rainier."

Edith Van Cleve was responsible for getting Grace to Hollywood for her first movie role in the summer of 1950. Henry Hathaway was directing *Fourteen Hours* (1951) for Twentieth Century-Fox, a film based on a real-life drama of 1938 when a young man jumped to his death from a ledge of the Gotham Hotel. Grace was cast as "Mrs. Fuller," a neatly dressed young woman discussing divorce plans with her lawyer when the suicide takes place across the street. After witnessing the tragic event, she changes her mind about the divorce.

Actor Richard Basehart played the jumper, Agnes Moorehead portrayed his mother, Barbara Bel Geddes was the sweetheart, and Paul Douglas played a good-natured cop. Grace could not have been in more talented company. They had all been in the theater, with the exception of Miss Moorehead, who made her debut on Broadway a year later.

Hollywood did not impress Grace. She had the same opinion as Ava Gardner, who said in 1941, "Hollywood is just a dreary, quiet suburb of Los Angeles, with droopy palm trees, washed-out buildings, cheap dime stores, and garish theaters, a far cry from the razzle-dazzle of New York."

Conversely, Joan Crawford said, "Everything was so bright and cheerful." Myrna Loy commented, "Hollywood was fabulous! It is when you come upon it." Lauren Bacall, another graduate of the American Academy, said, "Hollywood is so clean. I had never known there were cities as pure-looking. Beautiful!"

Grace's reaction was based, primarily, on her love for New York City and the theater. She turned down an offer from MGM to sign a stock contract because it represented to her nothing more than a string of small parts in films. A producer at Twentieth Century-Fox thought Grace had no sex appeal and that it would be a waste of time to give her a screen test. Director Sidney Lumet said, "She has no stove in her belly."

Grace returned to New York, bought a mink stole with her earnings from *Fourteen Hours*, and joined Sanford Meisner's acting classes at the Neighborhood Playhouse. One day she received a call at school from her agent: "Meet me right away at Gregory Ratoff's office!"

"Who is he?" Grace asked.

"A director at Twentieth Century-Fox, and he's testing for the leading role in a movie called *Taxi*."

"I have to go home and change," Grace said. "I have on an old skirt and blouse. I'm not wearing any make-up and . . ."

"You haven't time for that. Leave this minute and I'll be waiting for you."

When Grace walked into Ratoff's office, he knew that she was right for the part of the plain Irish immigrant girl in *Taxi* (1953). "She's perfect!" he exclaimed. "I like her because she's not pretty." Grace perfected her Irish brogue and made the screen test. She was excited about *Taxi* because it was going to be filmed in New York and would not involve a studio contract, but the English actress Constance Smith was chosen instead.

"Grace wasn't only disappointed," Brian said, "she was stunned. Someone closely associated with *Taxi* in New York convinced her that she was a cinch for the part, but the final decision was made in Hollywood. Grace was going out with casting directors, producers, and agents, and it paid off to some extent. She was making good money doing commercials and acting on television, a very competitive business."

I asked Brian if he knew anything about Grace's relationship with "Philippe of the Waldorf."

"They were lovers," he replied. "Claude Philippe was the general manager of the Waldorf and the originator of the April in Paris Ball. He knew everyone in the Social Register by their first names. Philippe was a married man in his early forties when Grace met him. He was her entrée to exclusive parties. That's how she met Aly Khan. Claude Philippe was a discreet ladies' man or, to put it bluntly, a royal cocksman. Grace mentioned him in such a way that I knew damn well they were intimately involved, but Grace truly enjoyed sex. She was very warm, loving, giving, and emotional. There was nothing cheap or phony about her passion. I had more respect for Grace than most girls who slept around and hated every minute of it. I'm defending Grace but not condoning her frivolousness because word got around she could be had."

Claude Philippe's first three marriages ended in divorce. He was survived by a fourth wife when he died in 1978.

*   *   *

Though *Taxi* was well-received by the critics, Constance Smith was not convincing as the young Irish immigrant girl, and her brogue left a lot to be desired. By the time the film was released in January 1953, Grace was on the brink of Hollywood stardom. Her screen test for Gregory Ratoff was put to good use by her agents at MCA, and what appeared to be a setback for Grace was actually a blessing in disguise.

In the spring of 1951, Grace was asked to join the prestigious Elitch's Garden Theatre in Denver, Colorado, for a season of summer stock. At the same time, Hollywood director Fred Zinnemann was considering Grace for a small part in *High Noon*, a low-budget Western with Gary Cooper, that was supposed to begin filming in August. The two projects conflicted, but Edith Van Cleve advised Grace to go ahead with summer stock because Hollywood production schedules were unpredictable.

Grace flew in from Denver to see Zinnemann, who had never interviewed an actress wearing white gloves before. He never failed to mention this, but added, "It wasn't the white gloves. She was a very, very pretty girl." Grace was shy during the interview, answering "yes" or "no" to his questions. Not much for small talk, Zinnemann told her, "You should learn to speak to people when you meet them." It was a strained meeting, but her shyness convinced the director that she was right for the part of Gary Cooper's sweet Quaker wife in *High Noon*.

The summer of 1951 was one of the happiest for Grace. She was thrilled with the prospect of acting in a film with Gary Cooper while working with one of the best directors in Hollywood; but Grace returned to Denver with just as much enthusiasm over her participation in summer stock at Elitch's Garden Theatre.

"We had a grueling schedule of eleven plays in ten weeks," she said, ". . . closing in one, opening in another, and rehearsing something else. But we were too busy to be anything other than gratified." She was acclaimed in *The Man Who Came to Dinner* and *Ring Around the Moon*, to name a few. When the Kellys came to Elitch, Grace exclaimed, "I could stay here forever!" Margaret recognized the glow on her daughter's face and waited for the inevitable. This time the love of Grace's life was a tall, reserved Irishman with reddish blond hair. "I'd like you to meet Gene Lyons," she beamed. Margaret did her homework discreetly and found out Lyons was in the process of getting his marriage annulled. "What bothered me most," she said, "was Gracie's marrying someone in her own profession. He was a pleasant fellow, but not stable enough." Margaret did not express her opinion because she felt Grace was in love with love, not Lyons. With *High Noon* about to start shooting in California, the couple would have to separate anyway. This was some consolation to Margaret.

While Grace was enjoying the applause and her romance with Gene Lyons in Colorado, Gary Cooper checked into St. John's Hospital in Santa Monica for a hernia operation. He was legally separated from his wife, Rocky, and was seriously involved with actress Patricia Neal. Though Mrs. Cooper was a Catholic, the press indicated her attorneys were ready to negotiate a financial settlement in preparation for divorce. Rocky was dating millionaire Bob Six, who, according to close friends, was about to propose marriage.

When Gary checked out of the hospital, he drove to La Jolla Playhouse in San Diego to see Patricia in T. S. Eliot's *The Cocktail Party*. Because he appeared so pale and tired, reporters did not inquire into his personal life. Cooper was fifty years old and not in good health. An old injury to the hip made him limp in pain, and his recurring ulcer was giving him trouble. Professionally, the Montana cowboy was considered over the hill. He was offered *High Noon* after John Wayne, Charlton Heston, Marlon Brando, and Gregory Peck had turned it down.

The script was written by Carl Foreman after he was blacklisted by the House Un-American Activities Committee. He left the United States and settled in England. Producer Stanley Kramer approached John Wayne about playing Marshal Kane, who faces four outlaws alone when the townspeople refuse to support him. Wayne was bitterly opposed to the script and said a few years later, "I'll tell you about Carl Foreman and his rotten old *High Noon*. Everybody says it was a great picture because Gary Cooper and Grace Kelly were in it. It's the most un-American thing I've ever seen in my whole life! The last thing in the picture is ol' Coop putting the U.S. marshal's badge under his foot and stepping on it. I'll never regret having helped run Foreman out of this country!"

Though Gary agreed to do *High Noon* for a low salary, he was getting a percentage of the profits, making it possible for Kramer to produce the movie for only $750,000. Despite Cooper's ailments, he held on to the magnetism that women had found enormously attractive for more than twenty years. Perhaps he was more imposing with salt-and-pepper hair. His face, usually described as craggy, was considered rugged and strong in his middle years. If Cooper was over the hill in films, he was still true to the nickname "Studs" that Clara Bow had given him in 1927.

Though he would play opposite younger women in the late fifties, Gary wasn't feeling well and was not up to facing the camera with the likes of Grace Kelly. "They'll laugh at me," he scowled, looking at her photograph. Kramer assured him that she would be insignificant in the film.

CHAPTER
FOUR

Hollywood

Production on *High Noon* began in September of 1951 on location in California's Sonoma Mountains, where Gary Cooper had done many Westerns. In 1929, he had costarred and fallen in love with Lupe Velez during *Wolf Song* in Sonoma. Their stormy affair lasted for several years, but Gary's domineering mother saw to it that they never reached the altar. Lupe instead married Johnny ("Tarzan") Weissmuller and Cooper wed New York debutante Veronica ("Rocky") Balfe. However, Lupe and Gary never fell out of love, and when she became pregnant after her divorce from Weissmuller, there was only one solution. A devout Catholic, Lupe swallowed seventy-five Seconals on December 14, 1944. She left a suicide note to her boyfriend, Harald Ramond: ". . . I prefer to take my life away and our baby's before I bring him shame." Hushed about in Hollywood was that Lupe was protecting Cooper, whom she had been seeing on the sly. A few years later, he told a close friend, "I don't know if she was carryin' my baby. Coulda been."

Cooper was a notorious womanizer, but he was not immune to sorrow when his affairs with Clara Bow, Lupe, and Ingrid Bergman collapsed. In the fall of 1951,

Gary was living alone and facing another heartbreak over Patricia Neal.

"In my first talkie," Cooper recalled, "I said only two words, 'I do,' and that was the beginning of *High Noon*. Then the marshal kisses his pretty Quaker wife." It was not quite that simple, however. Hollywood kisses never are. They had to shoot the wedding scene over and over again. Gary took Grace in his arms and kissed her at least fifty times. He was tired and she was nervous, but it was the beginning of her first affair with a leading man. That Gary was twenty-eight years older than Grace only enhanced her attraction to him. The truth became apparent to the crew when she was going over her lines with Zinnemann one day. Cooper ambled over to them and offered to rehearse the dialogue with Grace. She smiled at him fondly.

Established stars of Cooper's stature rarely volunteered their time to assist a newcomer. It wasn't a case of being aloof or high and mighty. They did not want to play favorites or clash with the director's interpretation of the dialogue. There was time enough for that during rehearsals. Gary was a sweet and humble guy, but he indicated from the beginning of *High Noon* that he needed plenty of rest. Every day, however, he coached Grace or sat on the sidelines watching her rehearse.

Gary had invited screenwriter Bob Slatzer to drop by and discuss a fishing trip. The two men were sitting by themselves on the set. "Coop had just finished a scene with Grace," Slatzer said. "She was getting ready for some close-ups. Coop's eyes were fixed on her although we were a safe distance away."

"What do you think of that filly?" he asked Bob.

"She's all right. Good little actress."

"Yep. She's got a lot goin' for her."

Slatzer said the sparkle in Cooper's eyes revealed more than just admiration of her acting talents. When Grace finished her scene, she plopped herself on Gary's lap and kissed him on the cheek. He smiled and looked a little embarrassed, his face flushing red under the make-up. He wiped the lipstick off his cheek with a handkerchief. She was about to plant one on the other cheek, but he whispered, "Not here."

Grace listened intently while the two men talked about their fishing trip. "Going to take *me*?" she teased.

Cooper swallowed hard.

She pressed him for an answer and placed her hand on his knee. He blushed again, looked down at her hand, and tried to be casual. With a smile, he said, "Well, a . . . I don't think you'd enjoy fishin'."

There was a pause. Slatzer, sensing Gary's nervousness, asked her, "Have you ever been fishing?"

"Sure I have," she replied, then she winked and looked at Cooper. "I was just kidding about going along with you fellows."

"I figured," he sighed.

Slatzer stayed to have lunch with Cooper, but Grace did not sit at their table. When she threw a kiss in their direction, Gary mumbled to Bob, "That was for you."

"She was looking your way, Coop."

"Why don't you do something about that? I hear she's available."

"And compete with you?" Slatzer asked, laughing.

"I'm twice her age."

"I wouldn't let that stop me."

"It hasn't, but I don't need it."

Grace walked over to their table and looked at Gary. "You know that you don't act — you *react*!"

"Ain't that the way it's done?" he asked.

"We have a love scene to do later on. Are you ready?"

Again the silence was broken by Slatzer. "Coop, you're one lucky guy."

"Isn't he?" Grace said, smiling.

Gary was trying to finish his lunch. He chewed and swallowed hard, glanced over at Bob, and said, "Yep, guess I am."

Slatzer watched them film for the rest of the afternoon. Having been around Hollywood for a long time, he was not particularly interested in another one of Gary's flings. Bob was just as fascinated with the director, who was also paying a great deal of attention to Grace. "I was going over the script," he said, "and it seemed to me Fred Zinnemann was filming more of Grace than the script called for. His close-ups of her were endless. Katy Jurado had a heavier role, but he wasn't doing anything about it. She was ready to explode and I couldn't blame her. I thought Zinnemann had a thing going for Grace and found out later that I was right. Miles of her on film ended up on the cutting-room floor."

It was Grace and Gary who made the gossip columns. The frantic Kellys sent Lizanne to chaperon her sister, but when rumors of the affair persisted, Margaret rushed to California. Grace was not alone with Cooper on their last few dates to prove nothing but friendship existed between them. The Kellys would make a habit of chasing after Grace to give the impression she was properly chaperoned.

Gary told the press that Miss Kelly was very serious

about her work. "She was trying to learn," he commented. "You could see that. You can tell if a person really wants to be an actress. She was one of those people you could get that feeling about."

Grace had seen the rushes of *High Noon* and did not pretend she was pleased. "Everything is so clear working with Gary Cooper," she said. "When I look into his face, I can see everything he's thinking. But when I look into my own face, I see absolutely nothing." She was anxious to get back to her acting lessons in New York but spoke about Cooper all the time. He, in turn, constantly brought up her name in conversation. They loved each other for a brief time but were not "in love." Gary and Grace were too much alike — each was given to brief, intense affairs.

Bob Slatzer ran into Grace at the Polo Lounge in the Beverly Hills Hotel before she left Hollywood. "How about coming to a party?" she asked him.

"Will Coop be there?" Bob asked.

"He only comes around when I'm alone."

Slatzer went out with Grace on a few dates. Gossip travels fast in Tinseltown, and Cooper was curious. On a fishing trip with Bob, he asked about Grace. "I guess I'd kinda be out of school if I asked if you went to bed with her."

Slatzer grinned. "You would be."

"I shouldn't ask a thing like that."

Bob had never known Cooper to ask personal questions. "He was a very quiet and unassuming guy," Slatzer said, "and he minded his own business, but it took him a while to get Grace out of his system. He was being eaten up with the idea that she might have gone to bed with me."

Mrs. Kelly was asking questions, too, but Grace only

admitted to going out with Cooper a couple of times "because I'm in love with someone else."

"Not that boy I met in Denver?" Margaret wanted to know.

"He has a name, Mother. Gene Lyons."

"What kind of a courtship can it be? You'll be in New York and he'll be . . ."

"In New York, too," Grace interrupted. "Gene plans to study acting there."

"I wish you'd take more of an interest in your friends from Philadelphia."

"That's just it, Mother. They're not interested in the theater. Some of them told me they thought I was foolish to want to be an actress."

"Gracie, please be absolutely sure before you consider anything as final as marriage."

"Gene and I were apart for several months while I was in California. We survived it because of our love and our dedication to acting. We can help each other."

"He's a married man," Margaret reminded her.

"Gene's annulment will be coming through any day now."

"But you hardly know him, Gracie."

"He's highly regarded as an actor. One day he'll be one of the greats in the theater."

Grace accepted Gene's heavy drinking but she was not aware that he was an alcoholic. They acted out their doomed affair in *The Rich Boy*, an F. Scott Fitzgerald story adapted for the "Philco Television Playhouse" that aired in February 1952. Grace portrayed a debutante who leaves the man she loves because of his excessive drinking and who marries someone else. "You see, I am in love at last," she tells her former boyfriend. "I was only infatuated with you."

Grace, however, was very much in love with her shy, sensitive, and gentle Irish actor. It was no infatuation. Perhaps Grace described him best when she said, "Gene has a fragile psyche." Her close friends insist that he was the first mature love of her life, but they were not aware of Don Richardson, who, in turn, did not know Grace was involved with Lyons.

Brian did not get the impression she was interested in marriage because it might conflict with her career. "Grace undoubtedly fell in love quite often," he said. "She was a romanticist who wanted to belong. She envied her sisters and girlfriends getting married and having babies. At the time, it wasn't in the cards for Grace, and she knew it down deep inside."

Her desire to marry Lyons diminished with the realization that there was nothing she could do about his drinking. Grace tried to cope, believing that love would replace his inner conflict and the fears that made him self-destruct. A year after they met, her film career began to skyrocket, but she was still in love with Gene and continued to see him whenever possible. He got the part of the police commissioner on the popular weekly television program, "Ironside," with Raymond Burr. When the series ended in 1975, Lyons died an alcoholic down on his luck. There has been much speculation that Grace's stardom was the beginning of the end for Gene, but he was more depressed that she was interested in other men. Grace could only console herself knowing that he had chosen the bottle over her, hopeless as it was.

In the spring of 1952, Grace got her second role in a

Broadway play, *To Be Continued*. It opened at the Booth Theater on April 23 and flopped.

Meanwhile, the sneak preview of *High Noon* in Riverside, California, was such a disaster that Stanley Kramer wanted to shelve it. Bob Slatzer was right about Fred Zinnemann's obsession with Grace because she dominated the film. Journalist James Bacon said, "Whenever you see a preponderance of close-ups in a movie, you can always be sure that the director is in love with the star." Film cutter Elmo Williams begged for one weekend with the movie, and Kramer gave his consent. Simply stated, *High Noon* was edited into a classic. Williams took out most of the love story and all but a few close-ups of Grace. "I confined the action to the actual hour of high noon," Williams said, "and inserted more ticking of the clock. I could see that Coop's painful ulcer was an asset in the suspense of a man about to face four killers by himself." Williams also came up with the idea of using *The Ballad of High Noon*, which tells the story of Marshal Kane's lonely vigil. Elmo Williams won an Oscar for editing and Gary Cooper was chosen Best Actor of 1952 for *High Noon*. Backstage afterward, he said to a friend, "First time in the history of the Academy an ulcer ever won an Oscar."

Cooper's costars were praised for their fine support and teamwork by critics, but Grace went unnoticed. Zinnemann said she was very, very wooden, ". . . but it fit her part well." Alfred Hitchcock described Grace as "mousy." Director John Ford was bored with her performance. "All she did," he said, "was shoot a guy in the back. Cooper should have given her a boot in the pants and sent her back East." Ford was casting for *Magambo* and was looking for an actress to play the prim wife of an Englishman in this remake of

Red Dust, which had been filmed in 1932. MCA suggested Ford view Grace's *Taxi* test, and the director changed his mind. "That dame has breeding and class," he told MGM mogul Dore Schary, "but I'd like to see her in color."

Grace arrived in Hollywood on September 3, 1951, for the screen test, which was a complete success. Schary referred to it as "stunning." John Ford agreed. The reluctant one was Grace, who would lose the part if she did not sign a seven-year contract with MGM. Negotiations began with Lucille Ryman Carroll, the head of talent at Metro.

"I insist on time off to work in the theater," Grace said.

Mrs. Carroll agreed to give her one year off after three and the right to make her home base in New York.

"I also want it stipulated that I can choose my own parts," Grace spoke up.

"That isn't possible."

"Suppose the role doesn't suit me?"

"Trust me, my dear. We're the best judge of that."

Grace signed with MGM because she wanted to see Africa and work with Clark Gable. Much has been said about her contractual demands, but she gained nothing more than a reputation for being a gutsy lady. As for the studio's allowing her to work on the stage, this exposure could only benefit Grace and serve as free publicity for the studio. An executive at MGM said, "Nobody in Hollywood was interested in Grace Kelly because she hadn't done anything impressive. I think she knew this and accepted $750 a week instead of the usual $1,500."

Over the years, Grace stressed her overwhelming desire to go to Africa with Clark Gable and the legendary director John Ford. "Maybe if the movie was on location in Arizona," she said, "I wouldn't have done *Mogambo*." It appears, however, that the "King of Hollywood" was as much an incentive as the Dark Continent.

It was actor Stewart Granger's idea to do a remake of *Red Dust* following his success in *King Solomon's Mines* (1950). Schary, who had replaced Louis B. Mayer, went ahead with the script but decided it was Gable whose career was in danger. He sweetly told Granger that several months away from his wife, Jean Simmons, might jeopardize their marriage and "besides, Gable needs all the help he can get right now." It wasn't that simple, however. Schary told Clark he would get what he wanted — Ava, big-game hunting, and *Mogambo*. Gable was delighted, but Schary gave him the bad news. "The Mau Mau are rebelling," he said, "so there will be a delay."

"Don't you think we should get started before they go on the warpath?" Gable asked.

"Yes, but we haven't cast the part of Linda."

"Then I'll go fishing."

"No, you'll go to London and make *Never Let Me Go* [1953]."

"Why me?"

"Do you want *Mogambo*?"

Gable grinned. "Yeah, but I have to pay a price. Is that it?"

"Look at it this way, Clark. Gene Tierney will be your leading lady in *Never Let Me Go*, and I'm trying like hell to sign her for the part of Linda in *Mogambo*. See if you can change her mind. Meanwhile, get your goddamn divorce from Sylvia and don't miss the boat for France. Got it?"

"Yeah."

Gable was not always as cooperative, but he was an

avid hunter, a good shot, and eager to go on safari. He was also a single man after shedding wife number four, Lady Ashley. He had many women at home and abroad, but Gene Tierney's mother told her, "You could have Clark if you set your mind to it." Gene wasn't interested, having been introduced to the one man who was more charming than Gable and could back it up in the bedroom — Prince Aly Khan. She apologized to Clark for turning down the part of Linda in *Mogambo*, but Gene couldn't bear to leave her baby from a previous marriage to dress designer Oleg Cassini. "I didn't resent the role that could have been mine going to Grace Kelly," Gene wrote in her memoirs. "I thought Ava Gardner stole the movie. Not because she is more beautiful. She can act."

Ouch!

While Gable was driving his new custom Jaguar from Paris to Rome with the beautiful model Suzanne Dadolle by his side, Grace was back in New York calling family and friends. "I'm going to do a picture in Africa with *old* Clark Gable and *old* Ava Gardner directed by *old* John Ford." Her flippant attitude was soon cured by shots for typhoid, paratyphoid, tetanus, cholera, smallpox, and the deadliest of all, yellow fever. With a touch of all six, she sweated it out in bed. It was worth the agony until the phone rang. Her agent was calling with bad news. "Actors Equity won't grant you a permit to work in Africa."

"I don't understand," she said, moaning.

"*Mogambo* is an MGM British production, and aside from John Ford and three principal stars, the entire cast and crew have to be British. Due to your lack of film credits, Grace, you're not a principal star."

She was crushed. "Isn't there anything you can do? What about John Ford? He knows everybody."

"This is a union problem, Grace. If they want an English actress, that's the way it has to be."

"What about Clark Gable?" she asked. "He's in Europe and could use his influence."

"He doesn't know you, Grace. Besides, he's hiding out with some young girl near Lake Como."

"Where's that?"

"Northern Italy."

"I wish I'd known before I got those dreadful inoculations."

Gene Lyons was there to cheer her up. He wanted the best for Grace and did not seem concerned about her childish crush on "old" Clark Gable. They talked about how the strange African continent changed people. Some grew up, some grew old, and some went mad. Ernest Hemingway said there were no exceptions.

"I'm going mad and growing old right here in New York," she told Lyons. "Never, never would I have signed that contract if it hadn't been for *Mogambo*. I'm not anxious to act in films. You know I prefer the reality of the stage and performing in front of an audience. Hollywood thrives on freaks. Beautiful stories are dissected . . . filmed out of sequence. Actors are nothing but trained robots who stand on markers and perform for the camera. There's no feeling. It's strictly business. When I signed that contract, I became nothing but a puppet."

It was a gloomy day when Grace found out that Virginia McKenna, a well-known British actress who had originally turned down the part of Linda, was approached again.

Margaret Kelly hoped the African trip would be

cancelled. "How can I allow you to go over there all by yourself?" she asked her daughter. "What will people say? Do you think it's proper?"

"Oh, Mother," Grace said, laughing, "you've got such old-fashioned ideas."

Margaret recaptured her frenzy in an article a few years later: "Clark Gable was known as the King, and that meant not only King of the Movies but King of the Lady-Killers. I was only too well aware of the emotions that our Gracie could arouse in men simply by existing."

She reconsidered for one very good reason — Gene Lyons. "I thought a long separation would change Gracie's mind about him."

"Was Grace with Gene Lyons the night you introduced me to her at the Stork Club?" I asked Brian.

"Who knows? I didn't know one guy from another."

"She was getting ready to leave for Africa."

"As I recall, Grace was rambling on and on about making her first public appearance as a movie actress at an opening of *High Noon* somewhere in New Jersey. The worst part was sitting through the movie. Grace thought it was a wonderful picture except for her."

"She was very excited about *Mogambo*, remember?"

"And Gable."

"She was reading everything she could find about Africa."

"And Gable."

"And Swahili."

"And Gable."

"Did Grace correspond with you from Africa?" I asked.

"Yes. A few letters and postcards."

"What did she write about?"

"Her hunting excursions, the natives, the bad weather, and how much she adored Ava Gardner."

"And Gable?"

"In passing, and that was a clue. When Grace didn't mention someone, there was too much to tell."

"In an interview with Joan Crawford, she talked incessantly about Gable. Their affair lasted more than twenty years and she was still in love with him. After a few vodkas, she roasted his girlfriends, including Grace. Joan thought she was a phony."

"I can understand that," Brian said. "Crawford had to claw her way to the top and resented pretty rich girls getting the breaks."

"She thought Grace deliberately schemed to seduce Gable."

"That wasn't hard to do."

My interviews with Joan Crawford in 1971 were quite revealing, to say the least. I was writing a book about Robert Taylor, her costar in several films, but she talked about everyone else instead. Apologetically, Joan promised to discuss Taylor "next time," and it took three long sessions to get the information I wanted. She enjoyed talking about Hollywood and kept abreast of the latest gossip. Gable had been dead for eleven years, but she made him big as life. "If we hadn't helped each other through the bad times," she said, "neither of us would have survived Hollywood. He never got over the death of his wife, Carole Lombard, in that plane crash. The Kelly girl resembled her but didn't have Carole's sophistication, wit, salty tongue, and spunk. I was sure Clark would be attracted to the prim young thing. He had just gone through a dreadful divorce, and MGM wasn't going to renew his contract. He was a big lonely lug who drank too much. Clark was on a binge when he married Lady Ashley, and I was worried he might do the same damn thing with the Kelly girl. She got her hooks into him, all right. I saw her in *Mogambo* and wanted to scrub the righteous look of innocence off that prissy puss."

Joan Crawford was far more amusing than catty. She is still considered the ultimate star, but her life was no bed of roses. Whatever she achieved in films was a result of hard work and fighting for good roles. It was only natural that she resented Grace Kelly, "who got the breaks because her family was wealthy and influential."

Clark Gable was fifty-one when he made *Mogambo*. Like Crawford, he traveled a bumpy road through life. When he expressed an interest in the theater and his wildcat father called him a sissy, Clark, at the age of twenty-one, hopped a freight train from his home in Ohio to Portland, Oregon, where he met thirty-four-year-old Josephine Dillon, a drama coach. When she moved her acting school to Hollywood, Clark followed. Josephine said, "Our marriage in 1924 was in name only because I could no longer afford two residences. It had nothing to do with love or physical attraction." His extensive training under her strict tutelage was responsible for Gable's success on the Broadway stage. In New York, he met Ria Langham, a wealthy divorcée from Houston, who was eighteen years older than Clark. They were married in 1930.

He attracted the attention of a Hollywood agent in the stage production of *The Last Mile* at the Majestic Theater in Los Angeles, and on December 4, 1930, Clark Gable signed an MGM contract for $650 a week. Punished by the studio for his affair with Joan Crawford (then Mrs. Douglas Fairbanks, Jr.), MGM loaned him to Columbia Pictures for *It Happened One Night*, a low budget film with no script; in 1934, Gable won an Oscar for Best Actor in this Frank Capra comedy.

Clark divorced Ria and wed Carole Lombard while he was filming *Gone With the Wind* in 1939. It was the ideal marriage, supposedly, but Gable was not a faithful guy. He said many times, "One woman is pretty much like another." This was Carole's reason for flying home from an Indiana war bond rally rather than taking the train as planned. She had her reasons for not trusting Clark with his leading lady, Lana Turner. On January 16, 1942, Carole's plane crashed near Las Vegas. There were no survivors.

Gable was never the same. He joined the Air Corps during World War II and volunteered for five dangerous missions. His general told director Frank Capra, "That guy gives me the willies. Know what I think? Gable's trying to get himself killed. Yeah! So he can join up with his wife."

Clark was gray at the temples when he returned to the screen. Depressed and drinking heavily, he dated socialites and actresses who resembled Carole. One of these ladies was Lady Ashley (Sylvia Hawkes Ashley Fairbanks Stanley), who became the fourth Mrs. Gable in December 1949. They were divorced two years later.

Clark was a quiet man who rarely bragged about women and who caused quite a sensation when he was shown a photo of MGM's stable of gorgeous leading ladies and said, smiling, "They're all beautiful and I've had every one of them!"

Joan Crawford admitted Gable was not a great lover. "But he had a wonderful time living up to the reputation," she said.

Carole Lombard did not mince words. "Clark's a lousy lay, but I adore him!"

Vivien Leigh, who played Scarlett O'Hara in *Gone With the Wind,* complained about Gable's bad breath, which was caused by his false teeth. He didn't like her much, either, and ate onion sandwiches daily to prove it!

When he left for Africa, columnist Louella Parsons wrote that Gable was Hollywood's own king of hearts. "He not always agreeable," she said. "He's not a fast man with a buck. He is frequently lazy and doesn't like to give interviews or dress up for parties. He often takes a snort too many. But his warmth, charm, and simplicity make you forgive him anything. He's still the great lover on and off the screen."

CHAPTER
FIVE

Growing Up

Mogambo is the story about Victor, a white hunter (Clark Gable), whose dalliance with Honey Bear (Ava Gardner), an American showgirl who has come on safari for fun, is interrupted by the arrival in their camp of an English anthropologist and his pretty wife Linda (Grace). Honey Bear is the first to notice that Victor has melted the icy Linda, who decides to leave her unsuspecting husband, but Victor thinks twice about breaking up the marriage and tells a distraught Linda she was only a diversion. She shoots Victor, who isn't seriously wounded. The English couple depart on the next boat, and Honey Bear stays in Africa with Victor.

In *Red Dust*, the 1932 version of *Mogambo*, Gable had the male lead with Jean Harlow as the wisecracking trollop. Mary Astor was the elegant wife who falls in love with Gable, and Gene Raymond played the trusting husband. Each rendition held up under its own merits. Jean Harlow bathed in a rain barrel. Ava Gardner takes a shower with bare legs and shoulders showing. *Red Dust* wins the prize for love scenes between Gable and Mary Astor, but *Mogambo* has the advantages of being in color and on location in Africa with the animals, natives, and indescribable sunsets to support a beautiful cast of players.

* * *

Grace had to wait a week before her agent called with the good news that her permit had been granted. "I don't know how it was resolved by MGM," she said, "and I didn't ask questions. Before anything else happened, all I could think about was getting on that plane."

She faced a long and tedious journey from New York to Africa by way of England, Italy, and Egypt. Gable had gone on ahead of the others, but Ava Gardner, her husband, Frank Sinatra, and MGM publicist Morgan Hudgins met Grace in Rome. Photographers were falling over themselves trying to get pictures of Ava and Frank while Grace sat quietly reading a book about the adventures of an African white hunter. The "Battling Sinatras" had been front-page news before and after their marriage in 1951, but shortly before departing for Africa, they were involved in the famous Palm Springs incident that Hollywood insiders whisper about to this day.

Headlines in the *Los Angeles Mirror*: BOUDOIR FIGHT HEADS FRANKIE AND AVA TO COURTS.

And the *Los Angeles Times*: SINATRA-AVA BOUDOIR ROW BUZZES. TOO MUCH LEFT TO THE IMAGINATION.

There are several versions of what happened on October 21, 1952, in Sinatra's Palm Springs house. Ava said she drove to the desert after a quarrel with Frank and found Lana Turner and their business manager, Ben Cole, having a bite to eat in the kitchen. A few minutes later, Frank burst through the door and shouted, "I bet you broads have really been cutting me up!" Lana and Ben fled and returned later to find the Sinatras fighting and the place crawling with police. Lana wrote in her memoirs that none of them referred to that night again, but many vile rumors persisted, among them that Frank had found her and Ava in bed together.

Sinatra's accusation that the girls were talking about him appears to be the most logical explanation. He had been romantically linked to Lana, who was divorced from Ava's former husband, bandleader Artie Shaw. Frank went into a rage when the musician's name was mentioned because Ava and Artie remained friends.

The Sinatras had separated before, but this breakup was more serious than the others because Ava was going to Africa for six months, leaving him behind. Frank begged Earl Wilson to print an appeal for reconciliation, and on October 27, 1952, the columnist wrote, FRANKIE READY TO SURRENDER; WANTS AVA BACK, ANY TERMS. The plan worked, and on November 7, the Sinatras celebrated their first wedding anniversary on a stratocruiser bound for Africa. Because Frank's career was in a slump and his divorce had drained him financially, Ava paid for his airfare.

Grace was shy and standoffish on the flight. She knew her place in the company of such a celebrated couple. The exquisite Ava was one of MGM's top stars and was considered to be "the most beautiful animal in the world." Her fabulous figure — 36-inch bust, 20-inch waist, and 36-inch hips — was admired from Syracuse to Singapore. (Grace refused to give her measurements.) Ava Gardner was a lady with a spicy tongue, a torrid temper, and a wonderful sense of humor. She was a hearty drinker and a passionate thirty-year-old woman who, after her divorce from Mickey Rooney, had been involved with Peter Lawford, Howard Duff, Robert Walker, Howard Hughes, and bullfighter Mario Cabre.

Ava was balancing the glamour stigma with good reviews in *Show Boat* (1951) and *The Snows of Kilimanjaro* (1952), excelled only by her performance in *Mogambo*.

Frank Sinatra was anxious to play Maggio in *From Here to Eternity* (1953), but his chances of getting the part were very slim. He went to Africa with mixed emotions, wanting to be in Hollywood for the audition but also wanting to be with Ava, who thought she might be pregnant. Their nerves were at the breaking point.

Grace was delighted to see Clark Gable and John Ford waiting at the Nairobi airport. On the drive to the New Stanley Hotel, Ava invited everyone to her anniversary party. "Hey, this is the first time I've been married for a whole year!" she said, laughing.

"Aren't you tired from jet lag?" Gable asked.

"The only cure for that, honey, is a party! Don't bother unpacking."

Grace checked into her room and within minutes could hear Ava's phonograph blasting, cocktail glasses clicking, and people laughing. Still a bit shy and not sure she belonged with this close-knit group, Grace stood in the doorway. Gable asked her to sit down and relax. "Long trip," he smiled. "Bumpy?"

"Quite."

"Yeah, I flew into a storm. The hailstones were as big as my fist. The damn plane had dents all over. Scared the hell out of me."

One of the technicians sat next to Grace and told her that Clark got off the plane as white as a ghost.

"But you were in graver danger during the war," she said. "I would think you'd be immune by now."

"Almost turned down this project because I don't like to fly," Gable said.

"I was so anxious to get here, nothing mattered. This is

such a charming hotel."

"Yes, isn't it, but you'll only see it after dark, my dear. Every morning we all fly to the preserve at Mount Kenya, sixty miles from here, for shooting."

"Game?"

"No. *Mogambo*."

She laughed nervously and watched Gable pour himself a glass of Scotch. "I didn't mean to frighten you, Grace. The compound is very impressive. It ain't the Stanley, but for us, it's pretty fancy camping."

"I must confess here and now I fell in love with you in *Gone With the Wind*."

The technician sat back, crossed his arms, and watched the King operate. With a dimpled scowl, Gable said, "Everyone did, but for all the love in the world, I don't get a dime."

"Not a percentage?" she asked, gasping.

"Sad, but true," he replied, tapping his fingers to the tune of Sinatra's "All or Nothing at All" on the phonograph.

"Why didn't you *insist* before agreeing to play Rhett Butler?"

"Baby, I was under contract," he replied, "and besides, I had to get a fast divorce. That bastard [David O.] Selznick was afraid of scandal, you see, and my affair with Carole might have ruined his picture."

"Is it true Selznick was in love with her?" Grace asked innocently.

"I don't know where you heard that," he said, scowling, "but I'd rather not discuss it."

"I'm sorry . . ."

The technician shook his head, patted Gable on the back, and pointed to Sinatra, who was giving Ava a mink coat for their anniversary. When she tossed it aside, Gable's teeth almost fell out. "I'd never let a woman treat me like that," he said.

Ava laughed, "You would if she paid for it, honey."

At dinner that evening, Grace admitted that this was the first time she'd been away from home without a chaperone. When she spoke to the waiter in Swahili, Gable pretended to be impressed, but he considered the performance rather juvenile — even trite. The English-speaking waiter sighed, and Clark puckered his lips quizzically. The tall, slim blonde had class underneath that Swahili act, he said to himself, but no way is she Philadelphia Main Line. If anyone could tell the difference between the blue bloods and the nouveau riche, it was Gable.

The main topic of conversation was the Mau Mau infiltration. "Women carry pistols in their pocketbooks," he said. "The white residents can't trust their servants these days."

Grace was blasé about all that. She wanted to know why he had accepted the role of a man having an affair with a married woman since he'd turned down these parts previously.

"Because, my dear, the relationship between Linda and Victor does not go beyond infatuation."

"I didn't get that impression," she said, peeling a banana.

"Victor is a white hunter who plays by the rules on and off safari."

"In the script, he's described as a two-legged boa constrictor, Mr. Gable."

"Clark . . ."

"May I call you 'Ba'?"

72

He puckered up and grinned. "Did you say 'Pa'?"

"B-A. Ba . . . Swahili for 'father.'"

"I'm old enough to be."

"Ba has nothing to do with age, necessarily," she explained. "It refers to one who is admired and respected."

"Carole called me 'Pa,'" he said softly.

She nodded and paused for a moment. "Would you like my *ndizi*?"

"I've never turned down an offer like that in my life."

She handed him half of her banana.

"Thanks," he said, grinning.

"Do you plan any hunting while we're here?" she asked.

"I'm looking forward to it."

"May I tag along?"

"This is very dangerous territory, my dear."

"I don't frighten easily."

Gable looked into her aqua eyes. She didn't blink. Very interesting girl, he concluded . . . smooth tawny skin, perky lips, sculptured nose with sensuous nostrils, and soft yellow hair pulled back from her square jawline. She was very much like Carole. As if he cared, Clark asked, "Where did you learn to speak Swahili?"

"On my own. Do you know what *mogambo* means in English?"

"Tell me."

"It means passion."

"Does it!" He cheered, lifting his drink for a toast.

"So you see," she said smiling, avoiding his eyes, "there *is* more between Linda and Victor."

"That depends on one's interpretation of passion."

"You're rather old-fashioned about not playing a man

who makes love to a married woman on the screen."

"Maybe little girls from Philadelphia think it's old-fashioned, but I call it professional ethics."

"Referring to your image?" She laughed. "Hollywood amuses me. Holier than thou for the public and unholier than the devil in reality."

"How many films have you done, Grace?"

"Two."

"That explains it. After a few more, you'll be as holy as I am."

Gable recognized many facets in Grace. She was corny, innocent, brazen, flirty, childish, and seductive. Like a baby cobra, he told his technician friend.

The following day, they flew to the MGM location settlement near Mount Kenya. While the plane was making its descent, Gable told Grace, "This landing strip is eighteen hundred yards long. It was literally hacked out of the jungle."

"And what are all those tents?"

"Home, my dear. Home sweet home on the banks of the Kagera River, but those tents are upholstered and very comfortable. Thirteen of them are dining rooms. Over there is the movie theater, an entertainment section with pool tables, and a hospital with an X-ray unit."

He made sure she was settled in her tent, complete with hot and cold running water. "Around back are two large oil drums," he explained. "The one propped over the wood fire is the hot water."

"A fire near my tent?"

"The flames will keep the lions away at night."

"Very amusing, Ba."

"Nothing to fear. Roaming around someplace are a

hundred and seventy-five whites and three hundred and fifty natives at your service. All part of the film unit. Then there's a great guy by the name of Bunny Allen, a true-to-life white hunter. You'll like him."

"What on earth is that?" she asked, pointing to a truck coming into camp.

"Native women."

"I thought you said there were more than three hundred here."

"They're all male," he said, laughing. "You see their wives stay home and do the menial work. Earning a few shillings by just standing around is quite a treat for them and better than working in the fields. They're even allowed to speak in this film, and that's quite an accomplishment."

Grace looked around the MGM camp site with fascination. "This was worth it," she exclaimed.

"The long flight?" Gable asked as he checked over his rifles.

"No. Signing my life away to MGM."

"I've been under contract for more than twenty years and now they're planning to dump me after one more film."

Grace had heard the rumors but said nothing that might upset him. Gable was in a talkative but pensive mood. "They want to give me a two-year extension," he said, "but I'm getting out on my own terms, and if Metro ever wants me back for another film, they can shove it!"

"You aren't giving me much to look forward to," she said, forcing a smile.

"You didn't know Louis B. Mayer, but after he was squeezed out in favor of Schary, nothing was the same. Mayer and I never got along, but he *was* MGM. Yes, the old man made us all stars from Greta Garbo to our beautiful

Ava . . . which reminds me of something Spencer Tracy said when she complained that one of her sexiest scenes had been cut out of our film *Lone Star* [1952]. Spence said, 'Yeah, since Schary took over, nobody gets laid at MGM.'"

Grace's hearty laugh was contagious. Gable couldn't help himself. "I'm glad we had this talk," he said. "I feel better."

"Any advice?" she asked.

"Be on time, know your lines, say them the best way you can, take the money, and go home at six o'clock."

John Ford, however, expected more than that. He was a rough, gruff, and abusive bull who told John Wayne what he could do with his horse. A veteran director of Westerns whose rude and uncouth manner could not be ignored, Ford was not tactful or soft-spoken. He referred to Grace as "Kelly" and bellowed when she acted according to the script. "Don't you have any instinct, Kelly? We're doing a movie, not a goddamn script!"

He was unsympathetic to the palsied trembling of Gable's head and hands, particularly during love scenes. Clark knew when his timing was off and wanted another retake of a scene with Ava. Ford turned him down and was blunt about the actor's embarrassing affliction. Gable walked off the set and refused to talk to the director again until the production moved to England.

Ford criticized Ava unmercifully and used vile language. When she had had enough, Ava spun around and gave it all back to him, using blue words he hadn't heard. Then she, too, stormed off the set. Everyone was surprised when Ford followed her. "You're damned good," he said. "Take it easy. You don't have to try so hard to get the fun and gaiety out of Honey Bear. No other actress can play her but you."

Ford didn't care about the private lives of his star players, but he knew about Ava's bitter bouts with Frank and was aware that she might be pregnant. He wasn't going to pamper her, but if she came to him for help, Ford would be the first to give it to her.

Grace complained about the Sinatras. "They fight all the time," she told Clark. "I wish their tent weren't next to mine."

"I bet they have a great time making up."

"I hear that, too."

"Frank's down on his luck, you know. I hope he gets a chance to test for Maggio. That's all he thinks about . . . besides Ava, of course."

"He's such a grand singer. Why would he want a part like that?"

"Hollywood almost ruined Frank. All he needs is one juicy part. That's all."

"I shouldn't be gossiping like this," she sighed, "but I hear everything, and . . ."

"Look, if you want to come on safari with Bunny and me, it's okay as long as he doesn't object."

"And Ava?"

"She hates killing of any kind. Besides, she sleeps until cocktails." Then he looked at Grace and, in a serious tone of voice, asked, "Are you sure you want to go hunting with me? It's dangerous. Bunny and I have enough to do without worrying about you."

"I won't be in your way."

"Yeah, but you might get in the way of a lion. We'll see."

"What more can I ask?" she smiled, taking his hand. They strolled along the riverbanks and did not try to hide their growing attraction to each other. If Clark's last wife Sylvia hadn't soured him, he might have been more enthusiastic over Grace, who had already made up her mind that she wanted Gable. Since Ava was the only other white woman for miles except for a few technicians' wives, he had no choice; nor did Clark have anything to lose. Those in camp who knew him when Carole was alive were reminded very much of their happiness whenever Grace called him "Ba," which sounded so much like Lombard's "Pa."

They flew back to the New Stanley for the weekend. Clark gave a surprise birthday party for Grace. She was deeply touched despite his casual remark, "Any excuse for a party!" Ava was all for that because Frank was flying home to test for *From Here to Eternity*. Not long after his departure, Ava's health declined. She was nauseated every day and suffered from the heat. When she finally collapsed in a faint, Ava flew to London and checked into a women's clinic. MGM officials said she was suffering from a severe case of anemia. Ava told friends she had a miscarriage and was heartbroken not being able to have Frank's baby, but there was every indication that she had had an abortion. A cast member overheard her admit she had no intention of having Sinatra's child because their marriage was pure hell. Either way, it was a very difficult time for her. Ava was a time bomb, and Ford knew it. When British officials put in a complaint about Ava's bathing in the nude in front of the native boys, Ford tried to keep it from her, but Ava found out, took off her clothes, and ran through camp in front of everybody.

Grace glanced at Clark.

"Anything wrong?" he asked casually.

"No . . ."

He leaned back in his chair, put his feet up, and asked, "Do you remember that mama hippo charging our canoe in the river the other day?"

"How could I forget it?"

"You were a brave girl, too, but Ava was alone in another boat and might have been killed. And do you recall the rhinos that charged the truck? She didn't panic or scream or complain. Well, those are the things that we should remember about Ava. Right now, she's a bewildered girl having some harmless fun."

"I'm not so sure I agree, Ba."

"I'm not so sure I care," he said sternly.

"You're angry."

"No, but have you given any thought to how you looked the other night being carried from my tent to your tent — out cold from too much booze?"

"I wasn't out cold!" she snapped.

"You're right. Excuse me. You came to, threw up, and were *half*-carried back to your tent."

Grace found out it was Ava who was the sophisticate — the happy-go-lucky girl who wept inwardly but never gave up. She was also Clark's pal and had been close to him for a few years. Completely alone for the first time, Grace grew up fast in Africa. If Gable did not respond to her femininity, she'd find a new approach. Grace got up early to be with him even when she wasn't filming. "Why do you do it?" he asked. "It's hell to bounce around in a tin wagon with nothing but mosquitoes and heat and God knows what."

"I don't want to miss anything," she explained. "I want to have stories to tell my grandchildren. That's why I want to go hunting with you and Bunny."

"Do I have a choice?" he asked.

"No."

"That's your answer."

It was as if they were playing scenes from *Mogambo* — he the white hunter and she the proper young lady. She takes a walk into the jungle and he searches for her frantically. He finds her near a waterfall. She slips and he grabs her. They kiss. Unspoken love.

Grace thought she could reenact this scene. She stayed behind one day when he was on location. He returned and couldn't find her. She was not at the hotel. Told that she had gone for a walk toward the water, he wanted to know why someone hadn't stopped her. "We were told not to wander off alone with the Mau Mau guerrillas everywhere!" he shouted, taking the path in the direction she had supposedly gone. He found her by the river. She was sitting on a rock reading Hemingway's *The Snows of Kilimanjaro*. Clark wanted to shake the life out of Grace, but he noticed tears in her eyes. "It's so beautiful," she sighed. ". . . Hemingway's leopard in the snow, and then I saw a lion and . . ."

"A lion!"

"A beautiful lion . . ."

"And you weren't afraid?" he asked, sitting down next to her.

"No. It was so moving. I had no fear at all."

"Neither did the lion, my dear. Promise me you won't go off alone again. Do I have your word?"

She didn't answer.

"Then you'll come along with me," he said, putting his arm around her. "I don't mind. I don't mind at all. As soon as my other guns arrive, we'll go on safaris, but for Christ's sake, Grace, don't go out alone!"

They sat by the water until dark. Observers said this was a common occurrence. She read to him from Hemingway's book and he recited poetry for her. They were like an old married couple. A member of the cast said, "Gracie was very plain. She wore frumpy clothes and her glasses and no make-up. She and Clark had their meals alone or they'd sit in the lobby together. Grace kinda followed him around. He'd get up from his chair and she'd get up from hers. He wasn't very affectionate. Clark hugged her, but he kissed and hugged Ava, too. He was flattered, I think, that Grace was madly in love with him. He held her hand when they took long walks and she'd lean against him. Maybe Grace was only a passing fancy for Gable, but I thought it was more than that. It was taken for granted they were practically living together."

Louella Parsons wired Clark about the romance and he replied, "This is the greatest compliment I've ever had, but I'm old enough to be her father. She's only a kid."

Grace had no comment.

Neither did John Ford. He wasn't concerned about who was sleeping together. He wasn't concerned about the Mau Mau situation. He was concerned, however, about his party for the British Governor of Uganda, Sir Andrew Cohan, and his wife. For a laugh, Ford asked Ava, "Why don't you tell the Governor what you see in that hundred-twenty-pound runt you're married to?"

"Well," Ava replied, "there's ten pounds of Frank and there's one hundred and ten pounds of cock!"

Everyone, including the Governor and his wife, thought it was hilarious. Ford was the only one who was shocked.

He paled, in fact. Gable cherished Ava at times like this. He laughed the loudest at her description of him. "Clark?" she said. "He's the sort of guy if you say, 'Hiya, Clark, how are ya?' he's stuck for an answer."

Grace was finally fitting into the group. She remembered raunchy jokes and repeated them. Instead of following on Gable's heels, she walked by his side, went on safari, and proved to be pretty good with a rifle. He admired her sportsmanship and guts. If Grace said nothing about going hunting with him, he came to her. She no longer tried to drink whiskey like the others. One disaster at a candlelight dinner for two was enough. She learned to fake it by sipping and getting pleasantly high.

Sinatra returned in time for the holidays. He had gotten the part of Maggio in *From Here to Eternity*, which eased the tension and was cause for celebration. He surprised Ava with pasta and all the ingredients for a homemade spaghetti sauce. She and Grace borrowed evening gowns from the wardrobe tent for Christmas Eve. The generator broke down, but there was only laughter in the darkness. "We ate by candlelight," Gable said. "I thought it was a very warm and romantic setting. Ava's sauce was the cause of the breakdown, but worth it. On Christmas Day, I found one of my socks hanging on the tent. Grace had stuffed it. We trimmed the tree, sang Christmas carols with the natives, and had a holiday dinner flown in by MGM — turkey, Christmas puddings, champagne, and plenty of booze. Ford recited 'The Night Before Christmas' — something we never expected. We were family and it was a nice feeling. I'll never forget it."

Soon after Christmas, they finished filming at Kagera. While the new location was being set up, Clark asked Grace

if she'd like to spend a weekend at a beach
Indian Ocean. "It's cooler at Malindi," he s;
can swim without crocodiles. I've been tol(
beautiful spot."

"I'd love to," she replied. "Do you mind if Ava and Frank
come along? I think they're on the verge of reconciling, and
this might do it."

Gable had noticed the gradual change in Grace. Was
she actually giving up a rare opportunity to be alone with
him for a few days? Had she developed compassion for
those who had problems far beyond her comprehension?
Not one to delve into women's psyches, Gable liked the
new Grace and found himself getting involved more than
he expected.

The two couples were forced to take an old plane to
Malindi. "'Old' is a feeble word for it," Clark said. "The
damn thing was held together by baling wire, but it was the
only available transportation. The others didn't mind, but
I had a long talk with the pilot, who assured me there was
nothing to worry about. I kept thinking about the four of
us — maybe the hottest properties in Hollywood — taking
a chance like this. MGM would not have been pleased."

Frank and Ava took advantage of the peaceful setting and
kept to themselves. The hotel was small, cozy, and romantic,
the view of the Indian Ocean was soothing, and the cool
breezes were a refreshing change from the heat and humidity
of Tanganyika. Gable responded to Grace's love but kept a
cool head. His technician friend said, "Clark liked to date
a variety of women. If we had been in civilization, I don't
think he would have spent as much time with Grace. She had
absolutely no personality when she arrived in Nairobi. John
Ford made an actress out of her, and Gable made a woman

of her. Working in the jungles of Africa was a new experience for everyone, and this drew us closer together. But it wasn't glamorous. Our young assistant director John Hancock was killed when his Jeep overturned. We had many close calls, and Clark's expertise with a gun saved us more than once. The natives called him 'bwana' for boss. Grace was in awe of the man, but I recall one day she arrived on the set fifteen minutes late and Gable gave her holy hell right then and there. He was also annoyed that she and Ava were very cool to each other at the start. When Grace was snippy, Clark came down on her good and hard. He loved her in his own way, taking into consideration the time and the place."

They swam together in the sea, walked along the soft beach, and watched the sun rise from their veranda. Grace did not want it to end and neither did Gable, but he knew only too well that the tender moments in Malindi were not real.

Rumors persisted about the Gable-Kelly affair in gossip columns almost daily now. Whether it was the intimate trip to Malindi or their constant togetherness on location, word leaked out that they were definitely in love. MGM was giving Grace an enormous publicity campaign in preparation for the release of *Mogambo*. Her role in *High Noon* was built up, emphasizing her part as Gary Cooper's wife. Moviegoers began to recognize Grace when her pictures, many of which were with Gable, appeared in magazines and newspapers. MGM took advantage of the romantic gossip, and Clark no longer protested or denied anything.

From the lovely beach resort, the cast settled into the

desolate Isoila desert country in Uganda. The waterholes were safe for swimming and camel transportation was great fun. Sinatra reported for work in *From Here to Eternity*, which was filming in Hawaii, and Ava was in good spirits. She and Grace had become pals. The one difference between them was Ava's openness, especially about sex.

Gardner said what Kelly was thinking.

Gable loved to tell the story about the girls walking past a group of Watusi warriors. Ava said, "I hear their cocks are really big." Grace blushed and Clark grinned from ear to ear. Suddenly, Ava pulled up a native's loincloth and a magnificent penis gleamed in the sunlight. Grace stared despite herself but Ava shrugged — "Frank's is bigger."

It was almost time to leave the Dark Continent. Grace told Clark she wanted to make the most of it.

"Not in Samburu country," he said.

"Don't be silly."

"What do you know about these savages?"

"They're seven feet tall!"

"Yeah, and they live on blood and milk."

"Not human blood, I hope."

"I suppose they drink that, too, but their main diet is the blood of cattle. They shoot an arrow into the neck, drain some blood, plug the hole with mud, and go to the next animal."

"How interesting . . ."

"No long walks, Grace."

"I'll stay with you, of course. What I don't understand is why we're forced to go to Samburu country."

"Because of the setting and regardless of their strange eating customs, Bunny says the natives won't bother us, but I'm not so sure. Stay in camp. I don't want to lose you now after all we've been through."

She took his arm and put her head on his shoulder. "I don't want to lose you, either. Remember that, Ba."

"Things will be a little hectic around here, preparing to leave and all," he said in a businesslike fashion. "I'm not sure if we'll be on the same plane going back, but I'll call you in London."

Ava, sitting nearby, apparently noticed tears welling up in Grace's eyes. "Know what?" she chirped. "I think we should stop off in Rome for a few days. That's what we'll do, Gracie — fly to Italy with Clarkie and Johnny Ford. While Frankie's in hulaland, you and I will have some fun. It's all set!"

Gable scowled. "I'm not sure Grace wants to keep up with you, babe."

"Who asked you?" Ava teased. "Could it be you don't want her to keep up with me?"

"Possible."

Grace beamed. "I'm looking forward to it. How long will it take us to finish filming in London, Ba?"

"We should be through by April depending on the weather. At best, we'll be there three months, but I'm staying on to help with the film editing."

"And I'm staying on to make *Knights of the Round Table* [1953] with Bob Taylor," Ava said.

Grace looked bewildered and sad but tried to make light of it. "Everyone seems to have plans but me," she said.

Gable laughed. "You gotta be kidding! MGM will keep you busy every minute."

"Doing what?"

"Making you a star, babe. Making you a star."

CHAPTER
SIX

Stardust and Tears

The girls had a great time in Rome. Ava knew the right places to go — primarily out-of-the-way bars and cozy restaurants. Grace's eyes were opened a little wider. Gable's were, too, when she told him Ava had taken her to some whorehouses in Rome.

"What for?" he asked.

"She likes to exchange jokes and stories with the girls."

"What did you do?"

"I stayed outside and talked to the boys."

"Yeah? Well, I wouldn't write home about it," Gable said, growling.

"Don't be a fuddy-duddy. Nothing happened."

"The paparazzi take sexy pictures of things that never happened in Rome, my dear. Front-page stuff."

Grace wasn't sure if Clark was jealous or warning her not to make the same mistakes he had at the start of his career.

Gable usually stayed at the prestigious Dorchester Hotel in London, but he changed his mind and checked into the quaint Connaught Hotel to avoid reporters and the British MGM publicists, who booked Grace at the luxurious Savoy.

Ava rented a house in Hyde Park Gate and kept open house day and night. At almost any hour, someone famous was sitting on the floor having a drink, including Grace, who was already beginning to hate being a studio contract player with an endless schedule of interviews and meetings. She sought refuge with Ava and poured out her heart about the boring rigors of the star buildup. "I dread to think what I'm facing in Hollywood," she said, sighing.

"You've got it made," Ava exclaimed. "Clark is helping John Ford edit *Mogambo*, and they say it's good. Real good."

"Clark told me to enjoy every minute of it."

"If he's enjoying it so much, how come he's hiding out at the Connaught?"

"I think he's hurt — very hurt about his MGM contract. I don't want to leave Clark here in London. He's drinking too much. A whole bottle of cognac before dinner . . ."

"Honey, in this business, that's par for the course. I'll look after him. Bob Taylor's here. He and Clark are old buddies."

"I love him," Grace said with tears in her eyes.

"As I said, in this business, that's par for the course. How about another drink, honey?"

Because of their busy schedules, Grace and Clark did not see much of each other in London. Unbeknownst to her, he was anxious to see Suzanne Dadolle in Paris, but editing *Mogambo* had taken longer than expected. Grace finally got the chance to spend a relaxed evening with Clark. "Can we fly back to New York together?" she asked.

"I'm sorry," he said, "but I want to see more of France and Switzerland."

"Why didn't you tell me?" she asked, fighting back tears.

"Because I didn't think it was important."

"What a terrible thing to say!"

"Grace, this will probably be my last chance to see Europe, all expenses paid by Metro, and I'm gonna wring 'em dry. Might do a film with Lana in Belgium, too."

"Where?!"

"When I was a kid, I never heard of Belgium. A strange sounding place to me was in Oregon. I didn't know what it was like to live in a house, and now that I have one, well, it's meaningless. So you tell me, why should I rush back?"

"Because I'll be in Hollywood, too."

"Grace, this is not the time for you to be dwelling on us. Concentrate on being a good actress because at the premiere of *Mogambo*, you'll be a star, and remember the difference."

"I could stay in London for a while."

"That wouldn't work out," he said, pouring himself a stiff drink.

"I've always wanted to see France. . . ."

"Whatever happened to the girl who knew exactly where she was going and nothing was gonna stand in her way? C'mon, babe, now's the time to enjoy the spotlight and the press conferences and the mobs of people asking for your autograph."

"I was told you hated all that and refused to do it."

He laughed. "Because I couldn't speak the King's English without a script. My first interview was such a disaster, it was my last for a lotta years. But you've got style, Grace. Getting through the preliminaries will be fun."

"*Mogambo* is a rebirth for you, too. We'll promote it together."

"I'll continue making movies, but parading around and flaunting myself, no thanks. I want no part of it."

Grace tried to stand her ground. "You can't run away from the fact that you're Clark Gable and people have the right to see you in person."

"They did and they do," he said, taking out his false teeth. "And this is what I show them if they get too overbearing!" He dropped them into a glass of Scotch, stirred the drink with two fingers, and put them back in his mouth. "That, my dear, is the King!"

On April 15, 1953, Gable drove Grace to Heathrow Airport. Reporters were everywhere, but he ignored them as he led Grace to the gate and gave her a fond hug and kiss. She burst into tears and sobbed. He whispered something to her; she hesitated, kissed him again, and rushed to the airplane bound for New York. There were many accounts of this farewell in the newspapers, but it was unanimous that Grace Kelly was very much in love with Clark Gable. She did not want to leave him. He was understanding and kind but showed no emotion. A few weeks later, he and Suzanne Dadolle were doing the Paris scene together. In May, he received word that his divorce from Sylvia was final; friends held their breath. If he had sent Grace Kelly home and rushed into Suzanne's arms, was the French girl going to be wife number five? She told the press, "Oui."

And that was the end of Gable's affair with Dadolle.

Grace returned to New York and Gene Lyons. She was carrying a torch for "Ba." Though Grace was adamant about living in New York, she had a slight change of heart after meeting Gable.

"Before she left for Africa," Brian recalled, "Grace would get a little testy if there was any mention about her renting a place in Hollywood. Hughes said there was no way she could avoid it after signing a contract with MGM unless the studio would pay her hotel bills, and that was very, very unlikely. Howard's staff was always scouting around for apartments and small houses. I told him to keep Grace in mind. I expected her to say, 'Mind your own business,' but she was pleased. I inquired about an odd-looking bracelet that she wore all the time. It was made from the hair of an elephant's tail and was supposed to bring good luck. Grace was all wrapped up in Africa. I enjoyed hearing all about it and truly envied her taking this trip of a lifetime."

Earl Wilson asked Grace how often she had been out with Gable. "I never counted," she replied. "I wasn't the only girl he dated and he wasn't the only guy I went out with."

"Do his ears stick out so much now?" Wilson asked.

"They don't stick out at all as far as I could see."

"Did he give you a diamond bracelet as reported?"

"Maybe he forgot to give it to me."

"Clark said you were a very sweet girl. He must be more than twice your age."

"He turned fifty-two in February. We celebrated his birthday in Africa."

Grace continued to date Gene Lyons on a fairly regular basis, but the Kellys were no longer worried that they would get married. She was also seeing Don Richardson on the sly. In the early summer of 1953, Grace did a television drama, "The Way of an Eagle," a biography of American ornithologist, John James Audubon. Her costar was forty-four-year-old Jean-Pierre Aumont, the handsome French movie star whose actress wife, Maria Montez, had died of a heart attack in 1951.

Aumont was attracted to Grace on the first day of rehearsals, but she kept her distance. They were playing Mr. and Mrs. Audubon, and Jean-Pierre was disappointed that she wasn't friendlier toward him. His invitations to lunch were declined for the next few days, but most annoying was her calling him "Mr. Aumont." A ladies man, he was not accustomed to the cold shoulder. Then one day they were doing a scene in a dance hall and there was graffiti on the walls. Jean-Pierre told her there was something he wanted her to see. The graffiti read, "Ladies, be kind to your men — after all, they're human beings, too."

Grace's laughter was the beginning of a tender romance that lasted for several months. They were together constantly until he had to return to France. It was her affair with Jean-Pierre that ended Grace's close relationship with Gene Lyons once and for all. She corresponded with Aumont, hoping and planning to see him, but it would be two years before they were together again.

Another disappointment was Gable's not coming back from Europe in time for the premiere of *Mogambo*, but he'd been hinting on the telephone that he might not be home before the holidays. Grace was relieved that Ava and Frank were able to attend the New York premiere at Radio City Music Hall on October 2, 1953. They flew to Hollywood the next day, but Frank bowed out of the Los Angeles premiere; on October 27, MGM made the announcement that the Sinatras were getting a divorce.

If *Mogambo*'s two leading ladies were having their ups and downs with men, they had scored a hit in the movie. Both were nominated for an Oscar — Ava for Best Actress and Grace for Best Supporting Actress. Critics agreed that Ava ran away with *Mogambo*, but, in essence, this was Grace's major debut in films; she was on her way to stardom. *Newsweek* wrote, "Grace Kelly makes one of the loveliest patricians to appear on the screen in a long time. Her particular quality is the suggestion that she is well born without being arrogant, cultivated without being stuffy, and highly charged emotionally without being blatant."

Though *Newsweek*'s review was the only one that mentioned Grace in detail, *Look* magazine named her the Best Actress of 1953. *Mogambo* was a hit at the box office, and Gable was applauded for being "beautifully commanding." It was a year of outstanding films as Hollywood continued to challenge its arch rival, television. The public might have been devoted to staying home one night a week for "I Love Lucy," but they had no intention of missing *The Robe* with Richard Burton, *Shane* with Alan Ladd, *Roman Holiday* with Audrey Hepburn and Gregory Peck, *Julius Caesar* with Marlon Brando, and *Lili* with Leslie Caron. The movie that received the most Oscar nominations in 1953 was *From Here to Eternity,* starring Burt Lancaster, Deborah Kerr, Montgomery Clift, and Frank Sinatra, all of whom were nominated for an Academy Award, with Sinatra a Best Supporting Actor winner.

MGM once boasted that it had "more stars than there are in heaven." Grace Kelly was one of the last to shine before the studio contract player system disappeared. The odds were against her in a decade that thrived on women with big bosoms, plunging necklines, well-rounded hips, and heavy black false eyelashes. In February 1953, twenty-seven-year-old Marilyn Monroe, wearing a gold lamé pleated gown with paper-thin lining hand-stitched to her nude curves, accepted *Photoplay*'s award for the Fastest Rising Star of 1952. The Crystal Room at the Beverly Hilton Hotel in Beverly Hills was brimming over with celebrities. Columnist Sheilah Graham said, "I was shocked. I had never seen anything like it in public." Joan Crawford, who was sitting with Grace, Rock Hudson, and his date, Mamie Van Doren, hissed, "There's nothing wrong with my tits, but I don't go around throwing them into people's faces!" Looking around the room, Crawford cursed, "Pretty few fuckin' real stars here." When she had sobered up the next day, Joan said in an interview with Bob Thomas, ". . . the public likes provocative feminine personalities, but it also likes to know that underneath it all the actresses are ladies."

Alfred Hitchcock had the same philosophy. He was looking for a girl with the attributes of a debutante on the surface and the sexual appetite of a whore in her belly. Though Hitchcock was a director of suspense dramas — *Rebecca* (1940), *Suspicion* (1941), *Spellbound* (1945), *Notorious* (1946), and *Strangers on a Train* (1951) — his mind was spinning new characters and plots all the time. Finding the actor or actress to fit the role was more difficult. If Hitchcock was a genius, he was also a perfectionist who would not compromise.

Born in London in 1899, Hitchcock's first job was a designer of title cards at the Islington studios of Famous Players-Lasky. Four years later, he rose to scriptwriter and tried editing and art direction. In 1926, he married

Alma Reville, a continuity girl and editor who would work closely with him throughout his life. In 1939, Hitchcock left England for Hollywood and won the New York Film Critics directing award for *The Lady Vanishes* (1938). During the forties, his favorite leading lady was Ingrid Bergman, who gave up Hollywood for Europe to marry her Italian lover, Roberto Rossellini.

In the early fifties, Hitchcock organized his own production company and signed with Warner Brothers to produce and direct *Dial M for Murder*. The film was based on Frederick Knott's play about an aging tennis player (Ray Milland) who discovers his rich English wife is having an affair with another man (Robert Cummings). The husband hires a school chum to kill her, but in the struggle, she stabs him in the back with a pair of scissors. The wife is arrested for murder but is saved at the end by a detective who solves the mystery when he finds a duplicate key to the couple's apartment.

Although the part of Margot was relatively dull, she had a dual personality, that of a staid wife and an adulteress. Any number of actresses could have handled the role with ease, but Hitchcock wanted a girl who would fit into his future projects. He spent more time than most directors with character development, making the role as fascinating as the star playing it.

In the spring and summer of 1953, Hitchcock was casting the part of Margot in *Dial M* while viewing the latest movies, including film clips of *Mogambo*, which had not been released yet. He was not impressed with Grace's performance because her voice was too shrill, but he took the time to view her screen test for *Taxi*; the intrigued Hitchcock arranged to meet Grace. The interview was a repeat of the one she had with Fred Zinnemann. "I could not think of anything to say to him," Grace said. "In a horrible way, it seemed funny to have my brain turn to stone." Hitchcock, however, thought she would be perfect for the part of the English wife, and arrangements were made for MGM to loan Grace to Warner Brothers for *Dial M*. It is interesting to note that the Buddha-like director made his choice before the success of *Mogambo* and her nomination for an Oscar.

Hitchcock knew he could afford to be more colorful in love scenes with a lady than he could with a hussy. Grace exuded sexual elegance, but she didn't flaunt it. "Actors often make the mistake of giving too much of themselves at the start and winding down," he said in a 1975 interview. "Grace, as young as she was, had the ability to pace herself."

Howard Hughes had another approach with his discovery, Jane Russell: "All eyes are on her from the beginning to the end. She's both sexy and aloof. It's more frustrating for a man to get the cold shoulder from a woman who's been around. Hitch does it the hard way."

Van Johnson said, "Hollywood went for Kelly in rebellion against a broadside of broads."

Still, Grace had yet to prove herself as a refined femme fatale on the screen. A few stolen kisses in *Mogambo* were mild compared to Deborah Kerr's torrid beach scenes with Burt Lancaster in *From Here to Eternity* and Elizabeth Taylor's "tell mama all" kiss from Montgomery Clift in *A Place in the Sun* (1951).

Hitchcock would bring Grace to the forefront with what he referred to as "sexual elegance." He lowered her voice and taught her how to exude passion. It helps, of course, if the director is in love with his leading lady, and Hitchcock was a Grace-watcher — a smitten voyeur. He was obsessed with the way she moved and walked and laughed. For the screen, he supervised her wardrobes, her hairdos, and her make-up. Everything had to be perfect because she was perfect.

Hitchcock studied Grace so intently that he knew what she was thinking despite a cover-up of casualness toward her leading men. He took advantage of mutual attractions, adding fuel to the fire.

It has often been said that to work with some movie stars is to love them. The old pros in Hollywood, however, give fair-warning, "It's all right to fall in love, but don't get married until you've fallen in love again in your next two films."

Many actors believe it betters their performance to have a romance with their costars that begins and ends with the picture. Robert Mitchum, under contract to Howard Hughes, found himself attracted to his flirtatious leading lady, Ava Gardner. The only obstacle was her involvement with his boss. Finding himself in a ticklish situation, Bob called Howard and asked, "Should I go to bed with Ava?"

"If you don't, everybody will think you're a pansy," Hughes replied.

Joan Crawford had affairs with directors, giving her the advantage over everyone else in the film. Bette Davis knew this and refused to commit herself to *Whatever Happened to Baby Jane?* (1962) with Joan until she had a heart-to-heart talk with director Robert Aldrich: "Have you slept with Miss Crawford?" she asked. "No," he fibbed, "not that I didn't have the chance."

Crawford said it was difficult not to fall in love with

some of her leading men. "The first time Gable grabbed me," she said, "my knees buckled. If he hadn't been holding me up, I would have fallen on the floor. I was very attracted to Henry Fonda and thought he'd get the hint when I gave him a jockstrap with rhinestones, gold sequins, and red beads. He opened the box on the movie set, held up the jockstrap, and didn't know what it was!"

Crawford said there were too many Hollywood romances for recall. "During their first kiss in *Flesh and the Devil* [1927] Greta Garbo and John Gilbert clung like there was glue on their lips," she exclaimed. "Elizabeth Taylor and Richard Burton, of course. Cary Grant wanted to marry Sophia Loren. Bette Davis never got over George Brent. She wanted Franchot Tone, too, but I got him. Norma Shearer had the hots for Tyrone Power, who wasn't interested. She settled for George Raft. If that's weird, how about Merle Oberon and James Cagney? And how many people remember that Gloria Swanson was married to Wallace Beery back in 1916? That pretty little thing and that ugly bastard. . . .

"I knew an actor who was so taken with his leading lady during a scene that he got a hard-on and the cameraman had to focus on him from the waist up. He was a professional and very embarrassed, but nature takes its course even in Hollywood."

Clark Gable arrived home just before the holidays, loaded down with African mementos. Waiting for him was a tiny Mexican burro named "Ba," a gift from Grace, who was spending Christmas in Philadelphia. They spoke to each other on the phone and he promised to escort her to the Academy Awards in March.

Spending almost two years abroad had been good

therapy for Gable. It helped him face the day he packed his belongings at MGM, put them in the Jaguar, and drove through the studio gates for the last time. He declined a farewell party and had a liquid lunch with a few studio friends of the lower echelon. "Strange how it all happened," he said. "I never should have gotten this far. Here I am, though. *Mogambo*'s a hit and I don't have a job. What I'd really like to do is produce my own stuff and I want Grace Kelly for my leading lady. I have good vibes about her."

Gable's feelings were stronger than that. He was in love with the girl who called him "Ba," but it took him a few months without her to face the truth. He told close friend Robert Taylor, who was going through a similar phase, "I want to retire in a few years and she's on the brink of a brilliant career. The press will say she married me for the publicity, and it might work against her."

"Marriage scares the hell outta me."

"You've only been divorced once, for Christ's sake."

"I don't ever want to go through another one," Taylor exclaimed.

"How old is your girlfriend, Ursula . . . Thiess?"

"Ten years younger than I am, and it's pronounced 'Teece.'"

"When Grace is thirty, I'll be ready for Social Security."

"Have you talked this over with her?"

"The subject of marriage hasn't come up but I know it will."

"Maybe you should have hashed it out in London."

"There wasn't time," Gable said, frowning.

"Your farewell scene at the airport was better than *Casablanca*." Taylor laughed.

"It was unexpected. Grace couldn't stop crying and I didn't know the right thing to say. I still don't. . . ."

"If you're really in love with her, get out of town — out of the country."

"I just got back!" Gable exclaimed.

"See what I mean? You're in deeper than before."

"Thanks."

"I'm headin' for Egypt to do *Valley of the Kings*."

"Have fun, but I'm predicting you'll marry the beautiful Ursula anyway 'cause you're running from yourself."

Gable's prediction came true six months later.

Grace rented a small apartment on Sweetzer Street in North Hollywood. Her occasional roommate was actress Rita Gam, but both girls were constantly on the move. When Grace was in Los Angeles in early 1954, the press reported she was staying at the Bel Air Hotel, but it was Gable who had a permanent suite there with his own private entrance. They spent many hours weighing the possibility of sharing the future, but Clark could not overlook the age factor. "It would be all right for a few years," he said, "and that's all — at best. I'd rather not pretend it will work out and risk losing what we have right now."

Gable confessed his love for her but wanted to trade marriage for a lifetime of friendship. Grace accepted the offer without shedding a tear.

They attended the Academy Awards together and the press went wild. Even though Grace lost to Donna Reed in *From Here to Eternity*, she said Frank Sinatra's winning an Oscar was such a delightful surprise that ". . . I didn't feel so bad." The award Ava hoped to get for Best Actress went to Audrey Hepburn for *Roman Holiday*.

Grace and Clark dated occasionally after they came to

a mutual agreement. She told the press that they had talked about marriage but that the age difference was insurmountable. One reporter wrote that Grace said, "His false teeth turn me off!"

CHAPTER
SEVEN

Dial M for Milland

Hitchcock wanted to film *Dial M for Murder* in black and white for dramatic effect but Warner Brothers went ahead with their plans for a three-dimensional picture in color. While the cumbersome equipment was being set up daily, the cast had plenty of time for chitchat. Hitchcock had expected his leading lady to let her hair down by now, but she remained shy and reserved. To throw her off, he exchanged raunchy jokes with the cast.

"Are you shocked, Miss Kelly?" Hitchcock asked.

"No, I went to a girls' convent school. I heard all those things when I was thirteen," she replied calmly.

That was the sort of answer Hitchcock wanted. It was the tip of the iceberg. Sitting nearby was Grace's costar, Ray Milland, who had been in a fog since the first day he set eyes on her. Like the unsinkable *Titanic*, he was hit hard.

Milland had been happily married for thirty years but was quite the ladies' man. He was, nonetheless, devoted to his wife, Mal, who had wisely given him a long leash. She knew only too well that Hollywood wives had the choice to either look the other way or marry an average guy who worked from nine to five.

The Millands were separated three times, twice due to

Ray's insurmountable career problems and once for the love of Grace Kelly, who was twenty-five years younger than her leading man in *Dial M for Murder*.

Before and after Milland won an Oscar in 1945 for his performance of an alcoholic in *The Lost Weekend*, he was often cast as the other man, someone's brother, or the hero's rival. Film historian David Shipman described Milland as ". . . the featured leading man — the actor who was never quite starred. . . . Real life rarely breathed into any of the films that he was given to do, and it is therefore somewhat difficult to assess him as a serious actor."

Ray Milland was named Reginald Truscott-Jones when he was born on January 3, 1905, in Neath, West Glamorgan, Wales. After his mother's second marriage, he was known by his stepfather's surname, Mullane. He studied at private schools, worked at his uncle's horse breeding farm, and attended King's College in Cardiff.

When he was twenty-one, Ray left home for London, where he applied for membership in the Household Cavalry, an exclusive regiment that guarded the royal family. He underwent nine months of punishing training in horsemanship, shooting, fencing, and boxing, won the British Army championship in both handgun and rifle marksmanship, and enjoyed a frenetic social life. Guardsmen had to have an independent income and, after three years, his stepfather stopped subsidizing him. Nearly penniless, Ray was forced to resign.

At a party, he met popular film star Estelle Brody, who invited him to her studio for lunch. A producer spotted Ray and hired him for a bit part. He appeared in several British films billed as Spike Milland. In 1930, he signed a contract with MGM, settled down in Hollywood, and married Muriel

("Mal") Weber. A year later, MGM dropped Ray's option and offered to pay his fare back to England. Rejected, broke, and embarrassed, he left his young wife behind and tried to salvage his acting career in London. Two films later, he said, "England was beginning to pall and I was longing to see my wife." Ray returned to Hollywood in 1933 and signed a contract with Paramount Pictures, where he stayed for twenty-one years. In 1940, the Millands had a son, Daniel, and a daughter, Victoria, was adopted in 1949. (Daniel committed suicide with a bullet to the head in the bedroom of his Beverly Hills home in 1981.)

Filming of *The Lost Weekend* took its toll on Milland. He lacked the confidence to play an alcoholic and forced himself to spend one night in the psychiatric ward at Bellevue Hospital in New York City to observe the inmates. Alas, Milland could not bear the screaming bedlam. Wearing only a hospital gown and robe, he ran into the street in his bare feet. The police dragged him back, but he was released within an hour. Returning to the same ward for the actual filming of the first scene in *The Lost Weekend* was a painful and unexpected experience for Milland.

When production resumed in Hollywood, he was depressed and nervous. "Now the real work begins," Ray said, "the cerebral part, the part where the thought processes become vocal, where the camera comes so close that nothing can be hidden and fakery isn't possible."

According to Milland's memoirs, his home life was deteriorating. Minor irritations became big problems, and Mal had lost her sense of humor. He came home one night from the studio, refused to attend a dinner party, stormed out of the house, and rented an apartment in the Sunset

Towers for two weeks. "My wife thought my depression was dramatically staged," he wrote, "as an excuse to shack up with some blonde Hollywood dame, and not without reason. There had been a few previous peccadilloes, nothing serious, just the normal male revolt against his convenient chains. It was very easy to succumb in those days." When the picture was finished a few weeks later, Ray took Mal on a romantic Canadian holiday.

Paramount bosses didn't like *The Lost Weekend* and shelved it for a few months. Much to everyone's surprise, the film won three Academy Awards, including Best Picture of the year.

The movie had been released in New York with no fanfare, but the public waited in long lines to see it. Milland was shocked by his nomination for Best Actor. The competition in 1945 was not overwhelming: Bing Crosby for *The Bells of St. Mary's*, Gene Kelly for *Anchors Aweigh*, Gregory Peck for *The Keys of the Kingdom*, and Cornel Wilde for *A Song to Remember*.

Ingrid Bergman read off the names of those nominated for Best Actor, opened the envelope, and smiled, saying, "Are you nervous, Mr. Milland? It's all yours!"

Minutes later, he was all but forgotten when Charles Boyer gave out the Oscar for Best Actress. "And the winner is . . . Joan Crawford in *Mildred Pierce*!" She was home in bed with a mild case of pneumonia, according to her doctor. The real reason was the fear of losing, but her fans didn't know that. The morning newspapers featured Joan asleep in bed with Oscar, tissues, nose spray, and telephone. Crawford's miraculous comeback dominated the Academy Awards, but she told a friend in confidence, "I know this is the beginning of the end."

This applied to Milland, also. His career had reached its peak. Within a year, his name had little drawing power at the box office, and in 1947, his films played double bills. He was tall, dark, and charming and his sharp features blended into handsomeness, but there was nothing outstanding about his looks. This lack of individualism kept him busy making movies, however, because he was a good foil for Paulette Goddard, Lana Turner, Marlene Dietrich — and Grace Kelly.

Milland had never been publicly linked to another woman. That he played when an opportunity presented itself was hushed in the Hollywood gossip mills. Everyone in town liked his wife and respected him. Ray was a good sport and had a fine sense of humor. In his memoirs, he wrote about filmmaking, "I have been paid fabulous sums to frolic with and to make bogus love to the most beautiful women in the world, which on one or two cases turned out to be not so bogus. My life in those days was one long saga of agony and ecstasy."

Dial M for Murder was a good vehicle for Milland; as the loving husband planning his wife's murder, it gave him a chance to act with compelling insincerity. "In a good movie," Hitchcock said, "the sound could go off and the audience would still have a perfectly clear idea of what was going on."

The same could be said for the blooming romance between Grace Kelly and Ray Milland. No one had to overhear their conversation to know what was brewing. Hitchcock was aware that other men in the cast and crew were taken with Grace, whose dressing room was filled with flowers. The competition was apparent to Milland, who did some pursuing of his own. An observant Hitchcock could voice his disapproval with one sour expression, but Grace was careful not to alienate him. She was a regular weekend dinner guest at the director's home at Bellagio Road. "Alma Hitchcock was a gourmet cook," Grace said. "I dieted all week in preparation for her delightful meals. We began with a stiff dry martini and then the best wines were served with course after course of delectable dishes."

On these pleasurable weekends, Hitchcock found time to go over the script with Grace to discuss his interpretation of her role. She had little to do in *Dial M,* but he had already decided to use her in future film projects. Grace's one major scene was getting out of bed in the middle of the night to answer the telephone while the murderer hides behind a curtain near the desk. He grabs her around the neck from behind, but gasping for her last breath, she stabs him with a pair of scissors. Hitchcock had chosen an elegant red velvet robe for her to wear, but Grace asked him, "Why would I bother to put on a fancy robe? I'd get out of bed and simply go to answer the phone in my nightgown." Hitchcock agreed to try it her way and liked the idea of Grace, half-clothed, struggling in the clutches of a man. It gave a dash of sex to the scene, and Hitchcock spent more than a week shooting it until he was satisfied with every detail.

He spoke to Grace about his next film, *Rear Window* (1954), obviously trying to get her reaction. She was interested but complained about her Metro contract. "I can't do anything without their permission." Hitchcock said MGM made a very good profit by loaning her out to other studios. "They'll use you in some bit of trash eventually," he said, "after everyone else has turned it down."

Hitchcock was trying to undo what Grace had been taught in drama school, and she was receptive. Not only had he lowered her voice into softer tones and taught her the art of using subtle facial expressions, he was also changing Grace's image. The *Los Angeles Daily News* described her as a "blonde, sexy newcomer with an appeal that will give the boys something to think about."

Ray Milland was one of them. It wasn't his style to chase women, but he did just that with Grace, who made no attempt to escape. Falling in love wasn't part of his master plan, either. A close friend of his said, "Ray took what came along in regard to women. He was a fun-loving guy who enjoyed a good time. He met Grace when she was taking on a new identity. Maybe she was testing it out on him, but the truth is they fell in love. It was harder on Ray because he had more to lose. He was twice her age, and she possessed a quality of innocence. Those of us who heard about the Cooper affair found it difficult to believe after meeting her."

They were discreet in the beginning, but rumors started when Grace and Ray were seen dining frequently. They were also observed having a few drinks at a cozy little place late in the evening. Mal Milland was accustomed to rumors about her husband, but when they persisted, she decided to find out for herself if the gossip was true. When Ray said he was going away for a few days on business, Mal sought help from trustworthy friends, who saw him boarding a plane with Grace.

Mal confronted Ray and they separated. He got an apartment in Hollywood, where Grace was seen coming and going at all hours.

Confidential magazine, which was the *People* magazine of its day, gathered more than enough information for a major article about Milland's fascination with his leading lady: "After one look at Gracie he went into a tailspin that reverberated from Perino's to Ciro's. The whole town soon hee-hawed over the news that suave Milland, who had a wife and family at home, was gaga over Grace. Ray pursued her ardently and Hollywood cackled. Then Mama Milland found out. She lowered the boom on Ramblin' Ray, and there followed one of the loudest, most tearful nights their Beverly Hills neighbors can remember."

The Millands had issued a joint statement that "they have come to the decision that it might be best for both of us to separate temporarily. The problems which have ended in this decision are purely personal. There is no third party involved"; but *Los Angeles Mirror-News* columnist Kendis Rochlen wrote, "Miss Kelly's supposed to be so terribly proper, but then look at all those whispers about her and Ray Milland."

Henry Hathaway's widow told author James Spada, "I have nothing good to say about Grace. She had an affair with my best friend's husband, Ray Milland. And all the time wearing those white gloves!" When asked if Grace had affairs with anyone else in Hollywood, Mrs. Hathaway replied, "You name it. Everybody! She wore those white gloves, but she was no saint."

Jack Kelly told public relations executive Scoop Conlon, an old friend, to "keep an eye on Grace" and reverse the damaging publicity. Jack hinted to a reporter that he didn't think very much of Milland. "I don't like that sort of thing," he said. "I'd like to see Grace married, but people in Hollywood think marriage is like a game of musical chairs."

Jack Kelly should have had sympathy for Grace because he had been very much in love with divorcée Ellen Frazer, a socialite from Philadelphia. They met shortly after Jack was the defeated Democratic candidate for mayor of Philadelphia in 1935. The Kelly children did not know about their father's girlfriend, but Margaret would not consent to a separation or a divorce. Ellen Frazer moved to Palm Beach and married an heir to the Minnesota Milling and Mining Company fortune. Though Jack enjoyed the company of other ladies, Ellen was the one and only woman he wanted to marry.

It's possible he related to Grace subconsciously because one of his arguments against her marrying was Milland's strong and enduring attachment to Mal, which Jack knew in his heart was similar to the bond he had with Margaret.

To avoid arguing, Grace gave her parents the impression that she would go back to New York and give up Milland. Within a few days, Louella Parsons wrote, "Grace dropped Ray like a hot potato when she heard about Mal Milland's divorce plans."

The *New York Journal American* did an article about Grace entitled: KELLY HASN'T ANYBODY'S HUSBAND. SHE'S JUST GOT A COLD. "With claws sharpened for action, more than one Hollywood housewife's growling, 'Anybody here seen Kelly?' — meaning Grace Kelly, tall, cool-type blond whose on-screen specialty is being married to actors, and who seems to be an off-screen jinx domestic-wise to her leading men." The reporter wrote that Grace was not happy, dabbing her blue eyes with a tissue and sniffing. "I've heard of some pretty silly things," she said huskily, "but this thing about Ray and me takes the Oscar. We didn't even have lunch alone in the Commissary!"

Grace denied any romance with Milland to Aline Mosby of the United Press. "Certainly not on my side," she said with a dash of sarcasm. Mosby compared her to Audrey Hepburn "in a new school of stars with boyish figures." Grace retorted, "The public is tired of curves. Years ago, the fashion was for flat-chested women. Then came the trend for bosoms. Now they want something new, I guess."

Louella Parsons had more to say, too: "I happen to know when Grace began *Dial M for Murder* she thought Ray was separated from his wife. Later he did leave home, but it was not the first time he walked out on his beautiful wife, Mal. This time, Mal decided to teach him a lesson. The first time he was the most miserable man in the world and came over to pour out his troubles on my shoulder. The second time, I criticized him, and I believe I mentioned by innuendo the 'siren' Grace."

Brian was amazed that Milland's name was never brought up when he had lunch with Grace shortly after she returned from Hollywood. "So I called Hughes and got the lowdown," he said. "It seems that everything that Milland owned was in his wife's name. She was pulling the strings and if Ray got a divorce, he'd be one broke puppet. Grace did not drop him like a hot potato. She saw Milland for almost a year. It was a mistake, that's all. A heartbreaking mistake."

Grace's Hollywood friends remained loyal during the scandal. Alfred Hitchcock called her about getting started on *Rear Window* with Jimmy Stewart. She was very excited with the prospect of working for Hitchcock again. It also gave her an excuse to go back to Hollywood — and Ray Milland.

Everyone connected with her films claimed, ". . . to work with Grace was to love her." They spoke out in her defense and some confessed to having fallen in love with the adorable actress who was anything but a shrew. She had a compelling aura that attracted any man if he was still breathing, but Grace was young and had been sheltered most of her life. Despite her cool and worldly appearance, she was a sensitive and trusting girl who fell in love too easily, her close friends intimated.

MGM worked hard to polish Grace's image by publishing her background in Philadelphia, emphasizing the athletic achievements of the Kelly men, her Pulitzer Prize-winning Uncle George, and Grace's flying home for the funeral of her childhood sweetheart, Harper Davis.

One reporter referred to her as "the blonde Philadelphia socialite," allowing the reader to assume she was a Main Line debutante, pure and unsoiled. Moviegoers were fascinated with the stories of Grace's life because their favorite movie stars, Ava Gardner, Joan Crawford, Clark Gable, Marilyn Monroe, Cary Grant, Barbara Stanwyck, and Alan Ladd had come from poor families forced to live on the wrong side of the tracks. Indeed, Grace Kelly *was* different, they surmised, and "jealous tramps" in Hollywood were trying to drag her down to their level.

The public ran to see *Mogambo* for the first or second time, and anxiously awaited *Dial M for Murder*. No one had to tell Grace to watch her step. She was devastated by the article in *Confidential* and the comments made by upstanding Hollywood citizens who sided with Mal Milland.

Bette Davis told her close friend, author Roy Moseley, that there were two "round heels" in Hollywood — Ingrid Bergman and Grace Kelly.

Before leaving for California to make *Rear Window*, Grace had lunch with Brian.

"I don't want to leave New York," she said.

"You have three good reasons to be on cloud nine."

"And what are they?" she asked, looking him straight in the eye.

"A great part, Hitchcock, and Jimmy Stewart."

"There's a fourth," Grace said teasingly.

Brian was positive she would at last bring up the subject of Ray Milland. "A fourth being the weather?"

"No. My wardrobe. Edith Head's sketches are smashing."

"Then cheer up, Grace. Maybe the studio will let you wear Miss Head's creations out on the town. Any exciting social events planned?"

"I don't go out when I'm working, but I hope to see Clark. He wants me to do a film with him in Hong Kong."

"Good script?"

"I haven't the vaguest. If it's good enough for Gable, it's good enough for Kelly."

"Is it good enough for MGM?"

"They haven't used me in anything. If Dore Schary won't loan me out, I'll go on suspension."

Brian remarked that "she had a bee in her bonnet" about everything that day. He had seen Grace annoyed before, but it went beyond her dislike for Hollywood and her caged-in attitude toward MGM. Brian was just as frustrated that she held back about Milland. "I didn't care if she lied," he said. "Grace always talked casually about her leading men, but not Milland. She mentioned him only once, and that was when he retired to the French Riviera not long after she married the Prince."

Grace returned to the town she despised and had long but depressing discussions with Milland. They were still very much in love, but Grace confessed in later years that she felt like a streetwalker during the scandalous affair and that she would not give the press or her enemies any cause to talk about her.

Ray went back to his wife and two children. In his 1974 book, *Wide-Eyed in Babylon,* he does not mention Grace Kelly. It is an amusing, breezy book that reflects his good humor rather than the grueling details of his life.

Milland did two successful television series and continued making movies. In 1980, critic David Thomson hailed him as "one of the most interesting of Hollywood survivors. Only after fifty did he show how discriminating and imaginative he could be in films of his own and by picking parts in exciting B pictures."

Milland's philosophy on acting, he told an interviewer, was, "Do what you can with what you've got. I know actors from my generation who sit at home and cry, 'Why don't they send me any scripts?' I tell them, 'Because you still think of yourself as a leading man. You're sixty-eight, not twenty-eight. Face it.'" He backed up this statement by appearing bald-headed practically overnight. His final roles included the 1984 movie *Sea Serpent: Mask of Death,* a television movie with the late Anne Baxter; and a recurring role as Stefanie Powers's father in TV's "Hart to Hart."

Ray Milland died of cancer on March 10, 1986. There was no funeral. His body was cremated and the ashes scattered at sea.

CHAPTER
EIGHT

The Crooner, Golden Boy, and Others

Gable discussed *Soldier of Fortune* (1955) with Grace. He was very excited about his negotiations with Twentieth Century-Fox. "I'm asking ten percent of the gross and a guaranteed four hundred thousand up front. That's not unreasonable, but it's the old waiting game for now. I also told 'em I wanted you for my leading lady. Keep it in mind, babe."

"Would I miss out on a free trip to Hong Kong?" she asked.

"I've often wondered which you wanted most — Africa or me."

"It was a package deal," she said, smiling. "I couldn't lose."

Grace was one of many girls the King was dating, but he was growing tired of the variety of women waiting for him in Palm Beach, New York, Phoenix, and Palm Springs. He proposed marriage to socialite Dolly O'Brien and movie executive Anita Colby. They turned him down because he drank too much. Clark and Grace wanted to believe marriage was possible, but once they faced facts, each could give the other warmth and understanding without dwelling on what might have been. Now they concentrated on working together in another film, an adventure that was very appealing to Grace.

Rear Window (1954) is the story about a bored photographer (James Stewart), confined to a wheelchair with a broken leg, who spies on his neighbors with a telephoto lens and believes one of them has murdered his wife. Grace played Jimmy's wealthy and playful girlfriend who drops by every day with food and kisses. Once again, Hitchcock played the sex game with his audience. It is obvious the wheelchair-bound Stewart can't make love and it is very obvious that Grace is trying to keep him warm in the meantime. The theme is based on murder and clues and neighbor-watching, but Stewart is so obsessed, one gets the impression that he should put away his lenses, put his arms around a very inviting Grace, and solve the murder some other time.

Jimmy Stewart had married Gloria McLean in 1949. He said in an interview recently how lucky he was to have found this wonderful woman, whom he still cherishes. "What did I do to deserve her?" he asked with misty eyes. While he was making *Rear Window,* the press and Hollywoodites wondered if Stewart would succumb to Grace, who had a perfect score to date. When asked how he felt about her, Jimmy said, "Everything about Grace is appealing. I'm married but I'm not dead! She has those big warm eyes — and, well, if you ever have played a love scene with her, you'd know she's not cold . . . besides, Grace has that twinkle and a touch of larceny in her eye."

Jimmy did, however, break tradition by frequently bringing her flowers. In his own shy way, he was neither obvious nor secretive about the bouquets, mumbling that he had picked them from his own garden. Others in the cast didn't think so, but how else could he explain an otherwise romantic gesture? Jimmy did not fall in love with Grace but he put her on a pedestal. "She has class," he said. "Not just the class of being a lady — I don't think that has anything to do with it — but she'll always have the class you find in a really great racehorse." According to journalist Gwen Robyns, when Grace married Prince Rainier, Jimmy said, "I'd have slit my throat if Grace ever did anything that was not like herself. If she had married one of these phony Hollywood characters, I'd have formed a committee of vigilantes."

Hitchcock did not bring flowers for his leading lady but he got dress designer Edith Head to fashion Grace's wardrobe in *Rear Window*. He told Miss Head it was important that the clothes help to establish some of the conflict in the story. Grace was to be the typical sophisticated society-girl magazine editor who falls in love with a scruffy photographer. He is insecure and thinks that she thinks he isn't good enough for her. "Hitch wanted Grace to look like a piece of Dresden china," Head explained, "something slightly untouchable. Her suits were impeccably tailored. Her accessories looked as though they couldn't be worn by anyone else but her. She was perfect and carried it off as no other actress could."

Grace appeared in a nightgown and peignoir in Jimmy's apartment, yet it was still an innocent scene because his leg was in a cast. She was showing him what he was missing

117

by not marrying her — a perfect example of Hitchcock's off-beat sense of humor.

Edith Head recalled that on one occasion, Hitchcock took her aside and whispered, "Can't we do something about Grace's bosom? It's not right. We'll have to put something in there." Grace told Miss Head in the dressing room, "I'm not going to wear falsies. They're too obvious. We'll make some minor adjustments and I'll stand as straight as I can." Hitchcock was satisfied. He looked at Grace and said, "See what a difference they make?"

Grace usually related this story "because it was one of the few times I defied Hitch. I never wore falsies and had no intention of doing so in the future."

Hitchcock wanted Grace to play herself in *Rear Window* and asked screenwriter John Michael Hayes to work with her prior to filming. His job was to highlight the girlfriend with Grace's sensual elegance. Despite himself, Hayes was entranced by her. "I couldn't get over the difference between her personal animation and, if I may say so, her sexuality. There was an alive, vital girl underneath that demure quiet facade. She had an inner life aching to be expressed."

Grace spoke with a clipped British accent on and off the screen. To her close friends, she sounded somewhat affected, but her manner of speaking fit her roles in *Mogamba* and *Dial M for Murder*. She also had the ability to tone down the British influence and come across as a graduate of Vassar. Grace suffered from a chronic sinus condition and frequent head colds, and was allergic to the smog in Los Angeles. The mild British accent helped to cover up the nasality, as did Hitchcock's lowering of her voice.

*   *   *

Bing Crosby was one of many celebrities introduced to Grace Kelly in 1952. His wife, Dixie, was dying of cancer, but that did not stop him from seeing other women. The Crosbys lived next door to the Alan Ladds, who invited Bing to use their pool anytime. What they did not expect was his dropping by with women after dark. Sue Ladd was gracious even though Dixie was a close friend. The two couples had a few drinks and pleasant conversation until Alan invariably excused himself. "I have to be at the studio early in the morning. Enjoy yourself, Bing, but remember to lock the door when you leave."

One of Crosby's girlfriends was Grace Kelly. Sue or Alan would occasionally go downstairs after midnight to make sure the door was latched and would be embarrassed to find Bing and Grace caressing and kissing on their couch. Alan never said anything, but he thought Crosby should go to a motel. Bing was known to be "close with a buck," but, more important, he did not want to risk losing his "nice guy" image.

Dixie Crosby died in November 1952, when Grace was in Africa.

Bing ignored the traditional mourning period and dated Rhonda Fleming, Kathryn Grant, and Mona Freeman. After Grace's breakup with Ray Milland, she resumed her romance with Bing, who was the same age as Gable. Gossip columnists glamorized her dates with the Crooner and the King. That Grace's mother or sister occasionally tagged along as chaperone was always good for a snicker from Hollywood insiders. Gable was particularly amused. "Where were her chaperones in Africa?" he joked.

After twenty-two years of marriage, Bing Crosby wanted to come and go as he pleased, though he had managed to have a good time when Dixie was alive. Crosby was a cold and controlled man who did not have the ability to love. His biographers claim no one person knew him very well. Whatever his indiscretions, the press took pity on him because it was common knowledge that Dixie was an alcoholic. She abused him in public and probably for all the right reasons, but Bing was considered a lonely and pathetic man in the forties. The public adored him so much that they would not have believed he was anything other than a devoted husband and the perfect father. Though Dixie's days were numbered, he agreed to make a movie in Europe and deliberately took an extended vacation, arriving home only a week before her death.

When Bing was seeing Grace at his neighbor's house in 1952, she was one of many girls he was using for diversion. Grace's two-year affair with Crosby was sporadic. She did not have the same strong attraction to him as she had had for Cooper, Gable, and Milland, but Bing was the perfect escort for Grace when she needed an impeccable mien. As the saying goes, she loved him but she wasn't *in* love with him. It was Bing who lost his cold, cold heart and never recovered.

Dial M for Murder opened at the Paramount Theatre on May 29, 1954. Bosley Crowther, critic for *The New York Times*, wrote, "In the pliant hands of Alfred Hitchcock, master at the job of squeezing thrills, the coils twine with sleek and silken evil. . . . His actors unfold the drama in their very appearances as do their various attitudes. . . . Ray Milland as the machinating husband is excitingly effectual, and Grace Kelly does a nice job of acting the wife's bewilderment, terror and grief. . . . Excellent color and color combinations add to the flow and variety of the drama's moods."

GRACE KELLY — HOLLYWOOD'S BRIGHTEST AND BUSIEST NEW STAR was the caption under her photo on the April cover of *Life* magazine. It predicted 1954 would be "the year of Grace."

Jack Kelly did not know what all the excitement was about. Neither did MGM mogul Dore Schary, who agreed to lend Grace to Paramount for a small part in *The Bridges at Toko-Ri* (1954) at a fee of $25,000. Grace's salary for a few weeks' work was $10,000. William Perlberg and George Seaton were coproducers of this Korean War picture that featured William Holden as a Navy pilot with a dangerous mission to destroy vital Korean bridges. Much of *Toko-Ri* was shot on location in the Far East, but Grace's scenes, as Holden's wife spending a week in Tokyo with him, were filmed on the Paramount lot in Hollywood.

Perlberg said in an interview, "The part of the wife wasn't big enough to attract an established star, but there were a few spots in it which had to be right, and we needed more than just an ordinary actress who could get away with it. We interviewed a lot of girls, but Grace had the sense to wear a plain outfit, flat-heeled walking shoes and her glasses. She had already grasped an understanding of the pilot's wife and took the role seriously."

Bill Holden was in Japan when he heard that Grace Kelly had been cast in *Toko-Ri*. He had heard a lot about her and was anxious to find out for himself if the rumors were true or exaggerated.

One of their scenes together was in a Japanese bath

and the other in bed. They were instantly attracted to one another. *Toko-Ri* was a first for Grace in several respects. She is seen wearing a bathing suit, she appeared in bed with a man, and she fell in love with a costar who was only eleven years older than she.

William Holden was known as "Golden Boy" for the role that made him famous in 1939. He attributed his good fortune to Barbara Stanwyck, his leading lady in the movie; until his death in 1981, he sent her roses every year on April 1, the anniversary of the film's starting date.

He was born William Franklin Beedle in O'Fallon, Illinois, in 1918. The family moved to South Pasadena, California, where Bill grew up with the ambition of becoming a chemist like his father. For a lark, he appeared as Marie Curie's eighty-year-old father-in-law in the stage production of *Manya* at the Pasadena Playhouse. A talent scout from Paramount Pictures liked the voice behind the beard and arranged a screen test for the twenty-year-old Beedle, who signed a seven-year contract at a starting salary of fifty dollars. Paramount's publicity director Terry DeLapp thought the name "Beedle" sounded like an insect. "Yeah," Bill said, "they used to call me Bugs in school."

"I was just talking to an associate editor of the *Times*," DeLapp said. "His name's Bill Holden. Let me give him a call." He got the newspaperman on the phone and explained, "There's a young kid in my office who needs a new name. Mind if I give him yours?"

"Does he look like the kind who'll get me in trouble?" the editor asked.

"He's from South Pasadena. Does that answer your question?"

122

DeLapp hung up the phone and asked young Beedle, "How would you like to be William Holden?"

Bill shrugged, "I don't care."

Bill is best known for his roles in *Sunset Boulevard* (1950) with Gloria Swanson, *Born Yesterday* (1950), and for his Oscar-winning performance in *Stalag 17* (1953). Six feet tall, with wide muscular shoulders, slim hips, thick brown hair, and blue eyes, Holden was a stunning man. As a boy, he had been excellent at gymnastics and was able to balance himself on a telephone line. Bill terrified many a producer and leading lady when they found him hanging by his fingertips from a window ledge twenty stories off the ground.

Holden had married actress Brenda Marshall in 1941. They had three children, a daughter from her previous marriage and two sons, Peter and Scott. His marriage began to fall apart in the early fifties. If it ended in divorce, he had made up his mind not to marry again — until, that is, he met Audrey Hepburn. During the production of *Sabrina* (1954), they fell in love and spoke about marriage. There was only one problem. Audrey wanted children but Holden had undergone a vasectomy after his second son had been born. Audrey changed her mind about marrying Bill because she was only twenty-five and wanted to have children of her own. When she married Mel Ferrer, Holden took a trip around the world and pledged, "I'm going to screw a girl in every country I visit." Still in love with Audrey, he made a point of telling her about his exciting vacation; she shrugged it off

William Holden lived life to the hilt. He was a gentleman, a delightful tease, a hearty drinker, a womanizer, and one of the best-looking actors in Hollywood. Shelley Winters wrote in her memoirs that she had spent several Christmas Eves with Bill in his dressing room from 4:00 p.m. to 4:00 a.m. and that he had given her a diamond watch in the early fifties. When her book was released some twenty years later, Bill told a reporter that he was grateful to Shelley for the free publicity, but the gallant prankster went one step further at a dinner dance in the Beverly Hills Hotel. When the band stopped in the middle of a song and played "White Christmas," Bill walked over to Shelley's table and bowed with outstretched arms. The humor to this story is that they had not seen each other all year, but he was waiting for her faithfully during the studio's annual Christmas party.

Bill began *The Bridges at Toko-Ri* not long after completing *Sabrina* with Audrey. His falling in love with Grace Kelly might have been a rebound affair, but his friends say he had been serious enough to propose to both women, who were very much alike, according to Holden. In a Paramount publicity release, he said, "Women like Grace Kelly and Audrey Hepburn help us to believe in the innate dignity of man."

During *Toko-Ri*, Bill and Grace had a gratifying affair that was interrupted when she finished her few scenes and returned to New York. The reviews of *Toko-Ri* concentrated on the war heroes in the film, Mickey Rooney, Fredric March, and Holden. *The New York Times* called Grace "briefly bewitching" and the *New York Herald Tribune* said, "Everyone knows how nice it is to have her around."

Grace enjoyed doing *Toko-Ri* with Bill but she had no intention of playing small parts again. When she heard that Jennifer Jones was pregnant and had to withdraw from *The Country Girl* (1954), Grace told MGM she wanted the part of Georgie Elgin. The studio said every actress in

Hollywood wanted to audition for that role. Furthermore, Dore Schary was opposed to loaning her out to Paramount a third time. Grace's reply to MGM's opposition was, "I'll give up making movies and go back to the theater."

The once-powerful Metro-Goldwyn-Mayer had lost their great contract players of the Golden Era, a time when scandal could have ruined Grace's chances of making another movie in Hollywood. Not only did MGM need her in 1954, but she was one of the few stars getting a salary rather than a percentage of the gross. Schary, however, did not give in right away because he was sure Paramount would not consider Grace the type to play the dowdy Georgie.

Grace decided to wait it out in New York. The love she shared with Ray Milland was a lingering threat for both of them. Ray did not want to go home until Grace sent him back. How and when they saw or spoke to each other isn't known. By her own admission, she clung to the hope that a miracle would reunite them. For Mal's sake, Ray was not available to the press, and Grace put on a glorious front, refusing to mention Milland's name even to her closest friends.

Returning to New York was Grace's only salvation. She saw a good deal of Jean-Pierre Aumont, who, she hoped, would help her forget Ray Milland, the one man she could not get out of her system.

Grace spent the weekends in Philadelphia with her family. Peggy was married with two children and Lizanne, the youngest, was engaged. Jack Kelly thought it was time Grace settled down, too. He pointed to Peggy as the star in the family and, to rub it in, brought up Grace's losing the Oscar for *Mogambo*. She was low-key when Jack was around because he didn't appreciate her acting out parts for her sisters, who wanted to know what it was like to be kissed by Gary Cooper and Clark Gable.

Margaret remained leery of Grace's choice in men. She said in an interview, "Ray Milland, Bing Crosby, and Jean-Pierre Aumont were the ones, the columnists said, who captured Gracie's affections for varying lengths of time. She was seen with each of these men, and she was interested in at least two of them. For a time, she considered marrying one — until her reason and her practical side prevailed. But none of the columnists, not even the ones who claimed to know the inside story, knew exactly what did go on."

The Kellys frequently arranged dates for Grace in New York or Philadelphia. They still had hopes that she would marry a wealthy businessman from the East; to keep peace in the family, Grace went out with some. There were one or two she dated frequently, but a friend claimed they were "society flings," tennis, sailing, and parties on Long Island.

"She enjoyed these diversions," Brian said, "because Grace needed to get away from the acting crowd — to balance herself. She had made up her mind to be a great movie star. This may sound egotistical, but whatever Grace did, she had to be the best, just like Jack Kelly. Philadelphia was a reminder that she could not please her father or make him proud of her. At this stage in her life, Grace didn't have a real home. She loved New York but worked in Hollywood. It appeared glamorous, but not for a sensitive person like Grace, who needed roots."

Jean-Pierre Aumont was born of Jewish heritage in Paris in 1909. His father's surname was Salomons; his mother's

126

was Cohen. Jean-Pierre appeared in many notable film and stage productions. Among his close friends in the British theater were Vivien Leigh and Laurence Olivier.

Aumont joined the French Tank Corps in 1939 and won the Croix de Guerre. Medically discharged, he made films in Hollywood and married actress Maria Montez in 1943. The daughter of a Spanish don, she had become a fantasy movie queen as Scheherazade in *Arabian Nights* (1942) with Jon Hall, her frequent leading man in *White Savage* (1943), *Ali Baba and the Forty Thieves* (1944), and *Cobra Woman* (1944).

Aumont's movie career was interrupted when he served with the Free French Army, was wounded again, and earned the Legion of Honor. In 1946, he returned to acting, dividing his time between America and France. In 1951, Maria died of a heart attack at the age of thirty-one. When Jean-Pierre met Grace a year later, he was living at his countryside home outside Paris with his small daughter, Maria-Christine.

Aumont was described by journalist Gwen Robyns as having a "kind of wanton charm superimposed on golden good looks that defy age." Grace obviously had him in mind when she said, "I prefer European men." Aumont was, above all, a survivor and the perfect father-image for Grace. She corresponded with him and they tried to be in New York at the same time. The press was not as yet very interested in Grace and her Frenchman because they believed she was still very much involved with Ray Milland.

Jean-Pierre and Grace were having dinner at Le Veau d'Or on East 60th Street when fashion designer Oleg Cassini sat down at a table nearby. He had seen *Mogambo* that very night and had been captivated by Grace. To his delight, there she now was only a few feet away. Cassini described her as "gorgeous, not striking. She did not stand out in a room; her beauty was subtle, the sort that required a second look."

Oleg calculated his first move very carefully before approaching Aumont's table. The two men had only been introduced once or twice in Hollywood, but Cassini's charm would see him through. While he and Jean-Pierre engaged in meaningless conversation, Oleg deliberately ignored Grace. When he was introduced to her, he continued his game of pretending he had never heard of Grace Kelly. The following morning, and for the next ten days, he sent her a dozen roses and signed the card, "The Friendly Florist." When he called to introduce himself, Grace seemed reluctant to go out with him but eventually gave in to having lunch. A few days later, when she turned down his dinner invitation because her sister was in town, Oleg took them both out. Grace was interested in Aumont and annoyed by the persistent Cassini, who would not take no for an answer. "There are other people I would like to see," she complained.

"Then we will see them together," Oleg said, and he arranged a small party at El Morocco for Grace and her friends. That night she told him, "I want you to know I happen to be in love." Cassini suspected Aumont but persisted until he got the man's initials — R. M. He complimented her on having good taste but added, "I don't think his wife will divorce him." She said it didn't matter. Oleg predicted within the year that he, himself, would be engaged to her. Grace was disgusted and exclaimed, "You're crazy!" At the end of the evening, she thanked him and announced her departure for California the next day. It was Grace's way of saying, "Good-bye and good riddance, Mr. Cassini!"

CHAPTER
NINE

Marry-Go-Round

William Perlberg and George Seaton, producers of *The Bridges at Toko-Ri*, were preparing to film *The Country Girl* with Jennifer Jones in the part of Georgie when they received a call from her husband, David Selznick, telling them that she was pregnant. Perlberg and Seaton looked at each other with the same idea in mind — Grace Kelly. She had proven herself at the audition for the unpretentious Navy wife in *Toko-Ri*, and they knew she could handle the part of Georgie by further underplaying her attributes. Perlberg said, "*Somehow*, we let Grace know we were negotiating for her, and *somehow* she got a copy of the *Country Girl* script."

Dore Schary tried to get around loaning her out to Paramount with the excuse that MGM wanted Grace to do *Green Fire* (1954) for them immediately. This is when she gave them the ultimatum, "I'll tear up my contract and give up films." They finally compromised. Grace could play the part of Georgie providing she follow up with *Green Fire* and agree to do four extra films for MGM.

"I just *had* to be in *The Country Girl*," Grace said. "There was a real acting part in it for me. Sometimes I had to act before, but I had beautiful clothes, or beautiful lingerie, or glamorous settings to help me. Many times I was just the feminine background for the male stars who carried the action and the story on their shoulders."

The screenplay of *The Country Girl* was adapted by George Seaton from a play by Clifford Odets. It is the story of Frank Elgin (Crosby), a singer and actor who turns to drink as his career sinks into the doldrums. When a Broadway director, Bernie Dodd (Holden), offers him a comeback, Frank blames his decline on his wife Georgie (Grace), who is worn out by years of supporting a weak, self-centered man. Bernie tries to separate the couple until he realizes that it is Georgie who has kept her husband from total destruction. They fall in love and work together to rebuild Frank's career and his self-confidence. In the end, however, Georgie sacrifices her love for Bernie and remains with Frank.

In the beginning of the film, Grace as the drained and exhausted Georgie appears with greasy hair and wearing baggy, wrinkled clothes. She has no vitality. Her eyes are listless and she wears no make-up. As her husband makes his comeback, she takes more pride in herself, particularly when another man falls in love with her; but Georgie at her best is merely a good-looking woman, lending contrast in the love scenes with Bernie, who is handsome enough to have any girl he wants.

Grace won her battle with MGM, but she had one more hurdle. Bing Crosby had the right to choose, accept, or reject his leading ladies, and he thought Grace was too pretty for the part of his droopy wife. He also doubted she could act the part with conviction. Perlberg and Seaton suggested giving Grace a chance. Bing shrugged, saying, "If it's okay with you guys, it's okay with me." After the first week of filming, he said, "I'll never open my mouth to you two again. I'm sorry I had my doubts about her. She's great."

Crosby's opinion was justified. He hadn't seen Grace for a while and was stunned by her beauty. Whatever feelings he had had for her previously were now magnified. She had been very hurt that he hadn't thought her worthy of *The Country Girl* and cried when Bing expressed his blunt thoughts to Seaton and Perlberg. He might have been rude at the start, but very soon Crosby was romancing Grace and pressing for dates. Bill Holden had been looking forward to being with her again, but he noticed that she was staying late with Bing in his dressing room almost every night. Bill took this in his stride because Bing was a good friend. Grace had, for the time being, chosen the man who could do her the most good, but she did not want to lose Holden, either. Using discretion, Grace told Bing about her dates with Bill who, she thought, felt slighted. Crosby rose to the occasion and invited Holden to his dressing room.

"I don't mind telling you, Bill," he said, "I'm smitten with Grace. Daffy about her, and I was wondering if . . ."

"If I felt the same way?" Holden replied. "What man wouldn't be overwhelmed by her? But look, Bing, I won't interfere."

Crosby and Grace were soon making the rounds of nightclubs and were publicized as "Hollywood's Newest Romance." He fell deeply in love with her and proposed marriage. Grace handled the situation delicately by asking for time. She was caught by surprise and needed to discuss the matter with her family; but there wasn't time for that just now because she was leaving for South America to do *Green Fire* right after *The Country Girl* was finished. Bing was disappointed, but he went along with it for a while.

Meanwhile, Oleg Cassini was also biding his time. He had written to Grace and had spoken to her casually on the phone. Then one evening she called him at his Long Island home, which he shared with his mother and brother. Grace said that she was lonely and needed cheering up. Could he come to Hollywood?

Oleg was so excited that he ran out of the house and jumped off the diving board into the swimming pool with all his clothes on. "It was in midair," he said, "that I remembered the pool had been drained. I landed face first."

With two black eyes and a broken nose, he appeared at her door. She opened and then closed it, finally letting him in with a giggle. Cassini was confused when Grace announced that she did not date during the work week but that he could pick her up at Paramount the next day. Oleg visited the *Country Girl* set often but saw very little of Grace socially. When he was photographed on the nightclub circuit with Anita Ekberg and Pier Angeli, Grace was miffed.

"It's all very simple," Cassini explained. "You're busy and I enjoy going out with lovely ladies."

Grace had hoped he would be satisfied seeing her on the movie set, where she allowed him to kiss and hug her in front of everyone. Crosby assumed Cassini was her new love interest. Holden got a different message — Grace was no longer involved with his friend, Bing, opening the door for him. Oleg was being used, but he also found the *real* Grace, who demanded attention and loyalty from the men who pursued her. Cassini decided two could play that game.

* * *

Oleg Loiewski-Cassini, a Russian Jew, was born in Paris in 1913 but grew up in Florence, where his mother had a dress salon. He played tennis on the Davis Cup team and, after emigrating to New York with his mother and brother, set up his own design business. Oleg and his brother Igor, who wrote the Cholly Knickerbocker gossip column, were very much a part of New York and Palm Beach society.

After his divorce from heiress Merry Fahrney, Oleg married actress Gene Tierney in 1941 and mingled with the Hollywood crowd. Eleven years later, they were divorced. Gene fell in love with Prince Aly Khan, who courted her throughout Europe, but they did not marry, as the press had predicted. She was in and out of mental sanatoriums for a few years but eventually married Hedy Lamarr's former husband, Texas millionaire Howard Lee.

Oleg Cassini was tall and slim with dark hair and a mustache. He was known as an international playboy with a continental charm that women found irresistible. Gene Tierney said Cassini was not handsome but dangerous in a seductive way; thin-lipped and languid: "Perhaps if I had never gone to school in Switzerland I would not have found Oleg as interesting as I did. He represented all the things that were different, glamorous, and continental. He had a beautiful speaking voice."

The Cassinis had two children. Daria was born mentally ill and was institutionalized for life. Oleg also paid the expenses and assisted with their other daughter, Tina. In her memoirs, Gene Tierney wrote about Oleg: "Fortunate is the woman who has a loving husband and an ex-husband who remains her friend."

Today, Cassini is best known for designing Jackie Kennedy's White House wardrobe, which began a new fashion trend for women in America and put hats on their heads once again, particularly the famous pillbox style.

Grace managed to keep Crosby interested but at bay during production of *The Country Girl*. She and Bill Holden resumed a romance that was blooming again even though Cassini was courting her on the Paramount lot. Grace knew she was in danger of another scandal involving a married man, but she was in love with Holden, who found her magnetic. They were careful to avoid suspicion by not spending time together on the movie set or in their dressing rooms. They arrived and left the studio separately. When Grace and Bill managed to slip out of town by car, a third party went along. The very few people who knew about the affair assumed Holden was on the rebound after his breakup with Audrey Hepburn. He seemed to be satisfied with uncomplicated affairs and was not in any rush to get a divorce, but it was just a matter of time before Bill found himself in love with Grace. When they talked about marriage, she consulted the family priest, who said, "If a non-Catholic divorced man embraces the Catholic church, his previous marriage will be considered invalid."

Holden had difficulty with the idea of dismissing his wife and children as though they had never existed. He told Grace this was a decision he could not make in haste. They continued to see each other, hoping to find another solution.

Reporters for *Confidential* magazine knew about the Kelly-Holden affair but were waiting for pictures to back up their exposé. Reporters finally got what they were waiting for — Holden's white Cadillac Eldorado convertible parked outside Grace's apartment early in the morning.

The allegations in *Confidential* were true but the evidence was all wrong. Director Arthur Jacobson said, "Grace called me the night before and she wanted a limo to pick her up because her car had broken down. Then I remembered Bill passed by her place on the way to the studio and I asked him to pick her up. That's all there was to it."

Holden told columnist Hedda Hopper that he was demanding a retraction from *Confidential*. "I don't understand all this publicity about Grace," he said. "I like her but I don't think she's the femme fatale she's built up to be."

"She's pretty femme," Hedda said, smirking.

"But she's not fatale," Holden snapped back.

Hedda Hopper had warned Crosby before he made *The Country Girl* that Grace was a nymphomaniac. Whether he found it to be true or false, he carried a torch for her the rest of his life.

While Holden's attorney put the pressure on *Confidential* for a retraction, Jack Kelly and his son forced their way into the office of the magazine's editor, causing quite a rumpus.

Grace was devastated by this second blow to her pride and reputation. The damage had been done. A retraction would not ease her depression and shame. *Confidential*'s follow-up article read, "Memo: Hollywood wives stop biting your nails ... this new Hollywood heat wave wasn't grabbing for a guy who already had a ball and chain." The writer went on to say that Grace walked out on Milland and told Holden to stay at home where he belonged. But "Does she or doesn't she?" The answer implied she "did" for single men. In conclusion, Miss Kelly was an example of still waters running deep: "Behind that frigid exterior is a smoldering fire ... and what the older fellows go for. She looks like a lady and has the manners of one. In the Hollywood of the chippies and the tramps, a lady is a rarity. That makes Grace Kelly the most dangerous dame in the movies today."

Columnist Hedda Hopper snickered over Holden's story about picking up Grace to take her to dinner. "She's dined with my wife and me four times!" Then he added, "It was Mrs. Holden's convertible. Does anyone think I'm so dumb as to park my wife's car outside another woman's apartment all night?"

Brian recalls Grace's comment about Holden's disappointing visit to Philadelphia. "Did the relationship go that far?" I asked.

"Yes, indeed," Brian replied. "Bill deteriorated after that. A few years later he tried to commit suicide with pills and liquor." Holden told actor Broderick Crawford, "I loved Grace and wanted to marry her, but I'd be damned if I'd let any church dictate what I could do with my life."

Brian described Grace as shocked, humiliated and very depressed. He sent her a note to call if she needed someone. When he heard from her, she was still doing *The Country Girl.*

"I hate this town," she told him bitterly. "The people here are jealous and frustrated neurotics who love you one day and hate you the next, stabbing you in the back if they get half a chance."

"If it's any consolation," Brian said, "everyone knows that magazine is a rag."

"Is that why it's always sold out?"

"You've been through this before, Grace, and rode it out very well."

"Have you ever been to a psychiatrist?" she asked.

Brian was taken aback for a moment. "I'm seeing one."

"You? Why?"

"I'm not sure what it is I *don't* want."

"Is he doing you any good?" she asked.

"Getting a lot off my chest has helped tremendously."

"Brian, I'm about to burst. Nothing's going right. I wanted to make a film with Clark in Hong Kong, but I'm committed to a rotten thing called *Green Fire* in the jungles of Colombia."

"Look on the positive side, Grace. You need to get away for a while, whether it's the Orient or South America. In the meantime, unload your problems on a shrink."

"Some of my friends have been going to one for years," she said. "I don't want that."

"Neither do I," Brian said. "We'll keep each other in check."

Brian said they spoke on the phone a few times before she left for Colombia. "Grace and I felt the same way about seeing a psychiatrist," he said. "Today it's fashionable, but back in the fifties, therapy wasn't something you talked about. We discussed our problems and focused on the analysis and solutions. Grace was facing up to her guilt. The first scandal was a warning, but when she almost broke up another marriage, the affairs were magnified. She had to admit to herself that no one accused her of anything that wasn't true. Grace mentioned William Holden. She was still in love with him, and they were working things out. The other, referring to Milland, was the real thing but a terrible mistake." Brian asked her about the Holden situation.

"Only time will tell," she replied. "I have to get on with

my life. Did you ever hear the song, 'I Fall in Love Too Easily'?"

"Sinatra?"

"Yes. Jule Styne and Sammy Cahn must have had me in mind when they wrote it," she said with a faint laugh. "I'll drop you a note from Colombia."

Psychoanalysis was an awakening for Grace. The truths she was forced to confront came as a great shock to her. "I had chosen to ignore or suppress them," she confided to Brian. The attraction to married men was a way of avoiding commitments. Love is real in every form it takes but is very seldom lasting. Subconsciously, Grace had been able to condone her sexual dalliances because she "loved her lovers" and rarely participated in one-night stands.

"Grace compared herself to the girl in high school or college, and there was always one who supposedly 'put out' in those days," Brian said. "The others either didn't date or were going steady. The pretty coed who went out with several boys and 'did it' with more than one fellow was called a whore. Grace was considered that 'one' girl on the Hollywood campus. Analysis helped her acknowledge the fact that she was highly charged sexually. Grace said this was typical of those born under the sign of Scorpio, but her therapist thought she should forget astrology and practice self-control, owing to the fact that she craved a great deal of love and affection. Grace was ahead of her time because the use of astrology is one of the instruments used by some psychiatrists today."

Grace withdrew from the outside world for a while, refusing invitations except from very close friends; but she could not avoid her leading men in *The Country*

Girl. Holden was still smitten with her but carried on as if nothing had happened. If he could survive Audrey Hepburn's marrying another man, Bill could recover from almost anything. This is not to imply he went his merry way; because Grace was so similar to Audrey, it was almost like losing the same girl twice.

It's been said that Crosby had ice water running through his veins. Knowing this, Grace was very concerned that Bing's love would turn to hatred. Wanting to believe their romance could be revived, he chose to be an understanding and patient friend. Crosby did not ardently pursue Grace nor did he give her the impression that he was interested in marriage any longer. As a matter of fact, he was dating Kathryn Grant, who would become the second Mrs. Crosby in 1957 after many canceled wedding dates, some at the last minute. When Bing died in 1977, Kathryn told Grace, "I've been jealous of you because Bing always loved you."

Despite the personal hardships involving the major players in *The Country Girl*, Kelly, Crosby, and the picture were nominated for Academy Awards. The word got around Hollywood that Grace had given an Oscar-winning performance without relying on her beauty. The crew gave her a plaque that was engraved: "To our Country Girl. This will hold you until you get next year's Academy Award."

Costume designer Edith Head remarked, "I put Grace in housedresses and skirts and blouses and made her look dumpy. I realized immediately when I showed the costumes to her that Grace was not at all comfortable." However, Edith had a knack for saying the right thing at the right time: "You look extremely depressed, Grace. I congratulate you."

Oleg Cassini was no stranger to Hollywood. He had been a costume designer at Paramount Studios and had been married to a movie actress. Grace was not enthusiastic about his suggestion that she arrive and leave the studio dressed to perfection daily during production of *The Country Girl*. Her contention was "staying in character" while his was, "You're a star, Grace." Gradually, she saw it his way and did not drag the dowdy Georgie home with her. Oleg began to design clothes for Grace, and, to her amazement, she made the best-dressed list for the first time in 1954. Miss Head had never told Grace that her personal wardrobe left a lot to be desired, ". . . but she was very fastidious about the way she looked," Edith said. "She wore white gloves and very sheer hose and always carried a hankie."

Cassini thought of Grace as a "pale, delicate English rose." He created subdued, elegant dresses that set off her patrician good looks. "I told her that her beauty should be set off like a great diamond, in very simple settings. I created the 'Grace Kelly' look for her."

Their relationship remained platonic, however, and Oleg was disappointed that she did not appreciate him as much as her wardrobe. Grace was adamant about not mixing business with pleasure. The invincible Cassini appeared unruffled, like his designer sketches, and offered to tag along with her to Colombia for *Green Fire*. Thanks but no thanks was her reply. Oleg returned to New York and invited four hundred guests to his birthday party for the lovely Pier Angeli. Gossip columnists wrote about the lavish celebration and implied that the host and honored guest were discussing marriage. Before she left for Colombia, Grace told Oleg over the telephone that she had seen the item in the newspaper and remarked, "You don't waste any time, do you?"

Grace wrote to him from South America and they talked on the phone occasionally. Cassini had no intention of marrying anyone else but made sure he was photographed with beautiful women or mentioned in the society and gossip columns. Oleg was determined that Grace would come to him of her own accord when she returned home. He was bored with their game of fencing.

CHAPTER
TEN

The Year of Grace

Clark Gable was disappointed that Grace was unable to costar with him in *Soldier of Fortune*. Twentieth Century-Fox signed Susan Hayward as his leading lady.

"Who?" he asked.

When Gable met the stunning redhead, he said, "I used to stare you down at parties and never got a nod."

"I'm blind as a bat. Why didn't you come over to me and say something?" she asked.

"Not without some kinda look. Know what I mean?"

Clark filmed *Soldier of Fortune* in Hong Kong. Scenes with Susan were shot in Hollywood because she was having a custody battle with her estranged husband, Jess Barker, and could not leave the country. Gable adored Susan, but he said to a friend, "I guess we met too late. We've both been stung many times, and I understand Susan has the hottest temper in Hollywood. I'm too old for that."

Besides, there was another woman in his life — Kay Spreckels, whom he had known for a long time. She was waiting for him at the airport when he returned from the Orient, and seven months later, in July 1955, they were married.

*   *   *

Following *The Country Girl*, William Holden went to Hong Kong for *Love Is a Many Splendored Thing* (1955). His leading lady, Jennifer Jones, complained about the script, her hair, her make-up, and eventually even Bill because he failed to sympathize. The two stars made divine love in the movie, but off-camera they were not speaking to one another. This was a first for Holden, who attempted a truce by presenting Jennifer with a dozen white roses. She threw them in his face.

Bill and his wife separated in 1963 and divorced ten years later. After a romance with French actress Capucine, he met Stefanie Powers in 1974. Holden was fighting the bottle when he fell in love with television's leading lady in "Hart to Hart." They shared an interest in his Mount Kenya Safari Club and traveled the world together, but not even Stefanie, the great love of Bill's middle years, was able to cure him of alcoholism. Alone at home, he fell down, hit his head, and bled to death in 1981.

Green Fire, an MGM potboiler about emerald mining in Colombia, was the price Grace paid for the part of Georgie. "It was a wretched experience," she said in an interview with Robert Levin for *Redbook* in 1957. "Everyone knew it was an awful picture . . . nobody had any idea how to save it."

Grace's handsome leading man was British actor Stewart Granger, who was happily married to actress Jean Simmons. "I have the perfect wife," he said. "She can't cook. She can't make a bed. She will not pick up things. She simply lives for her work. She dotes on fan magazines and fish and chips."

Granger was one of the few Hollywood actors who

apparently remained faithful to his wife. He admitted taking many cold showers, especially while working with a determined Ava Gardner when they costarred in *Bhowani Junction* (1956). She came to his room late at night and asked him, "Don't you find me attractive?"

"You're one of the most beautiful women in the world," he replied, "but I'm married to Jean."

"Oh, fuck Jean!" Ava exclaimed.

"I'd love to, darling, but she's not here," he said in a sweat. The gorgeous Ava disappeared into the night and Granger took another cold shower.

When Jean left him for another man six years later, it was no laughing matter, but the actresses who threw themselves at Granger undoubtedly shared the same afterthought, "What a waste."

"The trouble with me," he said, "is that I did everything for Jean. I taught her how to read, how to walk, how to carry herself. I taught her art, literature, current events. She was such a child. Our entire relationship was like *Pygmalion* [1938]."

Granger, an imposing six-foot-three, had a striking profile and a well-trained resonant voice. His leading ladies found him charming and friendly, but they also considered him quite a challenge in their bed-hopping society.

Granger made more than seventy movies and says today, "I'm not proud of one." *Scaramouche* (1952) and *King Solomon's Mines* (1950) were his best, but film historians do not overlook his fine work in *Beau Brummel* (1954), *Moonfleet* (1955), and *The Prisoner of Zenda* (1952).

He was born James Stewart in London in 1913 and changed his name for obvious reasons. When he met sixteen-year-old Jean Simmons in 1945 during the filming of *Caesar and Cleopatra* (1946), Granger was married to actress Elspeth March, whom he divorced in 1948. Two years later, he signed a contract with MGM, moved to Hollywood, and married Jean.

Granger was not happy about doing *Green Fire*, but he did not show his displeasure, as Grace did. For the first week, he thought she was "looking down" on others in the cast, observing and not saying anything. "None of us wanted to do the film," he said. "I felt bad that Grace was seeing us in this lousy movie." Granger admitted he was "tempted a bit" by her and thought she had a "delicious behind." Grace was her usual flirtatious self. "She would look at me in a contemplative sort of way," he said. "She was very nice to kiss and was always cool and lovely and smelt nice."

Grace had proven herself during hazardous situations in Africa, so she remained calm on the Magdalena River in Colombia when the crew's boat was caught in a violent storm. They were rescued in dugout canoes. Granger said he was trembling, but Grace's attitude was, "What else can we do?"

Her letters to Brian described the wretched conditions in the jungle villages. "Grace wrote that she didn't feel sorry for herself after seeing the poverty and filth," he said. "She sent very brief notes, expressing her eagerness to get back home. What surprised me was the fine review that *Green Fire* received from *The New York Times*, the most critical newspaper of them all. I remember it well because they thought the only things lacking were animals. I got a charge out of it. Grace wasn't amused."

Contract players did at least one movie they wanted to forget and occasionally had difficulty remembering the title. Clark Gable had chosen *Parnell* (1937) to change his image in the mid-thirties. Instead of a gangster-lover, he played an Irish statesman. The film was terrible. His future wife, Carole Lombard, had stickers of *Parnell* made and stuck them everywhere as a reminder that Clark wasn't God. For Joan Crawford, one of the worst was *Hollywood Canteen* in 1944. "A very pleasant pile of shit," she said in an interview, "but forget that I even appeared in it. I don't think I did."

Elizabeth Taylor was involved in much the same situation as Grace. She owed MGM a film, and they demanded she do *Butterfield 8* (1960).* Taylor told the producer, "Nothing you can say will make me like this movie. If you think I've been trouble in the past, you just wait. I'll be late every day and I'll cost you a fortune. You'll regret the day you ever forced me into making this crummy film."

Grace knew that *Green Fire* was the beginning of a feud with MGM. She had read scripts that the studio thought might interest her and turned them all down. MGM announced she would appear with Robert Taylor in Sir Walter Scott's *Quentin Durward* (1955). "All the men can duel and fight, but all I'd do would be to wear thirty-five different costumes, look pretty and frightened," she said. "There are eight people chasing me — the old man, robbers, the head gypsy, and Durward. The stage directions on every page of the script say, 'She clutches her jewel box and flees.' I just thought I'd be so bored." Kay Kendall was cast instead. *Quentin Durward* was the

---

* Elizabeth Taylor won an Oscar for *Butterfield 8*, which was most likely awarded to her for *Cat on a Hot Tin Roof* (1958), released previously when Hollywood had ostracized her for taking Eddie Fisher away from his wife, Debbie Reynolds.

last of Robert Taylor's costume epics, and the worst.

Grace played her final scene in *Green Fire* embracing Granger in the pouring rain. He is presumed killed in an explosion but suddenly appears alive and well in the torrential downpour. The camera focuses on Grace running into his arms. Granger said they were both drenched and her wet slacks accentuated "that fabulous behind." He covered it with both hands. "Grace was surprised but so happy to finish the film she didn't object," Granger said.

MGM's public relations staff went all out to publicize *Green Fire*. Grace was mortified when they placed her head on a bosomy body poured into a tight green strapless gown and displayed the blown up "photograph" prominently in front of the Mayfair Theatre in New York. "It makes me so mad," she exclaimed. "The dress isn't even in the movie!"

Dore Schary expected *Green Fire* to make money, but it failed at the box office. Admitting the picture was a big mistake, he said, "Grace wasn't angry. She was very sweet about doing the picture." She was not very sweet, however, about the touched-up photo in Times Square and refused to walk on the same side of the street.

Green Fire (released in late December 1954) was insignificant in "the year of Grace." *Dial M for Murder* was released in May, *Rear Window* in August, and *The Country Girl* premiered in December. Grace was nominated for Best Actress of 1954 for her portrayal of Bing Crosby's drab wife, Georgie.

She was on the cover of *Life* magazine, a profile portrait with a wave of her shoulder-length hair brushing the corner of one eye. Underneath her name was the caption, "Hollywood's Brightest and Busiest New Star." In the article, *Life* wrote that "Movies will soon be full of Grace Kelly. . . . What will not be evident is her determination — what one producer called Miss Kelly's 'stainless steel inside' that has brought this all about." Included in the article is a section entitled "Kelly Is Fine Old Name." Jack is pictured with Kell, rowing on the Schuylkill River. Uncle George got special mention as one of America's most distinguished playwrights.

Shortly afterward, Grace made the cover of *Look* magazine, sporting an oversized sweater. For an inside photo, she wore Cassini's antique pink taffeta dress. A few months later, she was honored to be chosen by *Time* for its cover, captioned "Gentlemen Prefer Ladies," and the inside story entitled "The Girl in White Gloves." The article said that Hollywood was trying hard, "with an air of an ill-at-ease lumberjack worrying whether he is using the right spoon."

The *Saturday Evening Post*'s "The Luckiest Girl in Hollywood" (October 1954) tried to explain the Grace Kelly phenomenon by interviewing her friends and costars but concluded, ". . . when you have finished all this, she is still such an elusive subject that writing about her is like trying to wrap up a hundred and fifteen pounds of smoke."

Grace received good reviews for *Rear Window*. However, the critics devoted their columns to praising or criticizing Alfred Hitchcock. The players were secondary. Though Jimmy Stewart received top billing, many movie houses put Grace's name on their marquees to attract business.

Hitchcock and Paramount postponed *To Catch A Thief*

(1955) until Grace had finished *Green Fire*. MGM was reluctant once again to loan her out, but she consulted Edith Head about her wardrobe for *To Catch a Thief*. "No matter what anyone says," Grace emphasized, "keep right on making my clothes for the picture. I'll be in it."

In May 1954, MGM made a deal to "swap" Grace Kelly for Bill Holden, who was Paramount's hottest property. Contract players were nothing more than expensive merchandise under the studio contract system. The most famous loan-out story was MGM's giving Clark Gable to Columbia Pictures in 1933 for *It Happened One Night* (1934), a dreadful comedy with no script and a very low budget. This was Gable's punishment for being uncooperative. He said bourbon got him through the agony of doing the movie. Claudette Colbert was in it for the money and the opportunity to work with Clark. They both won Oscars, as did the picture, director, and screenwriter. MGM's attempt to spank Gable turned out differently than expected, but they could only benefit by having the Best Actor of 1934 under contract.

Grace, too, had achieved fame at studios other than MGM. She won the International Press Award for *Mogambo*, but the film was only a glimmer of stardom for her. Dore Schary told writer Arthur Lewis, "We didn't know what to do with Grace in the beginning because we had Ava Gardner, Lana Turner, Greer Garson, Deborah Kerr, and Elizabeth Taylor. We couldn't sell Grace."

In 1954, every major Hollywood studio was clamoring for her, but it was Hitchcock who knew how to sell Grace Kelly on the screen. The director could do the same with any good actress, but he was enthralled with Grace. Enchanted by her. It might have been unrequited love; Hitchcock was not above that as an imaginative and often sadistic writer. He had for some time enjoyed his harmless fantasies, and one of them was Grace. Kenneth Anger wrote in *Hollywood Babylon* that Hitchcock was a scopophiliac, one who achieves sexual gratification through gazing: "... the ice-blond ex-model from Philadelphia had consented to indulge Peeping Al's whim just this once. It would be over in a mere five minutes when she snapped off the lights." According to Anger, Hitch used a powerful telescope to watch Grace disrobe in her bedroom a mile away.

Her leading men vehemently deny that Hitch was in love with Grace, but his strong attraction to her was evident to observers on the set of *To Catch a Thief*, which was filmed on the French Riviera. Though it is almost certain they were never involved intimately, Grace and Hitch communicated like lovers, teased and flirted like lovers. They used each other selfishly but also gave to one another unselfishly. Hitchcock was often hypnotized in Grace's company, looking at her and beyond her simultaneously.

They played the courting game with silent fervor. Grace was delightfully cruel at tantalizing him in a manner that he relished. They were soulmates who were involved in a very intense love affair of the mind. Hitchcock's only way of possessing Grace was to set up his own production company and have her under exclusive contract. After she deserted him for marriage, he called her "Princess Disgrace."

Fifty-year-old Cary Grant and his wife, Betsy Drake, were in Hong Kong when he received the script of *To Catch a Thief*. He was contemplating retirement at this juncture but was intrigued with the story of John Robie (the Cat), a reformed jewel thief. During an attempt to clear his name after a series of cat burglaries in Cannes, Robie meets and falls in love with a beautiful heiress (Grace Kelly).

In 1938, Grant had been one of the British actors at the dock in New York to welcome Hitchcock to America. They worked together in *Suspicion* (1941) with Joan Fontaine and in *Notorious* (1946) with Ingrid Bergman.

Cary returned from the Orient and was delighted to find out Grace Kelly would be his leading lady if MGM gave its consent. He had been a contract player at Paramount and offered to use his influence. Grant was impressed by Grace's approach to acting, which was a great deal like his own. They were both in control of the parts they played, and Cary could appreciate her cool aristocratic air because he had been married to heiress Barbara Hutton and socialized with the elite.

Before leaving Hollywood, Grace mailed a postcard to New York that would precede her by a few days . . .

CHAPTER
ELEVEN

Secret Fiancé

The year of Grace was also the year of Oleg Cassini. In his 1987 memoirs, he did not mention his male competition other than Aumont and Milland. By not exposing Grace's love affairs, he failed to give himself due credit for having outlasted his handsome opponents, if, in fact, he knew about them. Cassini's book, *In My Own Fashion*, was published in 1987, a few months after James Spada's best-seller, *Grace: The Secret Lives of a Princess* (1987), a biography that well-documented her private life. Cassini denounced Spada and his book, claiming it was untrue.

The Russian couturier's attempt at gallantry by defending Grace's honor five years after her death is commendable. It was obvious that he chose to write about the women in *his* life while he waited for Grace rather than to mention the men in *her* life; but Cassini proved he was a proud and patient man in 1954 by keeping calm during the "race for Grace."

He knew she was going to film *To Catch a Thief* on the French Riviera and hoped to see her in New York before she left. To his surprise, he received a postcard in Grace's handwriting that read simply, "Follow me." Cassini was beside himself, his mind swirling for excuses to take a business trip to France. It was all so sudden because Grace had arrived in New York shortly after her tempting card and had prepared to leave for Europe right away. Oleg told her impulsively, "I'll fly over with you for the weekend." In the early fifties, one did not hop over to Europe for only two or three days. She was taken aback by his frivolity. Oleg showed up at the airport with an invalid passport and was left behind, feeling like a fool; but he had his instructions on a postcard and was in France a week later.

When Grace arrived in Paris, she called Hitchcock, who had been in Cannes with the Grants for almost two weeks. "I'm very tired," she said. "Do you mind if I stay here for a few days and get some rest?"

"I do mind," Hitchcock replied.

"I'm truly exhausted," Grace said, sighing.

"Of course you are. I can tell by your voice that you're all in, but continue on to Cannes now. If you're going to have a nervous collapse, have it where we can look after you."

Grace was stalling for time, hoping Cassini would get to Paris before she had to leave for the Riviera. He was trying frantically to get his papers in order so they would have time alone in Paris. Because the weather was bad in Cannes, Grace was sure Hitchcock would give in to her request, but he grumbled about being behind schedule already.

Grace's exhaustion was not feigned, however. She had done five films in one year, endured two major scandals, and lost Holden and Milland without dignity, only to find herself one of the most sought after movie stars in the world. She was hounded by reporters everywhere. Grace might have rested in New York but had chosen to go out with Cassini. They were photographed "doing the town," and he was now considered by the press to be her "one and only." An observant Hitchcock was like the wise old owl in a poem that the students at the American Academy recited:

> *There was an old owl liv'd in an oak,*
> *The more he heard, the less he spoke;*
> *The less he spoke, the more he heard,*
> *O, if men were all like that wise bird!*

More than likely, Hitchcock was aware that Cassini had had a ticket on the same plane as Grace at the New York airport because other members of the cast and crew were on that flight also. It was obvious that Oleg planned to follow. MGM braced itself, but with Paramount's cooperation, they were able to minimize the romance.

Grace was charmed by the Hotel Carlton at Cannes, and she adored Cary and Betsy Grant, who were in the lobby to welcome her. Hitchcock was testy and gruff, but casual about the work schedule, giving Grace a chance to relax. Within days, she was feeling much better and perked up when Cary extended a very special invitation. "Aristotle Onassis has asked Betsy and me to a breakfast luncheon on his yacht *Christina* moored in Monte Carlo Harbor," Grant said. "Ari told me to bring some friends along. I thought you'd enjoy it."

Grace tagged along wearing her horn-rimmed glasses. During lunch, she talked very little and stayed in the background. When the party was over, Onassis took Cary aside and invited him back anytime. "And please," the Greek billionaire said, nodding toward Grace, "bring your secretary along with you."

Within two years, Onassis would be referring to the shy blonde "stenographer" as Her Serene Highness, Grace Patricia Grimaldi, Princess of Monaco.

On her sightseeing excursions, Grace visited the palace gardens that she had admired from a distance. The royal guard told her that tourists were permitted inside the palace. "No, thank you," she said. "I'd rather see the grounds." She wondered why the Prince did not have a swimming pool. It seemed odd that he would go to all the bother of changing into his trunks, calling for a car, and driving to the beach. As Princess, one of Grace's first undertakings was to install a pool and beach house in a private part of the grounds.

Cassini called Grace from Paris. Assuming he was staying only for the weekend, she invited him to dinner at the Hotel Carlton that evening. It got off to a bad start when they met in the lobby. Grace insisted Oleg go back to his room and put on a tie. He explained that an open shirt, slacks, and jacket was the manner of dress for men in Cannes during the warm weather, but she would not change her mind; Cassini was the only man who was wearing a tie in the dining room.

Grace got tipsy on champagne, but she was a far cry from Brian's description of "an adorable and amorous python." Her chilly disposition confused Cassini, who wondered if it was Grace who had actually written the propositional postcard. He went to bed alone that night and made up his mind to leave Cannes after an outing with Grace the following day. Oleg packed a picnic basket with delicacies and found a secluded spot near the sea. Trying not to be overbearing, he expressed his innermost feelings. He had nothing to lose. As far as Oleg was concerned, the courtship was over. "Enough is enough," he said. "We're alone here, on a raft in the Mediterranean. The sun is warm; the waves are lapping gently against the wood. There is no need for artifice any longer."

When they returned to the hotel, Cassini had every good reason to stay.

He took Grace to cozy little inns on winding back roads in Cannes, Monte Carlo, and Nice. His fluent French enabled them to mingle freely with the residents. The rainy weather was in Cassini's favor, too, because filming was shut down and he had Grace all to himself. For her, it meant more pressure to get the job done — and done well — on sunny days. She was frequently short-tempered with Oleg, who thought about nothing else other than being with her. He understood the rigors and discipline of an actress, having been married to Gene Tierney, but Oleg did not realize that Grace needed time alone to concentrate, memorize her lines, and get a good night's sleep. Also gnawing at her conscience was Oleg's presence in Cannes — staying at the same hotel, accompanying her to dinner with the Grants and the Hitchcocks, and knowing that reporters were taking notes.

In 1954, the press did not print details of a sensitive nature. It was widely known, however, that Oleg Cassini had followed Grace Kelly to the Riviera, where she was making *To Catch a Thief*. The romance was not highly publicized, but Louella Parsons wrote her usual tidbit about the possibility of marriage. That Cassini was in Cannes with Grace for two months was not spelled out in black and white, yet they were seen shopping, gambling, dancing, dining, swimming, and attending church regularly. She had fallen in love with Oleg, but as with all her serious involvements, there was the problem of his being twice divorced.

He proposed marriage and she accepted, which made them unofficially engaged. Grace wanted to notify her parents before there was any hint of it in the newspapers. Cassini said she discussed their wedding "with the flushed enthusiasm of a typical American Junior Leaguer." Grace was not concerned about her mother but told Oleg, "I don't think you're my father's type. He might give us some trouble." Shortly before they were scheduled to leave Europe, Grace decided it would be best if Cassini took a plane and she would sail with the Grants to New York. This sudden concern about the press and the reaction of her family gave Oleg his first clue that trouble was ahead.

"Grace had a marvelous time making *To Catch a Thief*," Brian said, "but without Cassini, she would have been a fifth wheel with the Grants and the Hitchcocks. They all went to dinner several times a week and were like family. In her letter, Grace said Cassini was showing her a good time and that love was very contagious on the French Riviera. She thought working with Cary Grant was a most rewarding experience, and Hitchcock wanted them to take an active part in his proposed independent production company. It had been quite a while since Grace sounded so optimistic."

Edith Head created Grace's elegant wardrobe for *To Catch a Thief*. They enjoyed a shopping spree for accessories in Paris with an unlimited expense account. Hitchcock told Edith, "Style is created in France, so let's do it."

In the film, Grace's first appearance was on the beach. She is wearing a huge sun hat and a striking black-and-white sun costume. Hitchcock did not want her to wear one of the

French bikinis that were so popular in the 1950s because he would not allow Grace to bare that much.

Because she suspects Cary is responsible for robbing rich women of their jewels, Grace's character deliberately flaunts her valuable gems in his face. One of the most seductive scenes takes place in Grace's hotel room. Wearing a simple strapless gown, she tries to tempt Cary with a luxurious diamond necklace around her neck. Edith Head's job was to design an elegant dress that created a background for the jewelry. "There had to be enough fabric showing in the tight shot so that the audience knew Grace had clothes on," Edith said. "This may sound simple, but it wasn't. The gown had to have simple lines so that it did not detract from the necklace, yet it had to emanate an haute couture quality that matched the expensive jewels."

The dialogue was sophisticated, suggestive, and very provocative:

Kelly: If you really want to see fireworks, it's better with the lights off. I have a feeling that you're going to see one of the Riviera's most fascinating sights. (She walks toward him, her gown strapless and low-cut.) I'm talking about the fireworks, of course.

Grant: I never doubted it.

Kelly (As she reclines seductively on a divan): Give up — admit who you are. Even in this light I can tell where your eyes are looking. (Close-up of her necklace, revealing as well her inviting décolletage.) Look — hold them — diamonds! Ever had a better offer in your whole life? One with everything? (The fireworks begin in the background. She kisses his fingers and then places his hand beneath the necklace. Cut to more fireworks.)

Grant: You know just as well as I do this necklace is imitation.

Kelly: Well, I'm not! (The kiss, and cut to fireworks.)

Grace was a notoriously bad driver, but there was no way that Hitchcock could use a double or he most certainly would have done so. She had to speed around the curves on a hazardous road with a sharp drop on one side. Grace loved to tell this story ". . . because Cary turned dead white under his tan." He admitted being absolutely terrified, holding on for dear life when the car hugged the cliff and rocks disappeared over the edge.

"What are you doing?" he asked in a panic. "Where are you going?"

"I don't know," she replied. "I haven't got my glasses on."

Grace had a fear of driving and avoided doing so whenever possible. One would never know, though, watching her with one white-gloved hand on the wheel and the wind blowing through her hair, glancing fondly at Cary, whose eyes were glued to the road — where hers should have been.

Hitchcock's sole purpose of having a lavish masquerade ball at the finale of *To Catch a Thief* was to present Grace "as a fairy princess." Edith Head designed a balloon-skirted, strapless, gold lamé ballroom gown and golden wig crowned with matching doves. Throughout the picture, Hitchcock insisted Grace wear subdued colors so that the climax would be a startling contrast.

In July 1954, the cast and crew of *To Catch a Thief*

returned to Hollywood for interior shots of the film. Oleg Cassini was at the dock to meet Grace, who had a twenty-four-hour layover in New York. She was surrounded in her cabin by reporters, MGM officials, photographers, and press agents. She gave Oleg a peck on the cheek and suggested they meet later at her apartment. Peggy and Lizanne were in New York to see their famous sister, making it virtually impossible for Oleg to be alone with his "fiancée." Grace was caught up in a haze of publicity that was unexpected. She had been in France when *Dial M for Murder* and *Rear Window* had been released, and now her picture graced the covers of *Life*, *Look*, and *Time* magazines. She was annoyed by reporters before leaving the country, but she was not prepared for the onslaught that awaited her in New York.

Cassini observed with disgust the hangers-on who were fawning over Grace. He got the cold shoulder from some of her acquaintances, who obviously did not approve of him. Oleg said in his memoirs that one of her friends on the boat that day asked Grace, "How low in the sewer can you go? How can you associate with this type of man?" Cassini's one salvation was meeting the Kelly sisters. Lizanne was engaged to a Jewish fellow, Donald LeVine, who was under scrutiny by the Kelly clan. In his wildest imagination, Oleg did not realize the obstacles he would face with Margaret and Jack as a son-in-law candidate.

Leaving Cassini behind in New York, Grace flew to Hollywood for the completion of *To Catch a Thief*, where she spent her weekends with Cary and Betsy at the Hitchcock retreat near Santa Cruz. Grace was overjoyed and touched when the Grants presented her with a black miniature poodle named Oliver. She cherished the dog and carried him off the boat on her spectacular arrival in Monte Carlo Harbor as the future Princess of Monaco.

To Catch a Thief received good reviews. The *Los Angeles Times* thought it was "a high-polish job, with Cary Grant and Grace Kelly ideal in the romantic leads." The *London Daily Telegraph* wrote, "The mood throughout is one of cynical humor, with witty dialogue and amorous overtones. . . . Grant and Kelly dominate the film with easy charm." Bosley Crowther at *The New York Times* raved, "*To Catch a Thief* comes off completely as a hit in the old Hitchcock style. . . . Miss Kelly is cool and exquisite and superior. The picture does nothing but give out a good, exciting time."

Margaret Kelly thought it would be a good idea if she had lunch with Grace and Oleg in New York before he met the rest of the family. Grace was sure this would work out for the best and that her mother would approve of Cassini. Margaret, in the meantime, called her close friend, Dorothea Sitley, the director of publicity for Gimbels department stores, where Oleg had previously been employed. Ma Kelly explained the delicate situation: ". . . Jack will kill him if he walks in the door, but if you say Oleg is okay, Jack will let him come." Dorothea thought Cassini was charming, ". . . but he's not for Grace. He's careless, just like a child wandering around." She said they went out for cocktails and he forgot his wallet. "So I had to pay for the drinks. Then Oleg hugged and kissed me. 'Don't know whatever I'd have done without you,' he said."

Margaret was not surprised because she had heard similar stories about Oleg from other people.

The night before Cassini met Ma Kelly, he invited Grace to a lavish masquerade dinner ball at Joan Whitney Payson's estate in Manhasset, Long Island, which was one of the major events of the social season. Oleg designed Grace's Helen of Troy costume, a full-length gold toga with a golden laurel tiara. He wore a short Greek tunic, helmet, and sandals. Cassini hoped that Grace's mingling with the Vanderbilts and the Whitneys would be an impressive bit of conversation at lunch with her mother the following day.

Unfortunately, when Oleg was introduced to Margaret, her arctic eyes chilled the air and her firm jaw remained clenched on the taxi ride from Grace's apartment to the Colony. She got to the point before lunch. "Look here, Oleg. You're a charming escort, but in my opinion, you are a poor risk for marriage." When Margaret emphasized the many women in his past, Cassini made the mistake of pointing out that ". . . attractive men, including your husband, have been popular with the opposite sex. Why am I being punished?"

Ma Kelly proposed a moratorium: "We don't think you should see each other for six months. This will give Grace a chance to find out if she's really in love or was under the influence of your persuasive charms in Europe."

Cassini would not agree to that. Through it all, Grace said nothing. He was more upset with her than with Margaret, but a few days later, Grace invited him, on behalf of her family, to spend a weekend at the beach house in New Jersey. When Jack Kelly found out that Cassini was coming for a visit, he cracked, "Should I shake his hand or kiss it?"

Grace's brother, Kell, had already expressed his feelings to *Time* magazine: "I generally don't approve of these oddballs she goes out with. I wish she would go out with the more athletic type. But she doesn't listen to me anymore."

The Kelly men did not say one word to Cassini, who related to a friend, "Having dinner with Grace's father was like eating a chocolate éclair filled with razor blades." Oleg's bedroom was located down the hall from Mr. and Mrs. Kelly; thus, he could not make a move without their knowing about it. Grace wanted him to be more aggressive. "Talk to my father," she urged. Cassini tried, but Jack did not acknowledge his existence. Again, Grace remained silent while Oleg suffered alone. "Infuriating and humiliating," he said. The weekend was a waste of time anyway. Margaret Kelly had already spoken, and the terms were simple. Grace was not to see Oleg for six months.

Hedda Hopper wrote in her column, "With all the attractive men around town, I do not understand what Grace Kelly sees in Oleg Cassini. It must be his moustache."

He responded with a telegram, "Dear Hedda, I'll shave mine if you shave yours."

Grace had every intention of seeing Oleg and still considered herself unofficially engaged to him. To appease her parents, they dined at home or at a friend's place. At public functions, it appeared as if Grace came without an escort to avoid being photographed with Oleg, who arrived either before or after her. Cassini told writer Gwen Robyns in a 1976 interview, "It became a contest, the prize being Grace — between me, the studio, and all the organized resistance that the family could bring to bear. It shouldn't have been that way."

Grace was twenty-five, a famous movie actress, and wealthy in her own right, but she still felt obligated to her domineering family. Brian asked Grace why she did not stand up to her father on that horrid weekend or simply return to New York.

"I couldn't do that," she replied.

"Sounds like a ploy to me."

"What do you mean?"

"No one can blame your family for not extending themselves."

"I hoped my father would change his mind," Grace said, "but he made it clear I would not be welcome at home if I married Oleg."

"Now what?" Brian asked.

"All I know is that I haven't looked at another man since Oleg and I were together in Cannes."

That was the key. Grace had been faithful to Cassini, unlike her other lovers, and this was reason enough for her to believe they could be happy. Without any film commitments in the fall of 1954, Grace was able to stay in New York with Oleg. He had that much in his favor, but Dore Schary was getting impatient. She had turned down every script sent to her, including *Diane* (1956), *Something of Value* (1957), and *The Cobweb* (1955). When Grace put in her bid for the part of Leslie in Warner Brothers' *Giant* (1956), MGM loaned out Elizabeth Taylor instead.

Before putting Grace on suspension (a forced leave of absence without pay), Schary offered her a Western, *Tribute to a Bad Man* (1956), with Spencer Tracy, who was considered by his peers to be the best actor in Hollywood. The details about Grace's relationship with Tracy are sketchy. Anne Edwards, in her 1985 biography of Katharine Hepburn, *A Remarkable Woman*, wrote, "There had been some rumors in the European press of a growing romance between Tracy and Grace Kelly. He had been seen with Hollywood's newest beauty and she agreed to appear with him in a future project, *Tribute to a Bad Man*. Tracy claimed the friendship was more business than pleasure, but the fact that Kelly had a penchant for married men did not do a great deal to reassure Kate."

Spencer Tracy, a staunch Catholic who did not believe in divorce, had been married for thirty years. His wife and children lived on their ranch in the San Fernando Valley. Tracy had a suite at the Beverly Wilshire Hotel, where he stayed, occasionally going home to see his family. Before he met Katharine Hepburn, Spencer had had a serious affair with Loretta Young. In 1938, they were a popular couple on the Hollywood nightclub circuit. A year later, she formally announced to the press, "Because Mr. Tracy and I are both Roman Catholics, to continue our courtship would be impossible."

He also had a brief fling with Joan Crawford, who broke off their relationship when Tracy criticized her acting ability. "Spence was a very disturbed man," she said. "He was a mean drunk and a bastard."

Still, Tracy was a hero to Katharine Hepburn even before she met him in 1941 during *Woman of the Year* (1942). They were a remarkable team in films and in private life. Though she gave the impression of relying on him, it was Hepburn who was the strong one, but she did not take the rumors about Spence and Grace lightly. He had sought out Grace's company in much the same way he had chased after Kate's good friend, Joan Fontaine, who had refused to go out with him.

Grace wanted to work with a star of Tracy's magnitude and flew from New York to Hollywood for the sole purpose of making this possible.

Tribute to a Bad Man is the story of a callous horse breeder in the Old West who is tough and arrogant with animals and humans — until he falls in love. The movie had potential with fifty-five-year-old Tracy in the lead role, but Grace was not satisfied with the script. MGM wanted a commitment from her and agreed to work on the revisions while she was in town. This gave Tracy some time with Grace. That she was an Irish Catholic made as much of an impression on him as her beauty did.

"Grace was intrigued with Tracy as she had been with Cooper and Gable," Brian said. "She was not interested in doing a Western, but she had to be discreet about it until her problems with MGM were resolved. Again, Grace was in awe of a legend. She said Tracy was a charmer and observing him was the greatest acting lesson of all. She said the same thing about Cooper. I don't know what happened between her and Tracy, but Grace didn't go all the way out there to sit at a conference table talking about a movie that she wasn't going to do."

Grace flew back to New York without giving MGM her decision. Eventually, she refused to do the Western; MGM suspended her on March 7, 1955.

Spencer Tracy was a week late reporting for work on *Tribute to a Bad Man*, disappeared for days at a time, and showed up on the set drunk. He was replaced by James Cagney and fired from MGM. Hollywood thought Tracy's film career was over. His health was bad, and he continued to drink and smoke to excess. Hepburn arrived home in time to see him through the ordeal, promising herself not to leave him again for any length of time. "Acting was easy for Spence," she said. "Life was the problem."

Tracy fooled them all but Kate; he made *Bad Day at Black Rock* (1954), for which he received an Oscar nomination.

CHAPTER
TWELVE

Oscar and Other Strange Bedfellows

Grace tried to keep herself busy moving into a new apartment building on 80th Street and Fifth Avenue. She told the press that it was strange not getting a salary anymore. "I'll have to postpone decorating my new apartment for the time being," she said, sighing like any average working girl. About her suspension, Grace said humbly, "I'm disappointed and a little bewildered. It's my first experience with a thing like this, and I guess that there is nothing that I can do but sit here and wait until they want me back."

"Why were you suspended?" a reporter asked.

"I felt I had to turn down the roles because they're just parts that I couldn't see myself playing. I hope that they are not too mad at me. Perhaps I was spoilt by my loan-out pictures. Now Metro says that they won't lend me to other studios anymore. They feel it's time that I made one for them and, of course, they have a good talking point."

During the stalemate, Dore Schary commented, "We feel that Miss Kelly has certain obligations to us. After all, we were the first to give her a chance. All her offers came after she appeared in *Mogambo*. Maybe she has a few complaints, but we are all willing to discuss whatever is wrong."

When the Oscar nominations were announced and Grace Kelly was among them for *The Country Girl*, Schary knew that MGM faced an embarrassment if she won an Academy Award while on suspension. Ten days before the Oscar ceremonies, Metro announced that Grace was back on salary. To make it appear that they had won the dispute, Schary said she had agreed to do *The Barretts of Wimpole Street* (1957). Behind closed doors, he told his staff, "If she turns down *Barretts*, we can suspend her again." However, three days later, on March 21, 1955, MGM lifted her suspension without binding her to any film commitments.

Grace wanted to make peace before the awards because she was jittery over being nominated for Best Actress. Parts such as Georgie did not come along very often — maybe once in a lifetime.

Judy Garland felt the same way about Vicki Lester in *A Star Is Born* (1954). She was favored to win after a four-year absence from the screen. Judy had overcome personal problems with the help of her third husband, producer Sid Luft, and Hollywood was happy to have her back. A star was *reborn*, actually, and in addition to the sentimentality of Judy's amazing comeback, she was about to give birth to her third child and would be in the hospital on the night of the awards.

Grace was quite sure Judy had a better chance over her and the other nominees for Best Actress: Dorothy Dandridge for *Carmen Jones* (1954), Jane Wyman for *Magnificent Obsession* (1954), and Audrey Hepburn for *Sabrina* (1954).

On the day of reckoning, Grace lunched at Paramount and had a last-minute fitting on her gown that Edith Head had created for this special occasion. "That dress was the only personal one I ever made for Grace," the designer said. "It was an aquamarine satin with shoestring shoulder straps and a matching cloak. Of course, she wore a pair of long white gloves. We were getting ready to leave for the Pantages Theatre when a lock of Grace's hair fell from her chignon. We were standing near a vase of flowers and she tucked a yellow rose into the hairpiece. The next day, women everywhere wore a flower in their hair, too."

It was going to be a close race between Garland and Kelly. Both actresses wanted that statue desperately, each for her own personal reasons aside from the prestige and career benefits. Judy needed it for her self-respect. She had beaten the odds after her MGM-induced addiction to sleeping pills and amphetamines. She had attempted suicide dozens of times and had suffered from nervous breakdowns, divorces, and eventually her inability to cope before the camera; but Judy had rebound with a brilliant and flawless performance in *A Star Is Born*.

There was no sentimentality going for Grace. She had, however, pulled a Bette Davis in *Now, Voyager* (1942) by choosing to play an ugly duckling and by handling the role so convincingly that moviegoers forgot she was the wicked femme fatale who had tried to steal Ray Milland and William Holden away from their wives.

The award for Best Actress would be announced at the end of a long Oscar ceremony on March 30, 1955. Bing Crosby, nominated for Best Actor, and *The Country Girl*, for Best Picture, lost to Marlon Brando in the award-winning *On the Waterfront* (1954). Eva Maria Saint, Brando's costar, got the nod for Best Supporting Actress, and Edmond O'Brien was the surprise choice for Best Supporting Actor in *The Barefoot Contessa* (1954).

It was getting late and the young lady with a yellow flower pinned underneath her chignon had reason to be discouraged. *The Country Girl* had not won an Oscar other than by George Seaton for Best Screenplay. Finally, Grace's former lover, William Holden, walked onstage to present the award for Best Actress. Grace Kelly appeared cool, sitting up straight in her seat, one hand over the other in her lap, and with a brave but faint smile on her lips. Holden opened the envelope, looked directly at the woman he had almost married a year ago, and said distinctly, "Actress of the year — Grace Kelly!"

She rose from her seat slowly, glided majestically down the aisle, and then climbed up the stairs to the stage. Holden presented her with the Oscar and stood aside as the deafening applause dwindled into a hush. Grace was about to cry as she said in a whisper, "I will never forget this moment. All I can say is thank you." As Holden led her offstage into the wings, she was trying hard to fight back the tears.

In Philadelphia, the Kelly family had invited friends to their home for the evening to watch the Academy Awards on television. After Grace's name was announced, Jack shook his head and remarked, "I can't believe it! I simply cannot believe Grace won. Of the four children, she's the last one I expected to support me in my old age."

When the press interviewed him about Grace's winning the Oscar, Jack told them, "You ought to see Peggy. She's the family extrovert. Just between us, I've always thought her the daughter with the most on the ball. You can't figure those things, can you?"

In another interview, Jack said he did not know what all the excitement was about and he was "bewildered" over Grace's success as a movie star. One would think his Irish pride would have prevented him from telling the press about a phone call he made to his daughter at the studio:

"Who's calling?" the operator asked.

"John B. Kelly of Philadelphia."

"Who?"

Pause . . . "Grace Kelly's father."

The call went right through.

Judy Garland was giving birth to her baby when the Oscars were being handed out. She was exhausted, weary, and sick with worry that baby Joey might not survive. When she was brought back to her room, there was a flurry of activity. Reporters were scrambling for elevators and the television crew assigned to Garland in case she was the winner was so busy dismantling cables and wires that the crew paid no attention to poor Judy and her husband, who suddenly found themselves all alone.

Returning home with a healthy baby boy, however, was more rewarding to Judy than an Oscar.

Backstage at the Pantages, Grace was asked to pose with Marlon Brando. "Kiss him," one of the photographers said.

"I think he should kiss me," she replied, and Brando obliged.

After the party at Romanoff's, Grace confessed to close friends that she went home and cried for a long time. She had conquered Hollywood and had gained the respect of her peers, but not from Jack Kelly, whose less than enthusiastic remarks were in all the newspapers. On Grace's first visit to Philadelphia after winning the Oscar, family and friends gathered at the house on Henry Street to hear about the glitter of Hollywood firsthand. Jack arrived home and, with one stern look, told Grace that she was no different from anyone else in the Kelly family.

Brian thought she was *very* different from most stars who won the award. "Grace was not one to seek revenge," he said, "but it must have been a wonderful feeling to be applauded by people who not long ago had called her a whore. She needed love just as much as she needed Oscar and thought the award would make her father realize she had chosen the right profession and be proud of her. But she wasn't embraced by him literally or figuratively. Grace needed to be hugged and kissed by her father. In my opinion, this desire was stronger than any sex drive. I avoided any conversation with Grace about her father because she always said something like, 'He means well' or that he had an odd sense of humor."

Grace spent the Easter holidays with Cary Grant and his wife at the Sands Hotel in Las Vegas. On her first visit to the gambling capital of the world, she tried her luck at the tables with the excitement of a child in a candy store. Cary, as usual, was a most congenial host, making sure the Easter bunny did not forget to leave a basket at her door.

It was a busy springtime for Grace. The decorator had finished her new apartment in New York and she was anxious to entertain old friends. Grace was also mulling over an invitation by the French government to be the guest of honor at the Cannes Film Festival in May. She did not look forward to the crowds or being followed by photographers and reporters, but when Eric Johnson, head of the Motion Picture Association of America, told Grace that he wanted her to represent the United States at the festival, she considered it her patriotic duty to attend.

Oleg Cassini remained behind the scenes and saw Grace whenever possible during this hectic time of her life. Close friends thought she was playing a cat-and-mouse game with him, but her letters to Oleg that were published in his memoirs prove otherwise. The pressure put on their relationship by her mother and father turned out to be minute compared to the demands put on Grace Kelly, Queen of Hollywood, whose crown was an Oscar. Cassini now faced criticism from the public, who had put their blonde goddess up on a pedestal. It was not easy for Grace, either. In an interview with *Collier's*, she said, "One has different goals at different periods. . . . I'd love to get married and have children, but I hate to plan — for next year, even for next week. There's a superstition of the theatre that if you want a thing badly, you mustn't talk about it. It's a sure way to lose."

Cassini was lost in the maze of Grace's popularity, too, but she had not changed her mind about their unofficial engagement. He was forced to stay in the background as if he no longer played a vital part in her life. Grace asked his permission to have dinner with Bing Crosby, knowing it would make the gossip columns. Oleg was furious because she had once been linked romantically with the Crooner. Grace did not deny that Crosby had been in love with her but explained that they were not dining alone. In fact, Bing had a date for the evening, she said. Cassini was very upset nonetheless. He completely lost his temper when Grace asked permission to go out with her agent and Frank Sinatra, recently separated from his wife, Ava Gardner.

"I'll be in Los Angeles that night!" Oleg raged on the telephone. "What am I supposed to do while you're having a cozy dinner at Chasen's with Sinatra? Sit in my room at the Beverly Hills Hotel? That will *really* give Hedda something to write about. Yes, I mind. And, no, you do not have my permission!"

Grace went out with Frank anyway. Most likely, she had had every intention of doing so and had called Oleg to prepare him for the morning papers. Some biographers claim that her dates with Sinatra ended Grace's romance with Cassini, but this was not the case. It did weaken their relationship, however. If there were doubts about her association with Spencer Tracy, there were none about Grace and Frank.

Ava Gardner had settled permanently in Spain, and though she did not pick up the final divorce papers until 1956, her marriage to Frank was over. He dated scores of women — Judy Garland, Kim Novak, Natalie Wood, and Shirley MacLaine. Kitty Kelley, author of *His Way*, wrote that Frank dropped Judy Garland because she wanted to get married. Elizabeth Taylor received the same treatment.

Grace, however, brought back fond memories for Sinatra of when he had been one of a close-knit group in Africa. She had been an unknown at the time and he had been broke, but by 1955, they had both won Oscars and were the most sought after stars in Hollywood.

Cassini was not as concerned about the publicity as he was about Sinatra's reputation for being a magnificent lover.

Women found him irresistible, and Grace was not immune. She was a very curious and passionate young lady. Frank and Grace were old friends who had shared a special love for Ava Gardner, whether they discussed her or not. They were both going through a confusing phase in their lives. For Grace, it was whether she wanted to salvage the Cassini affair. For Sinatra, it was facing the realization that he would always love Ava but that divorce was inevitable. Grace, with whom he later became close, was able to communicate with him because she had been witness to their tears, fights, and kisses during *Mogambo*.

"What's important about the Sinatra interlude," Brian said, "is that Grace defied Cassini, who was nobody's fool."

David Niven almost gave himself away years later when Prince Rainier asked the charming actor which one of his beautiful Hollywood conquests had been the most exciting. Without hesitating, Niven had replied, "Grace." When Rainier paled, Niven quickly responded, ". . . er . . . Gracie . . . Gracie Fields!"

Their brief affair occurred when Grace was spending most of her time in New York before the Cannes Film Festival in 1955. David Niven was elegant, urbane, and witty. The happy-go-lucky English actor had had romances with many beautiful actresses in Hollywood, a town he referred to as "the Playpen." His delicious sense of humor and discretion appealed to women of all ages. Niven's first wife, Primmie, fell down the basement stairs during an afternoon party of hide-and-seek at Tyrone Power's in 1946. Oleg Cassini, who was then married to Gene Tierney, had carried Primmie upstairs. She died the next day. After a rebound affair with

Rita Hayworth, David married Stockholm model Hjordis Tersmenden in 1948. In the early sixties, the Nivens bought a villa on Cap Ferrat in the south of France, a short drive from Monaco.

David Niven and Frank Sinatra remained Grace's lifelong friends.

Oleg Cassini knew when to fall back during his pursuit of Grace. It would only be a matter of time before she dropped him a loving note or telephoned. Yet he needed an influential ally and thought he had found one in Joseph P. Kennedy, the father of the future President of the United States. Oleg poured his heart out to Joe, who said, "Don't worry about a thing. Set up a meeting and we'll settle everything, I promise you."

Cassini was confident when they met for lunch at La Côte Basque. The stage was set, and Joe reached out for Grace's hand. "My dear," he said, "the Kellys, the Kennedys, people like us, we have to stick together." Joe glanced at Oleg and then back to Grace. "This fellow's a nice boy, but you'd be making a terrible mistake by marrying him."

Cassini laughed nervously, "He's kidding, Grace."

Joe looked into her blue eyes and said, "We Irish have to stick together." He might have been teasing, but Kennedy never did get around to helping Oleg. Instead, he flirted with Grace on his *own* behalf.

As the official couturier for First Lady Jacqueline Kennedy, Cassini was invited to private parties at the White House. Jack Kennedy loved to tease him at these gatherings: "Oleg, tell them about how Dad screwed you up with Grace Kelly."

Cassini's sense of humor measured up to the Kennedy

men, who were also enthralled with Grace and perhaps more flirtatious than the debonair couturier.

Grace Kelly arrived in Paris on May 4, 1955. On an overnight train to Cannes she met Olivia de Havilland and her husband, Pierre Galante. He was the movie editor of *Paris Match* magazine and wanted to do a spread on Grace. "How would you like to meet the Prince of Monaco?" Galante asked her. "It would be a change of pace."

"I guess it will be all right."

However, when she arrived in Cannes, Grace looked at her schedule and knew there was no time for a trip to Monaco because she was the official hostess at a 5:30 p.m. reception the following day.

Galante pleaded. "It's only a fifty-mile drive. We'll be back in plenty of time."

"Pierre, you know that would be impossible. I'm sorry."

An embarrassed Galante called the palace with his sincere apologies. "Is it possible," he asked the Prince's secretary, "to arrange for a three p.m. appointment?" Annoyed, she asked him to hold on for a moment. "His Serene Highness will try to be back at the palace by three p.m." was the reply.

Grace changed her mind again but the next morning regretted it. There had been an electricity strike, which meant her wrinkled clothes could not be pressed, nor did her hair dryer work when she plugged it in. She called her good friend, Rupert Allan, *Look* magazine's West Coast editor. "My hair is wringing wet," Grace fretted, "and I haven't anything suitable to wear."

Allan said, "Well, don't do it. I'll tell *Paris Match* to drop dead."

"No, no," Grace replied, "you can't get someone like the Prince of Monaco waiting there and not do it."

The only dress that was unwrinkled was a gaudy taffeta with large red-and-green cabbage roses splashed on a black background, long sleeves, a dropped waist, and a skirt that billowed to the midcalf like an umbrella.

In *The Bridesmaids*, a 1989 book about Grace and her six girlfriends, Judith Quine wrote, "The taffeta dress was a ghastly little item Grace had purchased that we all teased her about. She had tried it on for me one day with her hair pulled back. All you could see was the bombastic print. It made her look pinheaded on top and wide on the bottom. She looked like a pear wrapped for Christmas." When Grace told Judy about wearing the taffeta dress to Monaco, she laughed, "It's only for *Paris Match*. It's not like anyone will ever see those pictures again." Little did she know that the awful taffeta dress would be immortalized.

On that hectic May 6, Grace pulled her damp hair back in a bun and then realized she needed a hat. Mumbling to herself that it would not be appropriate for a lady to meet a prince without wearing one, she looked through her suitcases and found a headband with artificial flowers that she arranged around a chignon.

On the drive from Cannes to Monaco, Grace's chauffeur had to jam on the brakes to avoid an accident. Consequently, they were hit from behind by a car carrying photographers from *Paris Match* magazine. No one was hurt and there was little damage to either automobile, but Grace began to wonder if the trip was worth it.

Her entourage arrived at the Hotel de Paris in Monte

Carlo just in time for a quick lunch. Grace was still nibbling on a ham sandwich as their car approached the palace at 3:00 p.m. The Prince was delayed but had sent word for his staff to take everyone on a tour of the palace. Photographers followed Grace from room to room, taking pictures of her for almost forty-five minutes. She was getting nervous and asked questions about the tardy Prince. "Does he speak English? What do I call him? How old is he? *Where* is he?" Grace looked in a mirror, smoothed out her hair, dabbed some powder on her face, glanced at her watch, and turned to Galante. "It's getting late," she said. "Let's go." Annoyed and tired, she was ready to leave just as a palace guard announced the Prince's arrival. Grace was not prepared for his sudden entrance. He bowed and extended his hand. As she curtsied, he apologized for being late. Grace was expecting a stuffy, less attractive older man and was taken aback by the good-looking and friendly Prince Rainier. When he offered to show her around the palace, she declined.

"Perhaps you'd like to see the gardens?" He smiled at her.

She nodded and the photographers reloaded their cameras. The Prince showed Grace his private zoo, which consisted of several monkeys, two lions, and an Asian tiger given to him by Emperor Bao Dai of Indochina. To Grace's amazement, the Prince put his hand in the cages to pet the beasts. This impressed her most, she said. They walked through the palace gardens overlooking the Mediterranean and seemed to be completely engrossed in each other despite the presence of photographers. It had been a strain on both of them. Prince Rainier was expecting a glamorous movie queen with an ego to match but found himself with a shy, soft-spoken, and refined actress who was anything but haughty. Grace was relaxed for the first time that day and seemed in no rush to leave the palace until she was reminded of the time. Before their official good-byes, the Prince said he was planning a trip to the United States and hoped to see her again. Grace said, smiling, "I hope so."

Her visit to Monaco did not receive much attention. Those who knew she was meeting the Prince inquired about the visit. Grace said, "It was fine. Just fine."

"What was he like?" they asked.

"Charming," she replied. "Very charming."

It was not love at first sight for either Grace or the Prince, but he was earnestly looking for a wife. Without an heir to the throne, Monaco would be swallowed up by France. He mentioned Grace to his spiritual adviser, Father Francis Tucker, who thought she would be perfect and was pleased that Rainier had told her about a trip to the United States even though there was no such visit planned. Father Tucker took the reins from there.

CHAPTER
THIRTEEN

Countdown

Grace had corresponded with Jean-Pierre Aumont during the past two years and was anxious to be with him at the Cannes Film Festival. He telephoned shortly after her arrival in Cannes. Grace wanted to see him that day but said she was trying to get out of a scheduled meeting with Prince Rainier at his palace. "I have to see my hairdresser," she complained. "I'm going to cancel the trip to Monaco." Aumont advised her to keep the appointment and reminded Grace that she would be representing the United States in Monaco. If she broke her appointment with the Prince, it might be embarrassing.

Grace had many valid excuses not to meet Rainier. She had a very busy schedule prearranged for her at the Festival, her hair had to be styled, and all of her clothes needed pressing. She also wanted very much to spend time with Jean-Pierre before the film activities started. Grace was, however, destined to meet her prince despite no electricity, no hairdresser or tailor, an automobile accident, and Rainier's arriving almost too late for the introduction.

Two frustrating days later, Grace met Jean-Pierre at a dinner-dance given by Elsa Maxwell, the international hostess and columnist. Nobody, including the world press, noticed the couple until Aumont asked her to dance. Once she was in his arms, no one else existed for them. They looked into each other's eyes with love and passion, waltzing the night away. If they were not so very romantic, it might have been awkward to the observers. A photographer for *Time* magazine snapped a picture of the lovers on the dance floor. Underneath, the caption read, "Grace Kelly, commonly billed as an icy goddess, melted perceptibly in the company of French actor Jean-Pierre Aumont. . . . Has Aumont, who came and thawed, actually conquered Grace?"

Elsa Maxwell sharpened her pencils and wrote in her column that she asked Jean-Pierre if he was in love. "Falling in love!" he exclaimed. "I'm desperate. Grace is the most adorable girl I've met since Maria died."

"How does she feel about you?" Elsa asked.

"Oh, I don't think she feels that way about me at all."

Grace and Jean-Pierre (she called him "Pierre") were together every day and night but did not give the press much to write about until they slipped away for lunch to a cozy and very private little restaurant, the Château de la Galère. A photographer with a telephoto lens caught Grace and Jean-Pierre kissing and caressing each other. In one picture, she is holding Aumont's hand and nibbling on his fingers.

When the photos were published, a shocked Grace said, "How embarrassing." She immediately sent a telegram to her parents denying the romance.

Margaret Kelly told a reporter, "I thought the pictures were sweet. They're harmless enough . . . showing two young people having a happy time together." Margaret, however, contacted Grace and inquired, "Shall I ask Mr. Aumont to visit us in Philadelphia?"

"Mother," she replied, "that's entirely up to you."

Photos of the uninhibited lovers at lunch were in all the newspapers and *Life* magazine. Cassini's brother Igor wrote in his syndicated column that Aumont had arranged for the photographer to boost his sagging career. Igor added, "Grace was very upset but did not want to admit she was a guinea pig." When confronted with the accusation, Jean-Pierre admitted he had told a close friend who worked for *Paris Match* magazine that he was having lunch with Grace at Château de la Galère but thought nothing of it. "I'm extremely upset, too," he said.

Meanwhile, back at the palace, Prince Rainier was disappointed that Grace was seemingly on the verge of announcing her engagement to Aumont. He expressed his concern to Father Tucker, who sent a brief letter to Grace: "I want to thank you for showing the Prince what an American Catholic girl can be and for the very deep impression this has left on him."

Grace's reply expressed her regrets that she had missed Father Tucker on her visit to Monaco but hoped they would meet on her next trip to France. This was not encouraging to Rainier, who had heard firsthand about Elsa Maxwell's party and how captivated Grace was of Aumont. It reminded him of another dinner-dance at the Cannes Film Festival two years previously when his mistress, Gisele Pascal, and Gary Cooper had been photographed dancing cheek-to-cheek. The press reported that Gary had taken the lovely Gisele away from the Prince of Monaco. Rainier had sent a letter of protest to Cooper, who was hounded by the press about Miss Pascal. "I'm afraid I can't talk about that. My wife might not appreciate it," he said.

Rainier's nephew, Baron Christian de Massy, wrote in his 1986 book *Palace: My Life in the Royal Family of Monaco*, that a rift was caused when Gisele was seen dancing with Cooper and that the Prince had said it was like "a knife going through my heart."

However, it was Father Tucker who had had more to do with the breakup of Rainier's affair with Miss Pascal than Gary Cooper in 1953.

After the Cannes Film Festival was over, Grace and Jean-Pierre checked into adjoining rooms at the Raphael Hotel in Paris for a week of shopping, long walks, and quiet dinners alone or with friends. The European press hinted that the couple was secretly engaged to be married. What did Aumont have to say? "I adore her. She's wonderful."

When asked about the possibility of marriage to Jean-Pierre, Grace replied modestly, "A girl has to be asked first." Egging her on, a reporter said that Aumont's friends insist he *did* propose. Grace was flustered. "We live in a terrible world," she said. "A man can't even tell you he loves you without the whole world knowing about it."

Nevertheless, she and Jean-Pierre managed to leave Paris without anyone knowing about it. The press found out that Grace was still registered at the Raphael Hotel but would be away for a few days. This led to the speculation that she and Aumont had eloped. Finally, it was discovered that Grace was spending a quiet weekend at Jean-Pierre's country house at Rueil-Malmaison with his nine-year-old daughter, Marie-Christine, and relatives of his late wife Maria. Grace was photographed wearing her glasses while knitting peacefully in a homey setting with Jean-Pierre and his family sitting nearby. Again, the newspapers hinted Grace and Aumont were already married. Reporters caught up with them at the airport. "I'm flying back to New York alone," she said calmly and then struggled with the question of marriage to Jean-Pierre. "I don't know," Grace said, sighing. "I can't tell you at this time."

Her arrival in New York was also hectic. "I love France and the way Frenchmen's minds work," she replied.

A reporter asked if Aumont's age was a factor.

"Differences in age or nationality present no obstacles in marriage between two persons if they love each other," Grace emphasized; but a few days later, she made a formal statement about her relationship with Jean-Pierre: "We are just good friends."

Aumont explained the obstacles very simply. He lived in France and Grace lived in America. Though he often filmed in Hollywood and she in Europe, it could never have worked out. "We lived different lives," he said.

Six months later, Louella Parsons cornered Jean-Pierre at a party. "A little bird told me that you and Grace were supposed to get married once upon a time."

"Darling," he said, smiling, "don't tell me that *you* believe everything you read in the papers."

Hedda Hopper overheard and sharpened her fangs. "You must admit, Jean-Pierre, that it is more exciting to be Princess of Monaco than Madame Aumont."

Driving home from the party that night, Jean-Pierre had a minor automobile accident and fractured a rib. The next day, Louella Parsons wrote that Aumont had tried to kill himself. The article began with: "A little bird told me that Jean-Pierre drove his car into a ravine because of a broken heart. . . ."

Aumont was one of the few who received a telegram from Grace about her engagement before the formal announcement in the newspapers. He married Pier Angeli's twin sister, Marisa Pavan, on March 27, 1956, three weeks before Grace's wedding.

Grace had not worked in more than six months and MGM was anxious for her to make another film. She was prepared, once again, to go on suspension, but this was not necessary. The studio offered Grace the movie version of *The Swan* (1956). Her Uncle George was particularly fond of Ferenc Molnar's play and urged her to accept the part of Princess Alexandra, who must choose between love and duty. Casting Grace in the role of a princess was purely coincidental because the visit to Monaco was of little interest in comparison to her highly publicized affair with Jean-Pierre.

Grace did not have to report for work in *The Swan* until the fall. In June, she was maid of honor when Lizanne married Don LeVine in a big Philadelphia wedding. Grace spent the rest of the summer in New York or relaxing in Ocean City with Kell's wife, Mary, and with Peggy and her two daughters, Meg and Mary Lee.

Brian had lunch with Grace during the summer of 1955. "That's when she thought life had passed her by," he said. "Grace joked about everyone getting married — her sisters and girlfriends, most of whom had children old enough for school. She wanted a husband and kids, too."

"I can find the right movie script," Grace said, "but not the right man."

"Can you honestly say you haven't met the right man?" Brian asked.

"No, but . . ."

"Cassini?"

"I'm not sure."

"Aumont?"

"You can't blame my family for breaking up that one," she said, laughing.

"Then life's been fair after all."

"That's therapy talk," she said.

"The right man for you is the right man for the Kelly family."

"In a way . . . yes."

"Therapy teaches self-reliance, remember?"

"To a degree," she spoke up. "I could defy my family if I thought they'd come around eventually. We are very, very close and I love them very much."

"You make it sound as if it would be easier to give up your career than your family."

Grace thought for a moment. "If that's the way it sounds, that's the way it is."

Brian thought it was nonsense about Grace not finding the right man. "She had more than her share," he said, "but they weren't right for mama, papa, and the church. Grace was attracted to European men, but Jack Kelly thought they were effeminate and phony, one reason why Grace wouldn't allow Aumont to go through the torture of meeting her father. Cassini was still in the running, but if she made the next move with him, it would have to be down the aisle."

In an attempt to please her parents and maybe find a husband who was not in show business, Grace dated Philadelphia Main Liner William Clothier, who took her to the exclusive Piccadilly ball. Socialite Gordon White, a wealthy young British actor, was another escort. But Grace was never seriously interested in either man.

"I saw more of Grace that particular summer than I had since she began making movies," Brian said. "I was a good and impartial listener, and she was, too. I had problems of my own that Grace knew about. She'd call and ask, 'Is your private dining room available this week?' My secretary was the only one I could trust to set this up because Grace was so famous. These lunches were therapeutic, not romantic."

What was happening behind the scenes that summer was far more interesting than Grace's social life.

Invited to Lizanne's wedding were the Austins, who were like family to Jack and Margaret and known to the Kelly children as "Aunt Edie" and "Uncle Russ." When they mentioned a summer trip to Monte Carlo, Grace told them casually about her having met Prince Rainier. The Austins arrived in Monaco and hoped to attend the annual Red Cross Gala at the Sporting Club but were told that there were no tickets available. A determined Uncle Russ called the palace and got through to the Prince by mentioning the magic words — Grace Kelly.

Rainier said it was his pleasure to arrange a table and then got in touch with Father Tucker, who called the Austins about a tour of the palace. Once it was established that the Austins were close to the Kellys, Father Tucker said the Prince was planning to visit the United States and he asked the Austins if they could arrange another meeting with Grace. Aunt Edie and Uncle Russ promised to do their best.

There was a flurry of telephone calls between Monaco and Philadelphia. It was uncertain if Rainier would arrive in November or December. Knowing Grace did not appreciate surprises, Margaret consulted her about the Prince's visit. "It's fine with me, Mother. I'd like to see him again."

Brian, who suspected that Grace and Rainier had kept in touch, said, "When I read that he was planning his first visit to this country, I didn't think it was a coincidence. A prince is no different from any red-blooded man when it came to Grace, and I told her so. Looking back, she sort of gave herself away by saying, 'I won't allow the press to make a mockery of my private life again.'"

The Swan was the charming fable of a Ruritanian princess whose marriage to a rich prince (Alec Guinness) is arranged to save her father's kingdom from ruin. A handsome tutor (Louis Jourdan) is hired to teach the princess protocol in preparation for her marriage. The plan almost fails when she falls in love with her teacher, but duty prevails. Standing with the young princess on a balcony overlooking a lake, the compassionate prince explains, "Think what it means to be a swan . . . to glide like a dream on the smooth surface of the lake and never go on shore. On dry land where ordinary people walk, the swan is awkward, even ridiculous. So there she must stay out on the lake, silent . . . white . . . majestic. Be a bird but never fly: to know one song but never sing it until the moment of her death. And so it must be for you." The prince offers his arm to her and together they enter the palace.

Grace's period gowns in *The Swan* were designed by Helen Rose, who was given carte blanche by MGM. She used only the finest and most beautiful fabrics. A white chiffon ballgown was hand-embroidered with camellias on the background. When Grace tried it on for the first time and stood in front of the mirror, she said, purring,

"How simply marvelous. What talented people you have here at MGM."

After two weeks in Hollywood, the production company flew to Asheville, North Carolina, where *The Swan* was going to be filmed at the Biltmore, a French Renaissance-style château built by George Vanderbilt. Grace told her agent, "It's like a palace. I love it."

The setting was perfect for a young lady being courted by a prince whose letters to her were becoming more serious as the weeks passed. For Grace, it was beautiful but also frightening. Then word came that Rainier wanted to visit her while she was filming *The Swan*. *Look* magazine hoped to do a feature article on the reunion, but Grace thought better of it because Aumont was paying her a visit in Asheville. She told her parents that the filming schedule of *The Swan* was indefinite, and they decided Christmas Day in Philadelphia would be best for all concerned.

An interview with Prince Rainier appeared in *Collier's* magazine on December 9. He told journalist David Schoenbrun about a 1918 treaty between his great-grandfather, Prince Albert, and the French government that would recognize Monaco as an independent principality exempt from taxes; but should the Prince die without an heir, Monaco would become a protectorate, ruled by France.

Rainier said he wanted to get married for personal reasons, too, "because the life of a bachelor is lonely and empty." He was not shopping for a bride on his forthcoming trip to America, and he emphasized that he would marry only for love. Schoenbrun asked the Prince to describe his ideal. Rainier said she would be fair-haired with a light complexion, graceful, and feminine. He preferred natural-looking girls, not "highly charged sexy wenches."

As princess, she should be able to cook. Otherwise, she could not tell their chef what to prepare. A princess had to be a good hostess who was adept at setting a beautiful dinner table and who knew the art of flower arranging. "I want a wife more than a princess," Rainier said. The greatest difficulty, he confessed, was knowing a girl long enough and intimately enough to find out if they were really soulmates as well as lovers.

The Prince did not mention the importance of his future bride's dowry because Monaco was in trouble financially. Aristotle Onassis had purchased the casino in 1953 and was concerned about this and other investments in Monte Carlo. He talked to Gardner Cowles, publisher of *Look* magazine, about the sagging economy of Monaco and about how they might lure America's rich back there. One solution was to marry Prince Rainier off to a beautiful movie star; the first one that came to mind was Marilyn Monroe, whom Cowles knew personally. She did not know where Monaco was but asked if the Prince were rich and handsome. Cowles, who had once described Rainier as "a plump young man, but attractive enough," answered Monroe's inquiry with a question: "Do you think that the Prince will want to marry you?"

"Give me two days alone with him and of course he'll want to marry me," she had replied.

Cowles said he would arrange a meeting.

Kim Novak was second choice, but she wasn't interested.

Before Cowles had a chance to put his plan into motion, Prince Rainier was engaged to Jack Kelly's daughter.

Marilyn called Grace with congratulations, adding, "I'm so glad you've found a way out of this business." Oddly, the two actresses never met. They laughed about the time they had been on the same plane from New York to Los Angeles. Grace was in coach and Marilyn asleep in first class. Neither knew the other was aboard until disembarking.

Oleg Cassini was particularly riled over Grace's publicized affair with Aumont in Europe. He and Jean-Pierre were friendly enemies dating back to his marriage to Gene Tierney, when Oleg was in the army and Aumont had tried to date his lovely wife. Cassini was delighted, therefore, to break up Jean-Pierre's cozy dinner with Grace on the night they had first met. Forcing Aumont into an introduction had been Oleg's pleasure.

When she returned to New York from the Cannes Film Festival, Grace also returned to Cassini. She had not given up on the idea of marrying him, and Oleg believed that Grace truly belonged to him after all was said and done. They saw little of each other because Grace was busy with her sister's wedding and preparing for *The Swan*. The Kellys were disturbed over her weekend in Paris with Aumont, and MGM was angry about pictures of a bespectacled Grace knitting with Jean-Pierre sitting at her feet. The studio considered this in direct contrast to her image as an aloof sex goddess. As usual, Grace tried to placate her family and the studio by conducting herself with propriety. Even though Cassini did not fit into this mold, he was still on her mind.

One can only imagine how difficult it must have been for Grace not to confide in anyone about the Prince. It was easy for her to say years later that she had loved him from the beginning, but this hadn't dawned on her yet if, in fact, it was true. Knowing she would have to make the final decision alone if Rainier proposed, Grace became edgy when her three weeks at the Biltmore in North Carolina were over and filming resumed in Hollywood. She seemed almost relieved that *The Swan* was behind schedule and that the cast might have to stay in California over the holidays.

Brian flew to Los Angeles on business in December. He called Grace to wish her a Merry Christmas and she thought it would be nice to celebrate with some champagne. "I had no idea we were having a farewell drink," he said. "She was in another world and drifted off during our conversation. I knocked on the table and said, 'Earth to Grace. Earth to Grace. Do you read me?'"

"I'm sorry," she said. "Believe it or not, I was thinking about staying here for the holidays. It might be nice for a change."

"Christmas without your family?"

"Why am I always expected to live by the rules?"

"This old rebel is a sucker for tradition," Brian said. "When my sister eloped, I knew she'd regret not having a long white dress and wedding album."

"And?"

"I was right. Ten years later, she got married again in the church, but it wasn't the same."

"Did you ever consider eloping?" Grace asked.

"Yes. How about you?"

"With Oleg. He found a priest who would marry us and I almost went through with it."

"What stopped you?"

"I don't know," she said thoughtfully. "I wanted to, but there was always something standing in the way."

"So you're going through with it now?"

"No."

"What then?"

"There are some things one has to work out alone, but it's nothing I can't handle."

Brian was positive Grace had planned to elope with Cassini. "It all added up," he said. "For her not to go home on Christmas was like Santa Claus taking the day off. Grace was prepared to work over the holidays, but *The Swan* wrapped and she didn't have a valid excuse to stay in Los Angeles. Grace had not gotten over Cassini, and their so-called engagement was in limbo. I forgot about the Prince because he wasn't her type."

CHAPTER
FOURTEEN

"I Will Learn to Love Him"

The Swan was finished on Thursday, December 22, 1955. Grace could no longer procrastinate and so made reservations on a flight to New York the next morning. She packed her suitcases in a rush and barely made the plane on time.

A few years later in an interview for *Redbook* magazine, Grace admitted her reluctance. "I made up my mind I wouldn't go," she said. "And then — I can't remember how it happened — I just went and bought a ticket anyway."

She attended a party given by close friends in New York and arrived home on December 24. Christmas morning, Grace woke up wishing she had not left California. Meeting the Prince took all the courage she could muster. The day dragged until the hour of his planned arrival approached. Grace called her oldest sister, Peggy, begging her to come over right away for moral support.

Jack Kelly greeted Rainier, Father Tucker, Dr. Robert Donat, Rainier's personal physician, and the Austins at the front door. Grace was shy during the introductions, but Peggy noticed "sparks flying" between the Prince and her sister almost immediately. After dinner, Grace and Rainier went to Peggy's house. Jack drove Father Tucker to the rectory and returned home in a huff.

"The Prince wants to marry Grace," he told his wife. "He asked the good father to sound me out. How do you like that?"

"I wonder how Grace will take it," Margaret replied.

"Well, I told Father Tucker a thing or two."

"Like what?"

"Like I don't want any damn broken-down Prince marrying my daughter! Where the hell is he from anyway?"

"Someplace like Morocco."

"A place no one knows anything about. I think he's after Grace's money. Father Tucker says he can prove otherwise."

Margaret sighed. "Have you forgotten we invited the Prince and Dr. Donat to spend the night?"

"It makes no difference to me," Jack said, growling, "but I want no more talk about marriage. The Prince is a nice enough fellow, but I don't like the idea of him asking a priest to feel me out about his marrying my daughter."

Grace and Rainier did not come home until 3:00 a.m. He went to bed wearing a pair of Kell's pajamas that were twice his size. Before retiring, Grace spent a few minutes with her mother.

"What do you think of the Prince?" Margaret asked casually.

"He's most attractive in every way," Grace replied. "Yes, I think he's very nice."

The next day, she and the Prince took a drive to Bucks County. After lunch, he joined Father Tucker in

Wilmington, Delaware, where they were staying. Grace walked into the house on Henry Street wearing a gold chain ring studded with rubies and diamonds.

"What's that?" Jack wanted to know.

"It's only a friendship ring," Grace answered.

"Like hell," he barked. "Give it back!"

"Oh, Daddy . . ."

Grace kept the ring and spent the rest of the day and evening with friends. Jack's only salvation was the Prince's absence that night, but he showed up in Philadelphia the following night to meet Lizanne and her husband, who had been out of town on Christmas Day. Grace's sisters noticed a glow on her face that was different. In numerous interviews over the years, they admitted it did not appear as though Grace were head-over-heels in love, as she had been with Don Richardson and Oleg Cassini. She did not use the word "love" at the onset. Grace was happy being with the Prince wherever they went and whatever they were doing. "It was difficult to explain how I felt," she said.

The day after Christmas, Peggy told her mother, "The real secret of the Prince's courtship lies in what happened at my house last night!"

Jack Kelly wanted no part of it. He was not convinced that Rainier could support his daughter despite impressive financial statements provided by Father Tucker that proved otherwise. When Jack mentioned his first encounter with the priest, he told Margaret, "I don't want to get involved." Though he said his concern was Grace's welfare, Jack Kelly resented being upstaged by his daughter and replaced in her heart by a young, good-looking prince whose royal blood was more impressive than Kelly for Brickwork or a few Olympic Gold Medals.

On Wednesday, December 28, the Prince and Dr. Donat drove Grace to New York for a meeting with MGM about her next film, *High Society* (1956), a musical version of *The Philadelphia Story* (1940). In preparation, the studio arranged for her to take singing lessons, but Grace's mind was not on her career because that evening she had accepted Rainier's marriage proposal. Knowing this might be their last opportunity to be alone, Grace waited until the next morning to call home with the news. "Mother, we're in love and want to get married." This came as no surprise to Margaret. She calmly phoned Father Tucker, who was always one step ahead of everyone else in his role of Cupid. "The Prince has already asked me to come to New York," he said. "I'll see you on Saturday, Mrs. Kelly."

After accepting Rainier's proposal, Grace called her friends to tell them she was engaged to be married but hung up before telling them who the man was. The consensus was Oleg Cassini. No one suspected Prince Rainier, and it came as quite a shock to Grace's friends. A few were skeptical until she opened her heart. "I've been in love before," she told them, "but never like this." She described Rainier as a kind and gentle person — a good man with a wonderful sense of humor. Grace told close friend Judy Quine, "I don't want to be married to someone who feels inferior to my success or because I make more money than he does. The Prince is not going to be 'Mr. Kelly.' What he does is far more important than what I do."

Grace and Rainier stayed in New York for a few days. They went out for dinner, to the theater, and to supper clubs for dancing. They were mentioned only briefly in the gossip columns because reporters had never heard of

Prince Rainier. Within one week, these same reporters would be flocking to Philadelphia, begging for photos and interviews.

Father Tucker rushed to New York for a chat with Grace and Rainier, then he met with the Kellys and formally announced that the Prince wished to marry their daughter.

"Royalty doesn't mean anything to us," Jack said bluntly, but on New Year's Eve day, he gave his consent to the marriage. Margaret phoned Grace right away with the good news.

Grace called Oleg Cassini and asked him to meet her on the Staten Island ferry. "I have something very important to tell you," she said.

Grace explained that she had cared for him more than anyone she had ever known and would probably continue to do so. "However, for various reasons that should be apparent, I have decided to marry Prince Rainier of Monaco."

"But you hardly know the man!" Oleg argued. "Are you going to marry someone because he has a title and a few acres of real estate?"

"I will learn to love him," she said coldly.

Cassini could do nothing more than wish her happiness and say good-bye. About Grace's decision to marry, he wrote in his memoirs, "I thought it had tragic aspects. I saw it as a capitulation, a decision to avoid the wondrous turmoil of life."

He saw Grace only once more. It was on the beach at Monaco. He was jogging. She was lounging. He noticed her and stopped abruptly. She nodded, "Hello, Oleg." He replied, "Hello, Grace." And then he hurried on his way.

Oleg Cassini never married again. In his late seventies, with stunning white hair, he is still a dapper gentleman-couturier who grants an occasional interview about his lost love, Grace Kelly. "I was desolate," he said. "It took me a long, long time to get over the breakup, but I supported her and never said a word about how I felt."

Grace sent telegrams to Gene Lyons and Jean-Pierre Aumont about her engagement to the Prince before it was officially announced. Aumont was in California at the time and replied that he was delighted with the news. That night, he had an auto accident, described by Hedda Hopper as a suicide attempt.

Don Richardson told author James Spada that Grace had to take a fertility test to ensure an heir to the throne of Monaco. Her fear was the Prince finding out she was not a virgin. Richardson also said Grace told him on the phone that her father was being impossible about the dowry and that the last figure mentioned was $2 million.

Grace was not as candid with Brian, who called to congratulate her during *High Society,* but their conversation gives some credence to Richardson's version because Grace said marrying European royalty involved a generous dowry, proof that she could have babies, and giving up all rights to her children in the event of a divorce. "I didn't find anything unusual about this," Brian said.

Jeffrey Robinson disputed both the $2 million dowry and the fertility test in his 1989 tome, *Rainier and Grace: An Intimate Portrait.* The book consists of personal interviews with the Prince, who allowed Robinson to see the original marriage contract.

". . . while certain financial arrangements were made, a $2 million dowry was not involved," the author wrote.

Rainier explained there was no need for Grace to take a fertility test. "The law is quite clear," he told Robinson. "According to the treaty with France, should there be no natural heir to the throne, the ruling sovereign may adopt a child to perpetuate the reign."

This, then, brings up the question as to why the Prince did not marry Gisele Pascal, whom he loved deeply but had to give up because she had failed to pass a fertility test.

A close friend of the Kellys said the marriage agreement, including a dowry, was a complicated matter. "The private meetings were heated," he said, "because Jack felt he was being used. The Prince was wealthy on paper, but his funds were tied up in property and other assets. Monaco was suffering through a bank scandal and parliamentary crisis. Rainier was innocent of any wrongdoing, but not only was his good name at stake but his country's finances as well."

If Jack Kelly considered the dowry an outrage, he could easily have refused to pay it. The pressure put on him by his family was a flimsy excuse. They never had that much influence over Jack in the past because he reigned supreme in the Kelly household; *but* he was nothing more than a shanty Irishman to members of the Social Register and Philadelphia Main Liners. He could make them eat crow if his daughter became a princess.

Grace had the leading part in this fairy tale, but she was the one who would benefit the least. She was aware of the sacrifices but not the consequences. Though the Prince was one of her youngest suitors at thirty-two, he was the world's last absolute monarch and the ultimate father figure. Grace often said people were compelled to follow Jack Kelly — that he was a leader of men. Rainier's birthright gave him the same qualities. Both men were strong-willed, short-tempered, and unyielding. Jack had waited until he was more than thirty years old to marry the right woman, and so it was with Rainier. These similarities were obvious to Grace, if to no one else. The timing was perfect, too. "If I'd met the Prince two or three years ago," she said, "perhaps I wouldn't have married him — at least not so soon. It seemed right, and it felt right, and that was the way I wanted it. I knew that I was going to do it even if there was a chance that I was making a mistake. I would find out later."

It was a romantic three weeks. A prince had crossed the Atlantic to ask for her hand. Their courtship might have been a fast one, but it limped along for the amorous Grace, who was accustomed to caressing, kissing fervently, and being swept off to the bedroom. What might have taken a few hours or a day dragged on for months, and her passion overflowed into loving anticipation. It was a long prelude of hand-holding, embracing, nuzzling, and staring into each other's eyes that made her want Rainier all the more.

On January 5, 1956, the Kellys held a luncheon party for thirty relatives and friends at the Philadelphia Country Club. When the champagne was poured, Jack stood up, tapped his glass, and said, "We are happy to announce the engagement of our daughter Grace to His Serene Highness Prince Rainier of Monaco. We drink a toast to them."

Meanwhile, the local press had been alerted that Grace Kelly was coming home to announce her engagement to a prince. Don Lagado, a *Philadelphia Bulletin* photographer, rushed to the country club. Jack had said that his daughter did not want any pictures taken. Lagado was only one of many newspapermen, but he had known Jack for years and put it to him straight — "Do you know how important it is for a Philadelphia girl to marry a prince?" Jack finally allowed two pictures. Lagado rushed back to his office and explained the predicament to his editor, who exclaimed, "We got two pictures and no story! What does the Prince look like?"

Lagado said, "He's a fat little guy who comes up to Grace's chin."

Ted MacFarland at the *Inquirer* joked that the Prince was "titty high." This phrase was picked up by Jack Kelly, who mused, "The Prince comes up to Gracie's titties."

Rainier was five-foot-seven, the same as Grace in her stocking feet, although Margaret claimed her daughter was actually closer to five-foot-eight. If the Prince has been described as "stuffy," he proved his sense of humor by calling himself "Shorty."

On that January day in 1956, however, the Prince was short-tempered and impatient. After the luncheon, reporters were welcome en masse to the Kelly abode, where they asked questions and took pictures to their heart's content. Grace was used to the attention. She also knew how to pose and was not shy about asking, "Could you take another, please? I think my eyes were crossed in that one." Rainier was not relaxed and resented the attitude of the reporters, who were not above snapping their fingers at His Royal Highness and shouting, "Hey, Joe! Look this way!" or "Smile, Joe!" A hundred questions were asked, including how many children the couple wanted. Grace blushed. Margaret gushed, "I should say lots of children!" The annoyed Prince leaned over to Father Tucker and said, "After all, I don't belong to MGM." Jack Kelly put a halt to the hectic press conference by inviting reporters to the basement bar for cocktails.

The famous couple made their first public appearance at the "Night in Monte Carlo" Charity Benefit at the Waldorf-Astoria Hotel in New York. The Prince wore white tie and tails with his royal decorations. Grace was never lovelier in a Dior white strapless satin gown, pearls, and orchids. *Time* magazine reported, "They sat uncomfortably in the royal box and nibbled crystallized violets while the press howled at the door. Later at the Harwyn Club, Grace nibbled Rainier's ear and danced until four a.m."

The *Daily News* reported an incident at the charity gala that proved Jack Kelly's daughter was a chip off the old block: "If Prince Rainier thinks this girl is going to be the type who will sit idly by and let him have his own way, he had an inkling of things to come the other night at the Waldorf-Astoria.

"An unidentified woman came up to the Prince, gushing congratulations and then impulsively planted a kiss on his right cheek. Moments later, Grace's cool gaze found the red smear of lipstick. 'Wipe that off your cheek!' she hissed. It was not a request. It was an order. The girl's Jack Kelly's daughter, all right!"

Others who observed the occurrence said Grace demanded to know the woman's identity. The Prince insisted he had no idea, but the next day Graciela Levi-Castillo, an

Ecuadorean socialite, identified herself to the press as an old flame of Rainier's. "He knows who I am," she said, smiling.

Before leaving for Hollywood to make *High Society*, there was the matter of where the wedding would take place. It was assumed that Grace would be married in Philadelphia, but the people of Monaco were so outraged that Rainier changed his mind and the Kellys consented.

Worldwide reaction to the nuptials was negative. Grace Kelly was a legend — an untouchable, elegant, and sensual lady whose frigid exterior melted during a kiss from debonair Cary Grant, the velvety Frenchman Jean-Pierre Aumont, and in the arms of tall and handsome William Holden. Headlines in the *Chicago Tribune* were critical of the Prince: HE'S NOT GOOD ENOUGH FOR A KELLY because ". . . she is too well bred a girl to marry the silent partner in a gambling parlor." The *Denver Post* complained that Rainier was "beneath her station."

Hollywood's Hedda Hopper wrote that Grace's friends were completely baffled. "Half of them do not believe she and the Prince will ever reach the altar."

Margaret Kelly was not alone in her assumption that the Prince ruled Morocco. The buzz in Hollywood was how could the sophisticated Grace survive the sandstorms and riding camels. Dore Schary, trying to be helpful, suggested they have the wedding at MGM. Grace thanked him but said, "I don't think you understand, Dore." He gave a luncheon for his biggest star and her Prince, who told the MGM mogul that Monaco was five square miles. A stunned Schary blurted out, "That's not as big as our back lot!" It was an embarrassing blunder but proof that few people knew anything about the tiny principality famous only for its gambling.

High Society was the musical version of *The Philadelphia Story*, filmed in 1940 with Katharine Hepburn, Cary Grant, and Jimmy Stewart. Grace played the part of willful socialite Tracy Lord, who plans to marry the stuffed shirt, George Kitridge (John Lund). Complicating matters at the prewedding celebrations are Tracy's former husband, happy-go-lucky C. K. Dexter Haven (Bing Crosby) and *Spy* magazine reporters Celeste Holm and Frank Sinatra. Tracy has too much champagne the night before her wedding and embarrasses George by going for a midnight swim with reporter Sinatra. Dexter is on hand for the showdown and wins Tracy back.

Grace did her own singing in a duet with Crosby, "True Love," that was Bing's last big record hit. As a tribute to his leading lady, for whom he still carried a torch, Crosby named his fifty-five-foot fishing cruiser *True Love*. (Grace, incidentally, won a Gold Record Award for the romantic duet.)

High Society, released after Grace's wedding, was a smash at the box office but not with the critics. Bosley Crowther of *The New York Times* wrote that Kelly and Crosby walked through their roles. *Saturday Review* thought Grace "seemed preoccupied." To say the least, she did have many other things on her mind, but observers agreed Grace had never been so relaxed and that "she really let herself go."

Grace began filming on January 17, 1956. After a tour of the United States, the Prince rented a villa in Hollywood for six weeks. He presented his future wife with a twelve-carat solitaire diamond that Grace decided to wear in the film rather than an engagement ring provided by the studio. Making *High Society* was great fun for Grace, Sinatra, and Crosby. Huddled together on the set, they laughed at an abundance of jokes, Hollywood gags, and gossip, all of which were foreign to Rainier, who visited the studio almost every day. He knew very little about American customs and was less familiar with the camaraderie that movie people had. The touchy and chummy Grace was contrary to the shy and formal lady waiting for him in Philadelphia. The Prince took it in his stride, but he was uncomfortable even though everyone tried to make him feel at ease. That he and Grace came from different worlds was obvious to the Hollywood crowd, who gave the couple a short-lived engagement.

Rainier was relieved when his father, Prince Pierre de Polignac, arrived in Los Angeles to meet the future bride and discuss plans for the wedding. The tall and stately Prince Pierre was very fond of Grace from the start and would be her valuable ally in Monaco.

Winning over Rainier's father came at a time when she needed support. Without her knowledge, Margaret had granted a series of interviews to Hearst reporter Richard Gehman. The ten articles were entitled MY DAUGHTER GRACE KELLY — HER LIFE AND ROMANCES BY MRS. JOHN KELLY. Grace was mortified to see her private life exposed in the daily newspapers. She had overcome these scandals, had sought help from a therapist, and had risen above the horrible ridicule and gossip. Now her own mother had dug up Grace's romances with Clark Gable, Gary Cooper, Ray Milland, Gene Lyons, Jean-Pierre Aumont, and Oleg Cassini. Though Margaret denied that her daughter was ever involved with married men, blaming it on Hollywood publicity, the names mentioned in the articles reminded the public that the future fair-haired princess was no angel.

Margaret was so busy with plans for the royal wedding that she did not have time to edit the articles. Gehman tried to discuss the interviews with her but Margaret innocently told him, "I'll have to trust you, that's all." She was also too busy, apparently, to tell Grace, who later asked her mother, "How could you do this to me?" Margaret explained it was for a good cause. She was donating the royalties to her favorite charity, the Women's Medical College in Philadelphia. Grace did not forgive Margaret for a long time. She told a friend, "I've worked so hard and now my mother's going to destroy everything overnight."

The articles sold newspapers, but the general consensus was that a protective, loving mother would never think of exposing her daughter's private life in such a cheap way. If Mrs. John Kelly wanted to support her pet charity, she could have written a check. MGM was incensed but powerless. They did, however, edit the articles before they appeared in European newspapers.

It was not easy for Grace to face her coworkers on the set every morning when the series was running in the *Los Angeles Examiner*. The crew made sure there was not a copy of the newspaper around where Grace might see it. She was also embarrassed for Rainier because Margaret had described the courtship and engagement in detail. If he did not fathom Grace, the actress, he understood Grace, the woman, who was deeply hurt. Reporters showed compassion by not pressing her to comment on the articles. When they caught up with the Prince, he was asked to comment on Grace's cooking since they were spending quiet evenings together. He praised her dinners and jokingly said she was particularly good at barbecuing. Occasionally, a nasty newsman wanted to know if Grace expected her marriage to last, and the response was always the same: "A Catholic marries for life."

When she was asked about her film career, Grace said, "My contract with MGM is good for another four years. I've always been faithful to any agreement I've made." She was looking forward to costarring again with Jimmy Stewart in *Designing Woman* (1957), a movie based on the story of couturiere Helen Rose.

The Prince had other plans for his bride-to-be, however. "No more movies for Miss Kelly!" he exclaimed on his way back to Monaco in March. Rainier had managed to avoid the press when he left Los Angeles under an assumed name, C. Monte (for Monte Carlo), but reporters found him boarding the *Ile de France* in New York, where he announced Grace's retirement from the screen. The Prince said he was a "bit weary" of all the publicity and hoped his wedding would be a quiet one.

Grace had tried to reason with Rainier about fulfilling her contract with MGM. He was opposed, but apparently she held out hope. Nevertheless, the Prince was vehement at his unofficial press conference and she had no choice but to respond, "If that's the way he wants it, that's the way it will be."

Once again, MGM was in a dilemma over Grace. How could they sue a princess for breach of contract? Easing out of an awkward situation, they exchanged *Designing Woman* for exclusive film rights to the royal wedding. (Grace donated her share of the profits to the Monaco Red Cross.) No one, including MGM, believed she was giving up Hollywood for good. The studio kept Grace on salary until after the honeymoon, gave her a bonus of approximately $70,000 for 1956, paid a tidy sum of $7,000 for her wedding gown designed by Helen Rose, and assigned a publicity agent to manage the international press in Monaco. In return, Grace agreed that MGM could extend her contract until 1966.

The studio made one blunder. They waited until a week after the wedding to release *The Swan*, but the public did not want to pay for a ticket to see Grace Kelly as a make-believe princess when they could see the real one on newsreels. That critics liked *The Swan* was insignificant. Bosley Crowther's charming review in *The New York Times* ended, "The experience is a bit like eating the food at a wedding reception and sipping the light champagne, but that should be no discouragement to Miss Kelly's vast multitude of fans, who will no doubt welcome the opportunity to do just that with her."

Four months later, Grace's fans had more fun watching her getting tipsy on champagne in *High Society*, with Frank Sinatra and Bing Crosby.

Before Grace left Hollywood, there were parties given in her honor, but she had promised Rainier that she would not dance with anyone or drink until they were together again. Frank Sinatra took the initiative, phoned the Prince, and got his permission. Then there were the traditional bridal showers. Helen Rose arranged one of them and requested that the guests bring lingerie.

MGM asked Grace to attend the Academy Awards ceremony and present an Oscar to, as it turned out, Ernest Borgnine, who was voted Best Actor for his performance in the sleeper, *Marty* (1955). Afterward, Grace was adamant about not making an appearance in the pressroom, which was primarily reserved for Oscar winners. "They don't want to interview me," she said. "I haven't won anything." Someone in the crowd overheard and shouted, "Yes, you have. You've won a prince." Grace told an official photographer backstage that she had to catch an early plane for New York the next day, but she thought it only proper to pose for a picture with Ernest Borgnine. Then Grace Kelly left the theater, trying to avoid the crowds who gathered anyway. She smiled, slid in the backseat of a limousine, and waved farewell to Hollywood.

Alfred Hitchcock suffered a terrible blow when his sensual madonna jilted him. "Marrying a prince is in line with Grace's progression," he said. "Grace has bounced around with the ease of a girl on the trapeze. Whether the platform on which she has landed is too narrow, I don't know."

He tried replacing her with Kim Novak, Eva Marie Saint, Vera Miles, and Tippi Hedren, but when Hitchcock found a script that was perfect for Grace, he traveled all the way to Monaco, hoping to bring his smoldering goddess back to Hollywood.

It almost happened.

CHAPTER
FIFTEEN

The Prince

Rainier III, Louis Henri Maxence Bertrand de Grimaldi, His Serene Highness, the Prince of Monaco, was born on May 31, 1923. His ancestors, the Grimaldis, were Genovese buccaneers who fought for Spain and then France. In 1297, Francois ("The Spiteful") Grimaldi helped capture Monaco from a rival group by posing as a Franciscan monk seeking food and lodging at the fortress on Le Rocher, a headland on the Mediterranean coast of France where the palace of Monaco now stands. The two guards let Francois pass and were struck down by Spiteful's sword while his men swarmed the fortress.

Over the centuries, the Grimaldis lost and regained their power. In 1612, the Spanish moved in to the dismay of Monaco's ruler, Honoré II, who was compensated by Spain's recognition of his title as Serene Prince. He waited for almost thirty years to oust the Spanish.

Another hero in Monaco's history was Rainier's great-great-great-grandfather, Charles III, who restored his ravished country after the French Revolution. He was responsible for opening a casino in 1856, building Monte Carlo, and abolishing taxes.

When Charles died, his son Prince Albert I assumed the throne. His marriage to Lady Victoria Douglas-Hamilton of Scotland ended when she walked out during a violent argument, fled to Germany, and gave birth to a son, Louis II, heir to Monaco's throne.

Albert's second wife was the blond and beautiful Alice Heine, whose father was a self-made American millionaire. Her dowry to the Prince was $6 million. Princess Alice helped establish the Monte Carlo Opera and Ballet Russe, which were also Grace's pet projects. Albert and Alice had little in common, however, and their marriage ended in 1902.

Louis II was eleven when he met his father. Albert was never fond of the boy, who was a constant reminder that his mother had been cause for embarrassment by fleeing Monaco in the middle of the night. Albert also had doubts that he was the real father. Louis, who grew up missing his mother and hating Monaco, got himself posted in the French Foreign Legion. Some historians claim it was Albert's doing, but Louis thrived on adventure and was made Grand Officer of the Legion of Honor. While he was serving in Algeria, Louis fell in love with a divorced laundress, Marie Juliette Louvet, who gave birth to an illegitimate daughter, Charlotte, in 1898. Albert refused to give Louis permission to marry but twenty-one years later was forced to accept Charlotte in order to secure the Grimaldi dynasty. He arranged for her to marry Count Pierre de Polignac, an impoverished French nobleman. On the night before the wedding, Albert made the groom change his name to Grimaldi, making him Prince Pierre Grimaldi, Count of Polignac. In 1920, Pierre and Charlotte had their first child, Antoinette. Three years later, they had a son, Rainier Louis Henri Maxence Bertrand de Grimaldi. In 1929, Charlotte divorced Prince Pierre, who was granted an allowance and ejected from the palace by Louis II, who became the ruling prince when Albert died in 1922. Louis disliked Pierre intensely and tried to banish him from the Grimaldi family. Pierre fought for parental rights and had charge of his son's education. Rainier attended the Summer Fields School at St. Leonard's-on-Sea near Hastings in England. "It was dreadful," he said. From there he was sent to Stowe in Buckinghamshire, but to be a foreigner and a Catholic in a Protestant English public school was a lonely and degrading experience. The other boys called Rainier "fat little Monaco."

Louis found out his grandson tried to run away, petitioned the courts for custody, and won. From England, Rainier went to a Swiss school, Le Rosey, which he remembers fondly. When World War II started, the young Prince finished his education at the University of Montpellier and the École des Sciences Politiques in Paris. Rainier returned to the palace but was disgusted with his grandfather's decision to make Monaco off-limits to the American military. After a bitter quarrel, he volunteered as a foreigner with the French Free Forces, fought in the Alsace campaign, and was awarded the Croix de Guerre and the Bronze Star.

When the war was over, Rainier tried to make peace with his ailing grandfather and help rebuild Monaco after the Nazi occupation, but Louis was more interested in his romance with a French actress. He married Ghislaine Marie Dommanget, thirty years his junior, and Rainier promptly moved to an icy pink villa at Cap Ferrat, a short drive from Monaco. For the first time in his life, he was able to enjoy racing cars, skin diving, and sailing. The Prince shared his villa with French actress Gisele Pascal, who was the same age. They were remarkably compatible and very much in love.

Rainier met her in Paris while studying at Montpellier. He attended the theater one night to see a play called *His Lordship*, a comedy about a pretty commoner teaching a young lord about love. Rainier admired the stunning leading lady with auburn hair, big gray-blue eyes, upturned nose, and shapely figure; he went backstage to congratulate her. They were instantly attracted, but the shy Prince did nothing about it until he read in the newspapers that Miss Pascal was having a romance with popular singer Yves Montand. This was so upsetting to Rainier that he began to court Gisele, who became his constant companion. To be near him, she gave up her career and moved discreetly into his guarded villa.

In 1949, Louis died and twenty-six-year-old Prince Rainier became Monaco's ruler. He handled official business at the palace but lived in his Villa Iberia sheltered by palms and mimosa. It was taken for granted by the people of Monaco that he would marry Gisele, whom they referred to as the "invisible princess" and eventually their "uncrowned princess." Gisele refused to talk about the romance. "You will have to ask Monsieur," she told a reporter. "I am living in a dream and nothing must spoil it."

After a six-year affair, Rainier decided to marry Gisele in 1953. Palace advisers and Father Tucker wanted proof that Gisele was capable of producing a royal heir. Her personal physician said Miss Pascal was in excellent health and was able to have children. There were rumors, however, that she had failed two fertility tests administered by palace doctors; this has never been established. Though the law in Monaco allowed their ruler to adopt a child, it is doubtful that the Monegasques would have accepted an heir without the Grimaldi blood that had sustained their royalty for seven centuries.

With a heavy heart, Rainier gave up Gisele, who returned to Paris. He could not make a formal announcement about the breakup because he had never officially acknowledged their relationship. Soon after giving up Gisele, the Prince was crushed over her dates with actor Gary Cooper. The press and public were confused. One newspaper headline read: WILL GISELE LEAVE THE PRINCE, HIS CASTLE AND HIS CASINO FOR THE COWBOY? Cooper told reporters she was nice company. Correspondent Bernard Valery wrote, "That's a mess of an understatement even for a cowboy."

The press reported that Gisele was not Rainier's only headache. The Monaco Parliament wanted him to settle down "sensibly with some rich, titled woman. They even picked out an Italian princess with a three-million-dollar dowry for him, but Rainier would have none of it."

Palace insiders claim the Prince had considered giving up his throne for Gisele, and for a long time after their separation, he wore a ring she had given to him. Depressed and lonely, Rainier had to get away from Monaco for a while; he sailed his boat to French Guinea on the west coast of Africa, collecting animals for the palace zoo.

In Paris, Gary Cooper told reporters he did not want to talk about Miss Pascal ". . . because my wife might not appreciate it, and she's coming over here with our daughter next week." The Coopers, who had been legally separated for some time, reconciled a few months later.

Gisele finally granted an interview to clarify matters regarding the Prince. "It was a beautiful thing," she said.

"That's all I want people to know about it. We agreed to part so the Prince could fulfill his duty to his country. It was an affair of state." Appearing on stage in *Freres Jacques* and making a film, Gisele was working twelve hours a day. "You see," she said with a sad smile, "I have no time for love now."

However, in October 1955, Gisele married handsome French movie idol Raymond Pellegrin and later gave birth to a daughter, proving the palace doctors wrong about her ability to have children. Rainier never revealed his bitterness over this betrayal. By all accounts, Father Tucker was the one instrumental in breaking up the six-year affair. For reasons unknown (most likely dowry money, or lack of it), he did not deem Gisele Pascal an acceptable candidate for princess and used his persuasive power over the Royal Council to deny Rainier permission to marry Gisele.

The Prince's nephew, Baron Christian de Massy, claimed that Father Tucker "exerted a Rasputin-like influence over his uncle, constantly scheming." The Baron said his mother, Antoinette, fell victim to Father Tucker's gossip about her husband's infidelities, prompting the Princess to seek a divorce.

In the early sixties, the Prince arranged for Father Tucker's retirement in his native United States, where he subsequently died.

CHAPTER
SIXTEEN

Princess Grace

"I would like to tell my future compatriots that the Prince, my fiancé, has taught me to love them. I feel I already know them well, thanks to what the Prince has told me, and my dearest wish today is to find a small place in their hearts."

This message to the people of Monaco was broadcast on Radio Monte Carlo and the Voice of America by the future Princess of Monaco shortly after she boarded the liner *Constitution* in New York on April 4, 1956. Following the broadcast, Grace Kelly faced more than two hundred reporters and photographers at a press conference. When asked about her career, she said, "Right now, I'm too interested in my marriage career to think of the movies."

"What do you call the Prince?" a reporter wanted to know.

"I call him Rainier."

"How about your citizenship?"

"On my marriage, I shall become a Monegasque," she replied, "but it will not affect my American citizenship. I shall have a dual citizenship."

Grace was remarkably candid about not speaking to the Prince since his departure for Monaco three weeks ago. "We write to each other," she said.

Though the press corps would be sailing on the same ship, they were not allowed in the first-class section taken over by Grace's friends and relatives. In order to accommodate her group, sixty-six passengers previously booked in these staterooms were bumped. The only members of Grace's family not present were Kell's wife, Mary, and Lizanne, who were both pregnant.

This eight-day voyage was Jack Kelly's last hurrah, and he hosted the cocktail and dinner parties with great pomp and circumstance. Jack gave the impression that he was responsible for this historic event and had a fun time with his gregarious Peggy, who always managed to be the life of the party, laughing, dancing, and telling jokes. Like her father, she was the center of attention, the star of the show. In contrast, Grace kept up to date with thank-you notes, organized her wardrobe, and made sure friends and relatives were comfortable on board the ship. Peggy was to say that her sister's engagement was not a fairy-tale romance. Lizanne thought it was "just a nice agreement."

The Catholic news agency DIS wrote, "The romance, if not an imposed one, was certainly advised by experts who had watched the Monegasque tourist trade dwindling and badly needed some unexpected sensation to put it back in the public eye."

While the *Constitution* was sailing on a smooth sea in the warm sunshine, Rainier was handling all the arrangements for the wedding by himself. Tired and irritated, he was bothered by an infected tooth that was finally extracted; Rainier's temper still did not improve. He was annoyed with Father Tucker, who was enjoying his Cupid status by talking freely to the press. The Prince did not invite him to his stag party on April 8, and the rumor about their strained relationship persisted.

The Monegasques were excited over the forthcoming wedding, but the Grimaldis were less than enthusiastic about the family gathering in Monaco. Princess Charlotte detested her former husband, Prince de Polignac. The young widow of Louis II, Princess Ghislaine, was barely tolerated. Then there was Rainier's sister, Antoinette, who was not only estranged from their mother but resented transferring her rank in Monaco society to the new Princess.

Charlotte did not approve of Rainier's marrying an American movie actress and was prepared to dislike Grace before they met. That Princess Charlotte was the illegitimate daughter of a laundress was not important because she had inherited the royal blood of her father, Louis II.

On April 12 at 9:45 a.m., the *Constitution* sailed into the Bay of Hercules near Monaco, where the Prince was waiting at the bow of his white yacht, *Deo Juvante II*. Grace waved and he saluted. "I see him!" she exclaimed to her parents. Wearing a navy blue fitted coat over a matching dress, white gloves, and a huge white organdy hat, Grace held Oliver in her arms, his leash dangling loose, and walked down the gangplank. If this important part of the ceremony had been carefully planned, Grace would not have carried the dog because Rainier was thus unable to embrace or kiss her. Instead, she extended her gloved hand for the disappointing and unromantic greeting. Another major problem was her choice of hat for the occasion because the crowds waiting to get a glimpse of the future Princess could not see her face underneath the upside-down lacy white saucer.

The royal yacht circled the *Constitution* once and

sailed on into Monaco's harbor, where the celebration began with cannon salutes, fireworks, and bands playing "The Star-Spangled Banner." Onassis had arranged for a seaplane to drop red and white carnations on the harbor while boats blew their whistles and spouted fountains of water. Grace told Margaret, "I've never been happier in my life." Once off the yacht, she got into the Prince's green Chrysler, which he drove up the hill to the freshly painted pink palace of Monaco.

The Kellys were introduced to the Grimaldis at a small reception before lunch. If Charlotte was cold and expressionless with Grace, she was appalled when Margaret patted her firmly on the shoulder, shook her hand with gusto, and cheered, "Hi! I'm Ma Kelly!" Charlotte froze.

During the private luncheon, Jack Kelly looked around and commented, "The servants have so much braid, I can't tell them from the generals." Peggy thought that was hysterically funny. Kell did, too, but Charlotte's icy stare was difficult to ignore. If looks could kill . . .

Grace and Rainier made an appearance at the windows overlooking the palace courtyard, where a large crowd had gathered. This was the moment of truth when her family and friends realized she was actually going to be a princess. Her arrival in Monaco was spectacular, but as she stood over the cheering throng, the scene was reminiscent of Great Britain's royal family on the balcony of Buckingham Palace. A friend explained, "I was in awe but bewildered and sad. Grace said she was very happy but also a bit melancholy."

After the couple had dinner alone, Rainier drove to his Villa Iberia for the night and Grace joined her parents in the palace apartments. This would be their last chance to rest before five days of endless receptions, galas, and wedding rehearsals.

It was also a week of ordeals and tension brought about by Charlotte, who made no effort to conceal her hatred for Prince Pierre. When they argued in public, he got even by praising his future daughter-in-law, for whom Charlotte had yet to show any affection.

Grace was deeply hurt but hoped to establish a warm rapport with Rainier's sister. Her first gesture of friendship was asking Antoinette to be a bridesmaid. It was meant to be a surprise, and she succeeded in shocking Antoinette by presenting her with the organdy gown and matching hat. Grace had no idea she was breaking protocol and might not have felt so ashamed if Antoinette had explained that, as a member of the royal wedding party, she could not be a bridesmaid. Instead, her lady-in-waiting conveyed the message to Grace, who burst into tears. Rainier calmed her down by explaining that no harm was done.

Antoinette invited them for lunch at her villa on Saturday, April 14. This was the first day Grace emerged from the palace since her arrival, and the press was waiting. Rainier was at the wheel when he suddenly noticed someone lying on the road and jammed on his brakes. Thinking the man was hurt, Rainier got out of the car and was besieged by the press, including the reporter playing dead. In the backseat, Jack Kelly was flexing his muscles, ready to punch someone in the nose. Grace thought it was funny, but the Prince lost his temper. He had sense enough to get back in the car but was annoyed at Grace's amused smile. Maybe she was used to such nonsense, but Rainier was not. The hectic week had only begun and he was thoroughly disgusted knowing there were no less than sixteen hundred photographers and reporters in Monaco. Grace might have been amused at this one incident, but she would have preferred a simple wedding in a small church somewhere in the French countryside to avoid what was turning into a three-ring circus, with Grace as the main attraction. When she and Rainier were leaving a formal dinner-dance in the pouring rain, they ducked into a waiting limousine; a thousand drenched and angry reporters booed Grace. This was one of many disagreeable incidents that made her so nervous that she barely ate or slept. Still, the dark circles under her eyes and the loss of ten pounds did not detract from Grace's beauty or stance.

Jewel thieves were more organized than the press. More than $50,000 worth of gems were stolen from wealthy guests at the Hotel de Paris. Margaret Kelly's loss was kept a secret because she was staying at the palace. Insiders were suspicious of Charlotte's chauffeur and alleged lover, Rene Girier, a well-known "retired" jewel thief. She was appalled by the rumors, of course, and defended him vehemently.

One of the nightly festivities was a dinner-dance given by the Kelly family. Jack took advantage of the spotlight that was slowly fading for him. Supposedly, he had made some sarcastic remarks about Rainier's imperial attitude, but Jack was very chummy with him that evening because the Prince was *his* guest. Charlotte had to endure an obligatory dance with the bricklayer from Philadelphia; she did not pretend to enjoy it.

The Kellys were not hypocrites, either. Peggy drank milk with escargots and ran about the palace with her two children wearing shorts. Winston Churchill's son, Randolph, told England's Lady Docker in disgust, "I didn't come here to meet vulgar people like the Kellys!" Peggy's homespun frivolity would most likely have been refreshing to the press. Columnist Dorothy Kilgallen wrote, "The only really bright chaps here are the journalists for the sensational British papers. They solved the whole problem and haven't a care in the world. They just make up their stories — and believe me, they are a lot better than the stuff we conservative toffs are sending back home." It wasn't proper, of course, to write about Jack Kelly's predicament at the palace one day when nature called and he could not find a bathroom. Since the servants spoke only French, Jack phoned a Philadelphia reporter-friend at his hotel and took a limousine there for relief.

Jack told columnist Earl Wilson about the laundry service at the palace: "I took out a clean shirt and decided not to wear it. I put it down somewhere and when I looked for it again, it had been sent to the palace laundry and came back with the sleeves pleated!"

As Princess of Monaco, Grace could not wear jewelry given to her by other men. She gave each piece away in private to her girlfriends but was handsomely rewarded. Each day preceding the wedding, Rainier presented her with furs and jewels. Mistaken for a crown was the family coronet of diamonds often worn by Grace. The crown of Monaco had been stolen during the French Revolution and had never been replaced.

Grace received at least two diamond and ruby necklaces with matching rings, bracelets, and earrings. The people of Monaco presented their Prince and his bride with a new Rolls-Royce, and the list goes on. Queen Elizabeth did not attend the wedding but sent a gold tray. Cary Grant chose an antique writing desk and called to tell Grace he was filming

The Pride and the Passion (1957) in Spain and could not get away. Frank Sinatra backed out at the last minute because his former wife, Ava Gardner, was attending. Their recent divorce had been highly publicized and he was afraid the press might focus on them. "This is your day," he told Grace, who had been hoping to reunite Ava and Frank by strategically maneuvering the seating arrangements.

Because the films of Grace Kelly would not be shown again in Monaco's three movie theaters, friends in Philadelphia gave her a Cinemascope screen and two 35mm projectors for a proposed viewing room in the palace.

The night before the civil ceremony, Monaco turned off its lights for an hour of spectacular fireworks. Afterward, Grace retired to her rooms and Rainier to his villa, but the commoners danced until dawn.

At ten the next morning, eighty guests took their seats in the Salle du trône. Rainier, serious and tense, wore a morning coat and striped trousers. Grace was elegant and poised in a rose beige lace suit with a Juliet cap trimmed with matching silk roses and white gloves. The throne, used only for coronations, had been removed. Two cushioned and gilded chairs were placed a few feet apart in the center. Family and witnesses were seated in groups facing the uneasy couple. Judge Marcel Portanier read the civil marriage rites and then asked the bride, "Mademoiselle Grace Patricia Kelly, do you take as your husband His Serene Highness, My Lord, Prince Rainier III, here present?"

She answered softly, "Oui."

Turning to the Prince, who appeared restless, the judge

asked, "May I respectfully ask Your Serene Highness if he agrees to take as his wife and legitimate spouse Mademoiselle Grace Patricia Kelly, here present?"

The Prince perked up and said clearly, "Oui."

Grace sat erect as a statue throughout the hour-long ceremony, eyes forward, feet together, and hands crossed on her lap. In a frozen daze, she signed the official register with a trembling hand and went through the motions of greeting foreign diplomats while also waving to throngs of people from the palace balcony and posing for pictures. After a glass of champagne, Grace came to life. "Now I'm halfway married," she said. Even though Judge Portanier read the one hundred and forty-two titles she held as Princess of Monaco, Grace had been oblivious until later. She looked at the list and gasped, "I can't believe it!"

Sometime between the luncheon, lawn party, and Opera House gala, Rainier bestowed the Order on Grace. Rather than waiting until after the religious ceremony, he proclaimed that Grace was Her Serene Highness, Princess of Monaco. That evening at the Opera House, she wore the Order of Charles, a red-and-white ribbon, across her bodice.

Grace hoped this honor meant she would share the Prince's bed that night. He said it was impossible. She said it was a "Victorian" arrangement. He returned to his villa and Her Serene Highness retired alone.

On Thursday morning, April 19, six hundred guests assembled in Monaco's Cathedral of St. Nicholas. Among them were the David Nivens, Gloria Swanson, King Farouk of Egypt, the Aga Khan, Ava Gardner, Somerset Maugham, Conrad Hilton, and Aristotle Onassis with his wife, Tina. The altar was banked with white lilies, lilacs, and hydrangeas to hide a battery of cameras and microphones that would provide live television coverage.

At 10:30 a.m., Grace walked down the aisle holding Jack Kelly's arm. Ava Gardner turned to her escort, MGM publicist Morgan Hudgins, and whispered, "Look at Grace's father. How I envy her. If only I had a father like him to lean on." Ava, whose father had died when she was a child, did not know how much Grace yearned to be Jack Kelly's princess and how, on this day when the world revered her, she would have traded it all in for one minute of affection from her father.

Grace's white wedding gown, designed by Helen Rose, was a gift from MGM. The lace for the bodice and ten-foot train, made of antique Rose Point, was one hundred and twenty-five years old and had been purchased from a French museum. The skirt consisted of twenty-five yards of silk taffeta and one hundred yards of silk net. Thousands of seed pearls had been sewn into the veil and also decorated the petaled lace headdress. The gown had long tight sleeves with scalloped wrists, a pleated taffeta cummerbund, and a stand-up collar. Grace's hair was pulled straight back with a chignon, and the only jewelry she wore were pearl stud earrings. It would be redundant to describe Grace as a porcelain doll or the personification of beauty that day.

When father and daughter reached the altar, Jack was told to sit down. "No," he replied, "I'll wait until *he* gets here!" To the very end, Jack Kelly had no intention of being ordered around or of giving up his starring role in this spectacular event.

Outside, trumpets heralded the Prince's arrival. He had designed his wedding uniform to resemble those of Napoléon's marshals — a decorated black tunic with gold leaf on the cuffs, sky blue trousers with a gold band down the sides, and a midnight blue bicorne with white ostrich feathers. Rainier walked down the aisle followed by his three witnesses; Jack Kelly finally sat down.

The service went smoothly until the six-year-old page boy, carrying the rings, dropped one. Father Tucker picked it up, but Rainier was unable to get the ring on Grace's finger. She slipped it on by herself. When the ceremony was over, they did not kiss. He offered Grace his arm and they looked at each other affectionately. As they were getting into the car, she whispered something in his ear and he laughed. Sad, but true, it was a relief that the worst ordeal was over. Rainier told a reporter later, "There was such a lack of intimacy . . . cameras and microphones were everywhere. Such lack of dignity and solitude."

On the way back to the palace, Grace followed tradition and laid her small lily-of-the-valley bridal bouquet at the shrine of the martyred virgin Saint Devote and prayed for her marriage.

The wedding reception was held in the Court of Honor, where guests sipped champagne and nibbled on caviar, cold lobster, shrimp, and jellied eggs. The bride and groom cut a five-tier wedding cake with his sword and then disappeared to change their clothes for the honeymoon. Grace chose a simple gray suit and white hat for the short drive to the Prince's yacht.

As she said good-bye to family and friends in her bedroom parlor, everyone began to cry. Peggy came to the rescue and yelled, "See ya later, alligator!" A man's voice replied, "In a while, crocodile!" It was none other than Rainier, who put his arm around Grace and swept her out the door.

They waved from the bridge of the *Deo Juvante II* as it

left the harbor; to the delight of the crowds, Prince Rainier hugged Princess Grace at long last. They remained on deck until the royal yacht disappeared out to sea.

Variety reported the wedding with a notation: ". . . bride is film star, groom is non-pro."

CHAPTER
SEVENTEEN

Lonely Lady

Less than an hour after leaving Monaco, rough water forced Rainier to lay anchor. Grace, who was not a hearty sailor, had agreed to a yachting honeymoon for the privacy of hidden coves and secluded beaches along the Riviera coastline. She attributed her daily nausea to seasickness, unaware that she had become pregnant a few days into the honeymoon.

On August 2, Rainier made the formal announcement: "Her Serene Highness Princess Grace expects a child whose birth should take place in February. The significance of this awaited event is clear to all of you. . . ."

The people of Monaco did not see much of Grace during her pregnancy. She remained inside the dank and gloomy palace writing letters and making long-distance telephone calls. "They told me about morning sickness," Grace said, "but they didn't tell me you could be sick all day every day." She was also plagued with insomnia, sleeping late in the morning and napping in the afternoon. Estranged from her family and friends, the bewildered and lonely Grace was going through the most difficult and trying time in her life. She had crying jags and moods of deep depression.

"Grace had been cut off from everything and everyone,"

Brian said. "There was no transition. In later years, I asked her how she got through those few months and Grace said, 'I almost didn't.' She knew nothing about her husband's personal habits, his political affairs, or his friends. The language barrier was a serious handicap, too."

In September, Grace and Rainier visited New York to dispose of her Fifth Avenue apartment. Some pieces of furniture were shipped to Monaco, among them a love seat covered in blue brocade with "I love you" interwoven in golden threads throughout. To Grace, the apartment represented her achievements, independence, and her dream of returning to the Broadway stage. Giving up her roots in New York City was a sad task.

Rainier was perturbed over the crowds that gathered for a glimpse of the blond movie queen who had given up her Hollywood throne to become a princess. Grace's only concern was that her unborn baby might be harmed if she were jostled by throngs of people. The Secret Service handled these situations very well, and the royal couple dined at their favorite restaurants without incident.

Jack Kelly received the bill for one of their expensive meals at the Barclay in Philadelphia. "Ninety-five bucks!" he ranted. "My son-in-law must have ordered every expensive dish on the menu. What in God's name could four people have eaten for lunch that cost ninety-five bucks?" Jack took care of the bill, a large tab in those days, but it irked him to pay for luxury.

Grace returned to Monaco with a brighter attitude and thirty pounds heavier. She told a reporter her nausea had been replaced by a ravenous appetite, but added it was great fun after years of watching her diet.

Since Grace was expected to give birth earlier than

anticipated, Mrs. Kelly arrived in Monaco shortly after the holidays. Mother and daughter had been estranged over Margaret's newspaper articles; however, it took a keen eye to notice the strain that existed between them at the wedding festivities. During the last few weeks of Grace's pregnancy, they reconciled.

Reporters gathered in Monaco once again. Cameramen were staked out to televise the Princess on her way to the hospital. To their dismay, Grace decided to follow Grimaldi tradition by having the baby at the palace.

At 9:27 a.m. on January 23, 1957, the Princess of Monaco gave birth to Caroline Louise Marguerite, weighing in at 8 pounds and 11 ounces. Grace had been in labor for six hours and delivered the baby without anesthetic in the palace library, which had been converted into a delivery room.

In Monaco, a cannon announced the birth with twenty-one blasts. Church bells chimed, schools were closed, a holiday was proclaimed, and the Monegasques were treated to free champagne.

Rainier told his people, "Thank God and rejoice."

In Philadelphia, Jack Kelly said, "Aw, shucks. I was hoping for a boy."

Five months later, Grace was pregnant again, and on March 14, 1958, Monaco's cannon announced the birth of a male heir with one hundred and one blasts. Blond and blue-eyed, Albert Alexandre Louis Pierre weighed the same as his sister. Rainier said, "It was one of the most wonderful experiences of my life." Eighteen months later, he named Grace regent, declaring that in the event of his death, she would assume the throne until Albert was twenty-one. Though Grace was taking more of an interest in Rainier's affairs of state, she was happiest caring for the children and decorating their new country place, Roc Agel, a converted farmhouse in the mountains above Monaco. (Rainier had sold the villa that he had shared with Gisele Pascal.)

Roc Agel was Grace's hideaway nest where she could be simply mother and wife, puttering in the kitchen and arranging her flower garden. Rainier enjoyed cultivating the soil with his tractor, planting fruit trees, and tending to his wild and domestic animals on Roc Agel's sixty acres.

Grace said in a 1966 interview with *Playboy* magazine, "I don't look for happiness. So perhaps I am very content in life, in a way. . . . When I was acting, I wasn't a very happy person. It isn't much fun to have success and no one to share it with."

A good friend of the Kelly family, Bill Hegner, told journalist Arthur Lewis that Grace and Rainier were not close to each other. "They started out having problems; she cried a lot and called her friends cross-Atlantic and said Rainier was terrible; difficult to get along with. . . . They didn't communicate that well physically. . . ."

Madge ("Tiv") Tivey-Faucon, Grace's former lady-in-waiting, wrote an article for *Cosmopolitan* in 1964. Tiv had been hired as Rainier's secretary on the recommendation of Gisele Pascal and had been asked to stay on at the palace after his marriage. The article, tame by today's standards, related the Prince's criticism of Grace's wardrobe, which consisted mainly of old clothes. He told her that she looked like a "real emigrant" and "a prison wardress." Jack Kelly, the master of thrift, took a swipe at his daughter, too: "Gracie, I think you must buy your clothes at the Salvation Army!" According to Tiv, when the Princess was expecting Albert, she wore the same maternity clothes she had worn for Caroline.

In January 1960, Grace's beloved poodle, Oliver, was attacked and killed by another dog. Two days later, Rainier bought her another poodle, but Grace was inconsolable for a long time. Tragedy struck again in June of that year when Jack Kelly died of stomach cancer shortly before his seventy-first birthday. He had written his own will; it was such a masterpiece that copies were selling for $7 each from Boston to Bombay. Jack wrote in the will that he hated legal jargon and wanted to express his wishes in simple terms. To Margaret, he left all his personal property, insurance, and one-third of the residue, valued at around $2 million. The balance was divided among his four children. In the event of their death, Jack wanted the monies to revert to his grandchildren. "I don't want to give the impression that I am against sons-in-law," he wrote, "if they are the right type, they will provide for themselves and their families." He warned Kell about gambling and instructed his daughters not to deal in excesses. "As for me, just shed a respectful tear. . . . I had more than my share of success . . . my wife and children have not given me any heartaches, but . . . have given me much happiness and pardonable pride, and I want them to know I appreciate that . . . if I had the choice to give you worldly goods or character, I would give you character. . . . When I shove off for greener pastures or whatever it is on the other side of the curtain, I do it unafraid and, if you must know, a little curious."

That Jack did not have more money in his estate was a surprise to even his good friends. The bulk of his millions had been set up in trust for his children and grandchildren over the years, amounting to an estimated $8 million. A close family friend said, "If Grace's dowry was in the range of $2 million, Jack was the kind of guy to be just as generous with his other children."

Grace told friend Judy Quine in later years that her relationship with Peggy was strained after Jack's death: "Only once did she comment that I had never really understood our father, but I wonder if the fact that he and I made some peace with one another before he died doesn't make her resent me."

Jack's bond of love with Grace on his deathbed made it all the more painful for her. At the end, his deepest affection was for Grace, who somehow managed to be strong enough for both of them. Grief-stricken, she returned to Monaco and faced another heartbreaking crisis. A "well-meaning" friend thought Grace should know about Rainier's indiscretions during her absence.

The story goes that the Prince had been seen dancing at a nightclub with Zénaide Quiñones de León, Grace's new, young, attractive lady-in-waiting. Madge Tivey-Faucon had also been on hand to celebrate Rainier's thirty-seventh birthday. Grace confronted her husband, who said he had invited a few friends to a party and that's all there was to it. Tiv backed up his explanation, but the gossip that persisted in Monaco indicated there was more to the story. Grace had no choice but to fire Zénaide. There would be more tales linking the Prince with other women, but none that compared to partying and dancing while his wife sat by her dying father's bedside.

Grace's lingering depression and fatigue were cause for concern, but an offer to play the Virgin Mary in *King of Kings* (1961) made her come to life. Rainier was sympathetic but would not give his permission. Their discussions about her acting again ended with boisterous arguments or Grace's retreating into a shell.

To compensate for her loneliness, she invited friends from Hollywood to visit Monaco. Cary Grant and his wife, Betsy Drake, accepted her invitation to spend Easter 1961 at the palace. Grace met them at the airport, an honor she usually reserved for her mother, according to Tiv. The next morning Rainier was furious to see a picture of his wife kissing Cary Grant. It was unthinkable for Her Serene Highness to demonstrate affection for another man in public. Rainier was jealous of Grace's past and particularly of Grant, whose steamy love scenes with Grace in *To Catch a Thief* prompted the Prince to ban his staff from viewing the film in the palace cinema. During Grant's visit, Tiv claimed that Rainier sulked and did not speak to the actor. Grace, in turn, was cold to her husband. It appears that the Prince was more disturbed over her breach of protocol at the airport than anything else.

In 1962, Alfred Hitchcock sent Grace the screenplay of Winston Graham's novel *Marnie* (1964). She would play the title role of a frigid compulsive thief who is given a choice of marrying a rich man or going to jail.

"I have yet to understand why Rainier agreed to this particular project," Brian said. "If he was willing to let Grace act again, why not something more appropriate?"

Rainier had two reasons. He respected Hitchcock and he was very concerned over Grace's melancholia. Rainier thought it would be fun for the family to spend their fall vacation in New England during the filming. He made the formal announcement on March 18, 1962, making it perfectly clear that Her Serene Highness was not returning to the screen permanently. Rainier told a friend, ". . . it would be right for her to do it. Why should a talent like that go?"

But the Monegasques did not want their Princess kissing other men on the screen. They protested to the press and in writing to the Prince. MGM got into the act and threatened to take legal action if Grace violated her contract. Pope John XXIII sent a letter of objection to the palace, but Rainier did not change his mind. It was Grace who yielded to the people of Monaco and gave up all hope of acting again.

Tippi Hedren replaced her in *Marnie* and in Hitchcock's fantasies. "You're everything I've ever dreamed about," he confessed and then threatened Hedren when she rebuffed his advances. From then on, he referred to her as "that girl." In every respect, *Marnie* was a disaster.

In the early sixties, Grace was confronted with many tragedies and disappointments, including two miscarriages. On February 1, 1965, however, she had another daughter, Stéphanie Marie Elisabeth. The fear of not being able to have more children vanished with other doubts she had about her capabilities as a Princess. Grace was able to identify, at last, with the people of Monaco, who adored her. She had given them a male heir, chosen them over acting, and proven herself a political asset to the Prince, who gradually walked in her shadow. When she traveled, people congregated to see Her Serene Highness of Monaco instead of Grace Kelly, Hollywood movie star.

After ten years of marriage, she accepted Rainier's stubborness, moodiness, and bouts of temperament. They no longer pretended to share the same interests. He enjoyed his hobbies and she enjoyed hers. Grace said their belief in

Catholicism brought them together in difficult times. What was not generally known is that she had signed away all rights to the children if her marriage failed. The Prince's heirs to the throne belonged to Monaco.

Grace turned forty on November 12, 1969. "I'm an absolute basket case," she said in an interview for *Look* magazine. "I can't stand it. It comes as a great jolt. . . . For a woman, forty is torture, the end."

She mailed birthday party invitations with the heading "Scorpio" to a dinner-dance, with a swimming pool brunch the following day: "Hotel de Paris wholly converted for Scorpian occupancy. Your private nest awaits you. Courtesy of the High Scorpia. Other signs married to Scorpians tolerated."

Elizabeth Taylor chose this occasion to debut her fabulous Krupp diamond, a gift from Scorpian husband Richard Burton. A horde of security guards accompanied the famous couple, causing more commotion on this already exciting and noteworthy event.

The Burtons frequently escorted Grace to social gatherings that Rainier chose not to attend. With Elizabeth and Richard, she was a different person. European society considered the Princess too pompous and stiff with Rainier at her side. The Duchess of Windsor referred to Grace as a "boring snob." But in the company of the Burtons, Her Royal Highness let her hair down. At Elizabeth's fortieth birthday party in Budapest, Grace did wild Hungarian dances and kicked up her heels in a conga line that she probably started.

Leslie Bennetts, a reporter for the *Philadelphia Bulletin*, told biographer Arthur Lewis that Grace had less warmth and less spontaneity than anyone she had ever interviewed. "She's an awful stick. Her life revolves around the rituals of her position." She described Grace's accent as "stilted bastardized French in this incredibly affected voice."

Grace was puritanical in her role of Princess, but she let her hair down with the Hollywood crowd. Ava Gardner remarked that Grace was just another gal dishing the dirt after a few dry martinis.

Rock Hudson, a close Scorpian friend, attended a party in Los Angeles and stayed on with Grace after the other guests had gone home. "Her Serene Highness got ripped to the tits," he recalled. Hudson's good friend, Tom Clark, said, "Whenever Grace visited Hollywood, Rupert Allan always gave a party for her. Rock and Grace would wind up in a corner, laughing it up over who knows what silliness. They would collapse in a puddle of laughter."

Bob Slatzer, who was introduced to Grace by Gary Cooper, became a good friend of hers and they got together whenever she was in Los Angeles. Slatzer said William Holden mentioned Grace's romance with Cary Grant in the early seventies. "She hasn't changed much, has she?" Bill scowled.

Bob had heard the rumor before but kept it to himself until the next time he saw Grace. "How's Cary doing?" he asked her casually. "Do you get to see him as much as you'd like?"

"As often as I can," she smiled.

"You look like a woman with a guilty secret," he said teasingly.

"It's not a guilty secret. It's a glorious secret!"

Slatzer got the impression that Grace and Cary were brought together by personal torment rather than sexual gratification. Grant was depressed over his recent divorce from his third wife, Dyan Cannon. Grace was a lonely lady in need of love. "Cary is the one man who really understands my moods and passions," she said sincerely.

Slatzer said the affair was also known to intimates in Europe. "Grace would call close friends and ask them to let Cary know she was coming to Paris, New York, Los Angeles, or wherever he happened to be. This went on for six or seven years. Grant had other affairs, but he considered Grace the perfect woman. The undercurrent of passion that had been present during so much of their relationship never actually died, but after a while, both chose not to ignite it. They were content to talk over the phone."

At the age of seventeen, Princess Caroline rebelled against the strict tutelage in England. Grace remembered her own youthful spunk and independence and was determined to protect her daughter. In 1974, Grace decided to live in Paris for six months out of the year while Caroline attended school. Mother and daughter clashed over the basics — clothes, bad grades, and late-night parties. By now, Caroline had heard all about Grace's romantic life in Hollywood and used this as ammunition when her mother became overly strict and righteous.

Grace's futile attempts to restrain Caroline were minor compared to Margaret's brutal control over forty-nine-year-old Kell, who was seeking the Democratic nomination for mayor of Philadelphia. Separated from his wife and six children, Kell was linked in the gossip columns with a beautiful transsexual, Rachel Harlow. Knowing that the opposing party would use this against him, Margaret threatened to go on television and tell the people why they should *not* vote for Kell; *and* she would give financial support to his Republican opponent. Mother and son were never the same again. A few months after Margaret ruined forever Kell's chances in politics, she was felled by a stroke that crippled her mind and body. Nevertheless, the Kelly matriarch lingered until the age of ninety-one. She died of pneumonia in January 1990, unaware that both her son and Grace were dead. Kell had had a fatal heart attack in 1984 while jogging in Philadelphia. He was fifty-seven.

CHAPTER
EIGHTEEN

Sundown at 10:00 a.m.

"Caroline wants to fly with her own wings, live for herself. It's natural and normal. In one sense, she is more mature than I was at her age . . . but in another sense, she is more vulnerable," Grace said in an interview for the *London Daily Express* in April 1976.

Handsome Philippe Junot, a well-educated European playboy, was seventeen years older than Caroline. He came from a respectable upper-middle-class family, studied politics and business in the major capitals of the world, and was a consultant to an international investment bank when he proposed marriage to Caroline in early 1977.

Junot reminded Grace of the suave and sophisticated Oleg Cassini and Jack's threat to banish her from the Kelly home if she married Oleg. Grace remembered her own defiance and feared that Caroline might abandon Monaco and live with Junot in his Paris apartment. The paparazzi had already taken pictures of a topless Caroline kissing Philippe in a boat anchored off the Riviera coast.

Grace and Rainier consented to the engagement provided the couple wait a year before getting married. Nine months later, Grace had no choice but to begin making plans for the wedding that took place on June 29, 1978. The night before, Grace told Rainier, "Perhaps it's for the better. This way she'll have a successful second marriage."

Among the guests were Grace's loyal friends, the David Nivens, the Gregory Pecks, Barbara and Frank Sinatra, Cary Grant, and Ava Gardner. Stéphanie, who insisted on wearing jeans instead of a dress, was forbidden to attend.

As predicted by Grace, the marriage lasted two years. Caroline told Barbara Walters in a 1985 interview that her reason for marrying Junot was to escape the restrictions imposed on her. Caroline married wealthy Italian businessman Stephano Casiraghi in December 1983. They had three children and a happy union, but Caroline's life was shattered by the tragic death of Casiraghi in a speedboat accident in October 1990.

Grace accepted an offer to join the board of directors at Twentieth Century-Fox in 1976. She told a reporter, "There is too much crude sex and violence in movies and television today. I want to help change all that." Another reason was an excuse to get away from her daily routine in Monaco.

Robert Dornhelm, a young Hungarian director, convinced Grace to narrate *The Children of Theatre Street* (1977), a film documentary about the Kirov Ballet School in Leningrad. In 1979, Dornhelm also worked with Grace on a short film promoting Monaco and its Flower Festival. *Rearranged* had a comical plot about an astronomer who ends up by mistake in the bouquet contest. On behalf of her Garden Club, Grace produced, financed, and acted in the film. Whether it was Dornhelm's inspiration or her own awakening after the *Marnie* fiasco, Grace could no longer restrain her creative energies. She found this outlet by giving poetry readings that became so popular in the United States that she talked about looking for a New York apartment.

Rumors that the Prince and Princess of Monaco were having marital problems were more embarrassing than painful for Grace. Palace insiders claimed the royal couple had not slept in the same bed for a long time and were now occupying separate bedrooms.

Bill Hegner's interview with Arthur Lewis stressed the lack of physical communication ". . . even if they've had three children. She fulfilled her commitment and they've stuck it out because it's mutually beneficial. Now she can live in Paris and meet her friends again. She travels a lot; you don't see pictures of them together so often."

On a state visit to Bangkok, Grace and Rainier argued bitterly in the lobby of their hotel. She went to a dinner party by herself while he was spotted eating in the restaurant. There were also rumors about Grace and Robert Dornhelm. They spent a good deal of time together planning future projects, but it was her radiance and laughter when she was in his company that caused tongues to wag. Dornhelm told author James Spada that there was no romance and he doubted that she had one with anyone else. "But I'd like to think that she did have affairs because they would have been good for her."

Grace wanted more than ever to do a movie. *The Turning Point* (1977), the story of two aging ballet dancers, seemed to her the perfect comeback vehicle, but Rainier refused to give his permission.

Grace eased her frustration by drinking and overeating. She put on considerable weight but told a friend, "I'm fifty-two and the mother of three children. Why should I care?" Still, she cared enough to take off a few pounds for such occasions as the "Night of One Hundred Stars" in February 1982 at Radio City Music Hall to benefit the

Actors' Fund of America. For Grace, it was a touching reunion with people she had not seen in years.

On March 31, Philadelphia celebrated a "Tribute to Grace Kelly" at a banquet in the Annenberg Center. Stewart Granger, Frank Sinatra, and Jimmy Stewart were on hand to honor their favorite leading lady. "I am overwhelmed," Grace said in a brief speech, "and so filled with love I would just like to hug every one of you." A bad head cold did not prevent her from reminiscing all night with Hollywood pals.

On July 23, Grace told Pierre Salinger in a TV interview that she was lucky as an actress but had not done anything outstanding. Tactfully, Salinger skirted the possibility that her poetry readings were a prelude to making films again. Grace said it would be a difficult decision, adding, "I have tried to avoid saying never or always."

In August, Rainier, Grace, Caroline, and Albert cruised to Scandinavia on the SS Mermoz. Stéphanie stayed behind with her boyfriend Paul Belmondo, the eighteen-year-old son of the famous French actor Jean-Paul. Grace approved of the levelheaded young man but worried about Stéphanie, whose life revolved around Belmondo. Mother and daughter were at odds during the summer and quarreled bitterly. Stéphanie wanted to study dress design in Paris, where Paul lived. Grace was hesitant but decided to accompany her by train to Paris on Monday night, September 13. Stéphanie resented the idea of being chaperoned in Paris, and the angry discussions with her mother intensified.

Grace was going through a difficult menopause and, reportedly, she had high blood pressure but was not taking medication. After the cruise, a lingering head cold and bronchitis made her irritable, listless, and depressed.

On Monday morning, September 13, 1982, Grace's chauffeur parked her car, a Rover 3500, in front of the house at Roc Agel. Before leaving for Paris, she had an appointment with her seamstress and hurriedly laid out on the backseat dresses that needed altering. Grace dismissed the chauffeur because Stéphanie was going along and the car was packed with their belongings. Grace got behind the wheel and waved good-bye at about 9:30 a.m.

What happened during the next half hour has been told and retold so often that the details are as legendary as the fatal ride President John F. Kennedy took through Dallas.

Grace had a terrible fear of dying in an airplane or in a car. When she drove, which was seldom, it was erratic but at a snail's pace. She never wore seat belts because they were too confining or, as a friend said, "Grace felt trapped ... locked in." She was such a slow driver that her children loved to tease, "We could walk there faster."

In the late seventies, Grace was alone when she hit another car broadside at an intersection in Monaco. No one was hurt but the accident was her fault and she swore, "I'll never drive again."

Grace was, however, accustomed to the five-mile ride between Roc Agel and the palace, despite the winding roads. On this sunny September morning, she complained to Stéphanie about a headache. The driver of the truck behind them noticed the Rover swerving back and forth. Assuming Grace had dozed off, he blew his horn and the car got back on course. Doctors theorized later that she had had a minor stroke and was bewildered. If so, it could not have happened at a worse time. The Rover was on a decline headed for the sharpest turn on the Moyenne Corniche. In a panic, Grace cried out that the brakes did not work, but most likely she pressed down on the accelerator. The truck driver said, "The corner came up. I did not see it [the car] slow down . . . the brake lights didn't come on . . . she did not even try to turn and I had the impression that she was going faster and faster. . . ."

Stéphanie reached for the hand brake, but the Rover shot straight ahead off the edge of the hillside and into the air; it turned over and fell one hundred and twenty feet into a garden patch.

Stéphanie lost consciousness briefly and awoke crouched underneath the glove compartment, the only section of the Rover that was intact. The car door on the driver's side was ajar. She pushed it open with her feet and crawled out with the help of a gardener and his wife. Stéphanie told them who she was and to call her father. "My mother's in there!" she cried. "We have to get her out. Please get help!"

It took the gardener's wife a few minutes to realize the young lady was indeed Rainier's daughter and that the woman pinned in the backseat of the Rover was Princess Grace. Ambulance attendants had to break the back window in order to get her out. She had a wide gash on the forehead and her right leg was twisted. Although Grace's eyes were open, she did not respond.

While Grace and Stéphanie were being treated at Princess Grace Hospital, news bulletins from the palace made light of the auto accident, reporting that Grace had only suffered a broken leg and that Stéphanie had walked away with minor bruises. Caroline called from London and was told there was no need to come home until the next day. She returned to Monaco on Tuesday, September 14, a few hours before her mother died.

When Grace arrived at the hospital, doctors operated on her internal injuries, a collapsed lung, the head wound, and her fractured right leg. During the four-hour operation, she lapsed into a coma. Doctors suspected brain damage, but the hospital was not equipped with a scanner. The only one available was in the office of a Monte Carlo doctor, and Grace was taken there that night. The elevator was too small to accommodate the stretcher, and she had to be carried up to the second floor. The CAT scan revealed two brain lesions. Doctors theorized that Grace had suffered the small one in the car, a minor stroke that would not have killed her. The other lesion was a massive hemorrhage caused by the accident. This deadly stroke in conjunction with Grace's other injuries proved to be fatal. She was put on a life-support system, but on Tuesday morning, the encephalogram indicated that Grace was brain-dead. At noon, Rainier gave permission to have his wife taken off the life-support system, and at 10:35 p.m. on Tuesday, September 14, 1982, Princess Grace was dead.

The shock was intensified by the first palace bulletin that Grace had suffered only a broken leg in an automobile accident. How could she be dead? People around the world were dumbstruck, but they were also suspicious. Who was covering up? And why? The palace spokesman had mentioned brake failure in the original communiqué. If so, why was the Rover removed immediately and impounded by Rainier? And why was the Princess taken to a hospital that was not properly equipped to deal with her head injuries?

It was a long time before these questions were answered logically. Rainier had the car towed away before tourists could begin taking parts off the Rover for souvenirs; he did not want Grace's broken car on public display. A full investigation proved that there was no mechanical failure and that the brakes were not faulty. Either Grace did not have use of her leg after the stroke or she pushed down on the gas pedal by mistake.

She was taken to the Princess Grace Hospital because it was the closest facility and the extent of her injuries was still unknown. While she was in surgery, Rainier did not respond to the palace spokesman, who had no choice but to speculate. Grace's family was told it was "nothing serious," but the following day Rainier called them with the grave news that Grace was dying. The sad fact is that she was doomed before her ambulance reached the hospital.

There was talk that Stéphanie had actually driven the car because she was seen crawling out of the driver's seat. However, there were many reliable witnesses who had seen Grace behind the wheel.

To this day, though, rumors persist that Her Serene Highness had been murdered by the Mafia, who wanted to regain control of the gambling casino. It was Grace's influence that had kept the Mob out of Monte Carlo. Author Leslie Waller claims that an "executioner" posing as a nurse or doctor had injected lethal air bubbles into Grace's blood. "There was nothing political about it," Waller says, "and there was nothing personal. It was just another business move. She had to go. . . ."

John Scott-Walton, a former U.S. intelligence agent who lived in Monaco for twelve years, told the *Globe* that a man who knew of the plot to kill Princess Grace confessed on his deathbed. Scott-Walton says that organized crime figures had reason to believe that Grace's marriage to Rainier was over and that she was returning to the United States for good. "A few of the richest and most powerful men in Monaco agreed that a marriage breakup would be a 'public relations disaster and a financial calamity,'" Scott-Walton explained. "Instead of a scandal, her death left Monaco with a beautiful myth and a martyr." Still, the former intelligence agent claims that the brakes on the Rover were tampered with, but police were helpless against the "entrenched powers in Monaco."

Waller and Scott-Walton agree that organized crime had a contract out on Grace, but their motives are in direct conflict.

The most pathetic and disturbing theory was suicide, but Brian said, "Grace was afraid of cars whether she was driving or not, and if she had the sudden urge to do away with herself, I can't conceive of her taking Stéphanie with her. I read another account about Grace having such a bitter quarrel with Stéphanie in the car that day, she wasn't paying attention to the road, but that's fishy, too. I've driven around those curves sober, drunk, in the dark, in a hurry to catch a plane, or whatever, but unless you were crazy nuts, you paid attention. There were thirty or more curves and bends. It was almost impossible *not* to be aware every damn minute. I believe that a ministroke caused Grace to black out for a few seconds. Whether she was angry and upset, we'll never know."

"What about murder?" I asked.

"I was a big gambler at one time," Brian replied, "and met a few of the so-called big boys in Monte Carlo. They didn't like Grace, but she was more of a pest than a threat. Whatever she did to prevent the Mafia from taking over completely, she made up for by attracting high rollers and high society. Monte Carlo was never the same without her, but the latest gimmick is that a visit to Grace's tomb will cure disabilities and illnesses. A local priest has asked the Vatican to canonize Grace as they did Saint Bernadette, whose shrine at Lourdes attracts tourists by the millions."

CHAPTER
NINETEEN

Farewell

In the palace chapel, her body lay in state for several days to allow the people of Monaco to pay their respects. It was apparent that the beautiful Grace had been hastily prepared for burial. A cheap wig had been pulled down below her hair-line to cover the forehead wound. A friend remarked, "It's too bad that make-up experts were not consulted. They could have done miracles. The white velvet-lined coffin was a bit fussy, as was her white lace dress with ruffles on the high collar. Grace was not a frilly person. She no longer belonged to Hollywood, but any number of make-up artists and hairdressers would gladly have flown over and paid their respects at the same time."

Judy Quine commented that seeing Grace "gussied up" made her friend's death seem completely unreal.

On Saturday morning, September 18, 1982, silence reigned in Monaco as friends gathered for the funeral services in the Cathedral of St. Nicholas, where the royal wedding had taken place twenty-six years earlier. Princess Diana, First Lady Nancy Reagan, the Aga Khan, the King and Queen of Belgium, Prince Bertil of Sweden, and the Queen of Spain were among the dignitaries. Cary Grant and his fifth wife Barbara were Grace's only Hollywood friends in attendance. David Niven, who lived nearby, was seriously ill.

At 10:15 a.m., the eerie silence was broken by trumpets and the funeral procession began from the palace chapel to the cathedral. On television, the world watched Grace's family walk behind her casket. No one was more pathetic than Rainier. A broken and shattered man, his bowed head sank into his chest. He looked at no one — his eyelids drooped in despair. Rainier's only gesture was reaching out for Caroline's hand during the service. No one could forget his inconsolable torment, and sadly we asked ourselves, "Did he really love her that much?"

Stéphanie, who had suffered a cracked vertebra, was in traction at the hospital. She and Paul Belmondo watched the funeral on television.

"We weep for our Princess Grace," said the Archbishop. "The brutal suddenness of her death accentuates our sorrow. When she was among us, our Princess was always ready to help those who needed it. Now it is time for her, in return, to receive the help afforded by our prayers."

Cary Grant, weak with anguish, did not break down until he had left the church in his car.

On September 21, the Princess of Monaco was laid to rest in the Grimaldi vault behind the cathedral's High Altar.

On September 29, there was a memorial service for Grace at the Church of the Good Shepherd in Beverly Hills. Many of her friends who could not attend the funeral came to share their memories of "Gracie."

When Oleg Cassini was asked for a statement, he faced a

new and younger generation of reporters who were skeptical that he and Grace had once been very much in love. Cassini wrote in his memoirs that she had become a myth and that the press "seemed to resent the fact that Grace and I nearly married."

Ray Milland was said to be so grief-stricken over her death that he could not come to the telephone.

The other men in Grace's life had already passed on — Clark Gable in 1960, Gary Cooper in 1961, Gene Lyons in 1975, Bing Crosby in 1977, Alfred Hitchcock in 1980, and William Holden in 1981.

Jean-Pierre Aumont spoke to author Steven Englund about Grace a few months after her death. He referred to their relationship as a "very tender friendship."

William Holden's perspective of Grace Kelly was the most profound: "Her romances were always serious. She put her heart and soul into love affairs."

After her flings in New York, Grace thought she could distinguish sexual desires from emotional needs, but love addicts at any age are easy prey.

It is ironic that our two American princesses were obsessed with their fathers. Rita Hayworth had been physically abused by her father, according to author Barbara Leaming, whose source was Rita's second husband, Orson Welles.

Grace was emotionally abused by Jack Kelly, whose lack of depth and understanding was the cause of her rebelling not only against the Kelly code of ethics but particularly against her father. Knowing he would not condone divorced or married men, Grace taunted Jack by bringing them home. The manner in which he treated Oleg Cassini was rude, childish, and tinged with jealousy. A prince came along with the right credentials but Jack found fault anyway. He thought Rainier was too short. Outwardly, Jack was crass. Inwardly, he did not think any man was good enough for Grace. Neither knew the depth of their love for each other until he was dying.

Grace Kelly brought her own blend of magic to the screen. She was not a creation of MGM's dream factory or an illusion of make-up, bleached hair, padded bras, and false eyelashes. Her leading men, who were older, sophisticated, and blasé to romance, had never met a girl like Grace. She defined love for them and allowed her passion to bloom on forbidden ground. Grace's image as an untouchable goddess was more enduring than her love affairs. She had captured our imagination as the inaccessible and passive all-American girl. Grace's naturalness gave her an alluring quality that was refreshing and yet mysterious — a quality that was a vital attraction to men in her private life.

Grace Kelly belongs to a brief but unique chapter of Hollywood history. She will belong to us on film for all time — young, vibrant, and passionate.

CHRONOLOGY OF
GRACE KELLY'S FILMS

Fourteen Hours (Twentieth Century-Fox, 1951)
Producer: Sol C. Siegel
Director: Henry Hathaway
Based on a *New Yorker* magazine story by Joel Sayre
Cast: Paul Douglas, Richard Basehart, Barbara Bel Geddes,
    Agnes Moorehead, Debra Paget, and Grace Kelly
Black and white, 92 minutes

High Noon (United Artists, 1952)
Producer: Stanley Kramer
Director: Fred Zinnemann
Editor: Elmo Williams
Theme song: Dmitri Tiomkin
Based on the story "The Tin Star" by John W. Cunningham
Cast: Gary Cooper, Thomas Mitchell, Lloyd Bridges, Katy
    Jurado, and Grace Kelly
Black and white, 85 minutes

Mogambo (MGM, 1953)

Producer: Sam Zimbalist
Director: John Ford
Based on a play by Wilson Collison
Cast: Clark Gable, Ava Gardner, Grace Kelly, and Donald
Sinden
Color, 115 minutes

Dial M For Murder (Warner Brothers, 1954)

Producer and Director: Alfred Hitchcock
Based on a play by Frederick Knott
Cast: Ray Milland, Grace Kelly, Robert Cummings, and
John Williams
Color, 105 minutes

Rear Window (Paramount, 1954)

Producer and Director: Alfred Hitchcock
Based on a novelette by Cornell Woolrich
Cast: James Stewart, Grace Kelly, Wendell Corey, Thelma
Ritter, and Raymond Burr
Color, 112 minutes

The Country Girl (Paramount, 1954)

Producers: William Perlberg and George Seaton
Director: George Seaton
Based on a play by Clifford Odets
Cast: Bing Crosby, Grace Kelly (Academy Award), and
William Holden
Black and white, 104 minutes

Green Fire (MGM, 1954)

Producer: Armand Deutsch
Director: Andrew Marton
Cast: Stewart Granger, Grace Kelly, Paul Douglas, and
John Ericson
Color, 100 minutes

The Bridges at Toko-Ri (Paramount, 1955)

Producers: William Perlberg and George Seaton
Director: Mark Robson
Based on a novel by James E. Michener
Cast: William Holden, Grace Kelly, Fredric March, and
Mickey Rooney
Color, 103 minutes

To Catch a Thief (Paramount, 1955)

Producer and Director: Alfred Hitchcock
Based on a novel by David Dodge
Cast: Cary Grant, Grace Kelly, Jessie Royce Landis, John
Williams, and Brigitte Auber
Color, 97 minutes

The Swan (MGM, 1956)

Producer: Dore Schary
Director: Charles Vidor
Based on a play by Ferenc Molnar
Cast: Grace Kelly, Alec Guinness, Louis Jourdan, Agnes
Moorehead, Jessie Royce Landis, and Brian Aherne
Color, 112 minutes

High Society (MGM, 1956)

Producer: Sol C. Siegel
Director: Charles Walters
Based on the play "The Philadelphia Story" by Philip
  Barry
Cast: Bing Crosby, Grace Kelly, Frank Sinatra, Celeste
  Holm, John Lund, Louis Calhern, and Louis Armstrong
Color, 107 minutes

The Children of Theatre Street
(Peppercorn-Wormser, 1977)

Producer: Earle Mack
Director: Robert Dornhelm
Narrator: Princess Grace
Featuring the students and faculty of the Vaganova
  Choreographic Institute and Konstantine Zaklinsky of
  the Kirov Ballet
Color, 90 minutes

SELECTED BIBLIOGRAPHY

Anger, Kenneth. *Hollywood Babylon II.* New York: E. P. Dutton, 1984.

Arce, Hector. *Gary Cooper: An Intimate Biography.* New York: William Morrow, 1979.

Aumont, Jean-Pierre. *Sun and Shadow.* New York: W. W. Norton, 1977.

Bradford, Sarah. *Princess Grace.* New York: Stein and Day, 1984.

Bragg, Melvyn. *Richard Burton.* Boston: Little, Brown, 1988.

Cassini, Oleg. *In My Own Fashion.* New York: Simon & Schuster, 1987.

Clark, Tom. *Rock Hudson: Friend of Mine.* New York: Pharos, 1989.

Considine, Shaun. *Bette and Joan: The Divine Feud.* New York: E. P. Dutton, 1989.

de Massy, Baron Christian. *Palace: My Life in the Royal Family of Monaco.* New York: Atheneum, 1986.

Desser, Lloyd Fuller. *Who's Who of the Cinema.* New York: Macmillan, 1983.

Edwards, Anne. *A Remarkable Woman: A Biography of Katharine Hepburn.* New York: William Morrow, 1985.

Englund, Steven. *Grace of Monaco.* New York: Doubleday, 1984.

Granger, Stewart. *Sparks Fly Upward.* New York: G. P. Putnam's Sons, 1981.

Harris, Warren G. *Cary Grant.* New York: Doubleday, 1987.

Hart-Davis, Phyllida. *Grace: The Story of a Princess.* New York: St. Martin's Press, 1982.

Head, Edith, and Paddy Calistro. *Edith Head's Hollywood.* New York: E. P. Dutton, 1983.

Heymann, David C. *Poor Little Rich Girl: The Life and Legend of Barbara Hutton.* New York: Lyle Stuart, 1983.

Higham, Charles. *Ava.* New York: Delacorte Press, 1974.

"Interview with Princess Grace," *Playboy,* January 1966.

Kelley, Kitty. *Elizabeth Taylor: The Last Star.* New York: Simon & Schuster, 1981.

Kelly, Mrs. John B., as told to Richard Gehman. "My Daughter Grace Kelly," *Journal American,* January 15-24, 1956.

Leaming, Barbara. *If This Was Happiness: A Biography of Rita Hayworth.* New York: Viking, 1989.

Lewis, Arthur. *Those Philadelphia Kellys.* New York: William Morrow, 1977.

Milland, Ray. *Wide-Eyed in Babylon.* New York: William Morrow, 1974.

Moseley, Roy. *Bette Davis: An Intimate Memoir.* New York: Donald I. Fine, 1989.

Niven, David. *Bring on the Empty Horses.* London: Hamish Hamilton, 1975.

Parish, James Robert, and Ronald L. Bowers. *The MGM Stock Company.* New Rochelle, N.Y.: Arlington House, 1973.

Quine, Judith Balaban. *The Bridesmaids.* New York: Weidenfeld and Nicolson, 1989.

Robinson, Jeffrey. *Rainier and Grace: An Intimate Portrait.* New York: Atlantic Monthly Press, 1989.

Robyns, Gwen. *Princess Grace.* New York: David McKay, 1982.

Shepherd, Donald, and Robert Slazer. *Bing Crosby: The Hollow Man.* New York: Pinnacle Books, 1982.

Slater, Leonard. *Aly.* New York: Random House, 1964.

Spada, James. *Grace: The Secret Lives of a Princess.* New York: Doubleday, 1987.

Spoto, Donald. *The Dark Side of Genius: The Life of Alfred Hitchcock.* Boston: Little, Brown, 1983.

Summers, Anthony. *Goddess: The Secret Lives of Marilyn Monroe.* New York: Macmillan, 1985.

Swindell, Larry. *The Last Hero: The Biography of Gary Cooper.* New York: Doubleday, 1980.

Thomas, Bob. *Golden Boy: The Untold Story of William Holden.* New York: St. Martin's Press, 1983.

Tivey-Faucon, Madge. "Inside the Palace with Princess Grace," *Cosmopolitan,* March 1964.

Tornabene, Lyn. *Long Live the King: A Biography of Clark Gable.* New York: G. P. Putnam's Sons, 1976.

Wayne, Jane Ellen. *Cooper's Women.* New York: Prentice-Hall, 1988.

——. *Gable's Women.* New York: Prentice-Hall, 1987.

Wlaschin, Ken. *The World's Great Movie Stars.* New York: Harmony Books, 1979.

Other Sources

Academy of Motion Picture Arts and Sciences, Los Angeles
Beverly Hills Library
F. H. Goldwyn Library, Hollywood
Library of the Performing Arts at Lincoln Center, New York
New York Public Library
Seek Information Service, Glendale, California
UCLA Cinema Collection Library, Los Angeles
USC Main Library — Special Cinema Collection, Los Angeles

INDEX

LARGE PRINT

ISIS publish a wide range of books in large print, from fiction to biography. A full list of titles is available free of charge from the address below. Alternatively, contact your local library for details of their collection of ISIS books.

Details of ISIS unabridged audio books are also available.

Any suggestions for books you would like to see in large print or audio are always welcome.

ISIS
55 St Thomas' Street
Oxford OX1 1JG
(0865) 250333

BIOGRAPHY AND AUTOBIOGRAPHY

Eamonn & Grainne Andrews
For Ever and Ever, Eamonn

Chuck Ashman and Pamela Trescott
Cary Grant

Ronnie Barker	**It's Hello From Him**
Peter Brown	**Such Devoted Sisters**
Peter Coleman	**The Real Barry Humphries**
Joe Collins	**A Touch of Collins**
Peter Cushing	**An Autobiography** (A)
Peter Cushing	**'Past Forgetting'** (A)
Marlene Dietrich	**My Life**
Jerry Epstein	**Remebering Charlie**
Quentin Falk	**Anthony Hopkins**
David Fingleton	**Kiri**
Angela Fox	**Completely Foxed**
Angela Fox	**Slightly Foxed**
Michael Freeland	**A Salute to Irving Berlin**

(A) Large Print books also available in Audio

BIOGRAPHY AND AUTOBIOGRAPHY

Sir John Gielgud	**Backward Glances**
Hermione Gingold	**How to Grow Old Disgracefully** (A)
Joyce Grenfell	**The Time of My Life**
Rex Harrison	**A Damned Serious Business**
Ronald Harwood (ed)	**Dear Alec**
Helen Hayes	**Loving Life**
Stafford Hildred and David Britten	**Tom Jones**
Graham Jenkins	**Richard Burton, My Brother**
Teresa Jennings	**Patricia Hayes**
Joan Le Mesurier	**Lady, Don't Fall Backwards**
Maureen Lipman	**How Was It For You?**
Maureen Lipman	**Something to Fall Back On**
Joanna Lumley	**Stare Back and Smile**
Ray Moore	**Tomorrow Is Too Late** (A)
Alma and Ray Moore	**Tomorrow - Who Knows?**

(A) Large Print books also available in Audio

BIOGRAPHY AND AUTOBIOGRAPHY

Joe Morella and Edward Z Epstein	**Forever Lucy**
Sheridan Morley	**Odd Man Out: James Mason**
Barry Norman	**The Hollywood Greats**
Elena Oumano	**Paul Newman**
Harry Secombe	**Arias and Raspberries**
Gus Smith	**Richard Harris**
John Smith	**The Benny Hill Story**
Daniel Snowman	**The World of Placido Domingo**
Terry-Thomas	**Terry-Thomas Tells Tales**
Alexander Walker	**Peter Sellars**
Jane Ellen Wayne	**Ava's Men**
Ernie Wise	**Still On My Way to Hollywood**
Terry Wogan	**Wogan on Wogan**

(A) Large Print books also available in Audio

1052pM

1946